SMALL BATCH

Rowman & Littlefield
Studies in Food and Gastronomy

General Editor: Ken Albala, Professor of History, University of the Pacific (kalbala@pacific.edu)

Food studies is a vibrant and thriving field encompassing not only cooking and eating habits but also issues such as health, sustainability, food safety, and animal rights. Scholars in disciplines as diverse as history, anthropology, sociology, literature, and the arts focus on food. The mission of **Rowman & Littlefield Studies in Food and Gastronomy** is to publish the best in food scholarship, harnessing the energy, ideas, and creativity of a wide array of food writers today. This broad line of food-related titles will range from food history, interdisciplinary food studies monographs, general interest series, and popular trade titles to textbooks for students and budding chefs, scholarly cookbooks, and reference works.

Titles in the Series

SMALL BATCH

Pickles, Cheese, Chocolate, Spirits, and the Return of Artisanal Foods

Suzanne Cope

ROWMAN & LITTLEFIELD
Lanham • Boulder • New York • London

Published by Rowman & Littlefield
A wholly owned subsidiary of The Rowman & Littlefield Publishing
Group, Inc.
4501 Forbes Boulevard, Suite 200, Lanham, Maryland 20706
www.rowman.com

16 Carlisle Street, London W1D 3BT, United Kingdom

British Library Cataloguing in Publication Information Available

Library of Congress Cataloging-in-Publication Data

Cope, Suzanne.
Small batch : pickles, cheese, chocolate, spirits, and the return of artisanal foods / Suzanne
Cope.
pages cm—(Rowman & Littlefield studies in food and gastronomy)
Includes bibliographical references and index.
ISBN 978-1-4422-2734-7 (cloth : alk. paper)—ISBN 978-1-4422-2735-4 (electronic)
1. Food industry and trade—United States. 2. Cottage industries—United States. 3. Small
business—United States. I. Title.
HD9321.5.C588 2014
338.4'766400973—dc23

2014011222

∞ ™ The paper used in this publication meets the minimum requirements
of American National Standard for Information Sciences Permanence of
Paper for Printed Library Materials, ANSI/NISO Z39.48-1992.

Printed in the United States of America

CONTENTS

ACKNOWLEDGMENTS

Small Batch grew out of my dual love of true storytelling and food. While it came from a very personal place—I had been practicing home preserving and cheese making and urban gardening and had been devoting more than a reasonable portion of my time and disposable income to "artisanal" foods—I approached this project with the eye of an academic. My goal was to tell the stories of the artisans who graciously gave their time, and often samples of products, without bias. Although I will admit that my bias was inherent, in that I generally shared most producers' worldview regarding foodways. I encourage all readers to seek out these artisans—and others like them—to support these often barely self-sustaining businesses, as I truly believe that their collective presence is an important one in our continually changing food culture.

I must first thank the artisans who shared time and insight, in person, on the phone, or via the Internet. Many are noted by name here, as I used their stories and insights directly, but there are others whose feedback influenced this book less directly. I also want to thank my editor, Ken Albala, whose initial belief in my work led me to such an interesting project. And of course I must thank my family, especially Steve, who was my companion through much of this research and supportive throughout, and Rocco, who was with me from the beginning.

I

ARTISANAL FOODS

From Here to There and Back Again

Did it start with fresh mozzarella, with a handwritten sign that said it had been made that morning and sold, conveniently, just a few tables away from the heirloom tomatoes and bunches of fresh-picked basil? Or maybe it was the jars of pickles—flavored with garlic and a sprig of fresh dill, which I had only ever before seen my grandmother use—that lined the shelf of the new small grocer, who sold mostly locally made goods. I don't recall the first time I truly became aware of the growing offerings of "artisanal" goods that were for sale at the farmers market or specialty shop where I bought much of my food. But once I tasted them, I knew they were different from anything I had eaten in a long time. I finally remembered that mozzarella wasn't just for melting, and could taste of cream and salt and freshly mown grass. Pickles could crunch again—and they could be spicy and tangy and more than vinegar-soaked cucumbers. And I soon had my choice of offerings from a local chocolate maker and other handmade goods made by mostly small, start-up entrepreneurs as well.

I took the inherent narrative of these newly available foods for granted. I assumed that each was made by one person or by a small team, perhaps the same people selling them at the farmers market or whose name graced the label. Because I had been among those who had gotten to know the farmers who sold me much of my produce, I supposed that many of these new goods were made by folks with similar values: quality ingredients, environmental stewardship, perhaps a connection to the land and traditional preparation and preservation methods. And as I got to know some of these producers, I found that by and large I was correct. These small business owners were passionate about their products and had often started their business, in part, because of a desire to work with their hands, to make a product that upheld many of the same values that I held dear with my food sourcing. I found my favorites in my neighborhood, and I sought out others when I traveled farther afield. "Artisanal" goods, these were starting to be called. Sometimes "small batch" or "craft." These descriptions made sense—the mozzarella I often purchased was made by an artisan who learned her craft from her grandfather. The pickles I preferred were certainly made in small batches by one skilled pickler. The chocolate and the spirits and the other products as well exhibited a level of craft—nuanced quality and skill of production—that their mass-produced counterparts lacked.

But then there were more and more of these products, proudly defining themselves as "artisanal," some seen in glossy advertisements and on supermarket shelves and seemingly far from the craftsmen and -women of the farmers market just a few years prior. The idea of an "artisanal food revolution" was being bandied about, and as I read the write-ups and tasted the offerings of many of these new businesses I was soon left wondering what the term meant to those who, I knew, were pouring their heart and soul into every bottle of bourbon, every round of cheese.

Artisanal has become one of the newest buzzwords used to describe food and beverage products like chocolates, cheese, and gin that have been showing up on shelves of specialty shops and on tables at farmers markets within the last decade. Like so many monikers before and since—such as "natural" and "healthy"—the word is not regulated and has since been adopted by behemoth companies like Frito-Lay and Domino's Pizza to describe their (by most accounts decidedly non-) artisanal goods. Why the sudden interest in "artisanal" as a product descriptor?

The word itself comes from the Italian *artigiano*, which means "artisan" or "craftsman," and refers to someone who makes a specific product or provides a specialized service with a high degree of skill, similar to the English word *artisan*. *Artisanal* thus describes, in its broadest sense, a product that is made by an artisan, and most properly, something that is handmade, unique, and of high quality—the very opposite of what we mean by *mass-produced*. Many believe it was the industrialization of the American food system, with its cheap meat and dairy, bland vegetables, and proliferation of processed foods, that sparked a growing revolution back to personal gardens, small farms, and traditional forms of food preparation and preservation. Counterculture and "back-to-the-land" movements from the 1960s through the 1980s, and the rising environmental concerns of the early 2000s led to interest in organic foods and small farms, eventually coining the term *locavore* in 2005, and strengthening a movement toward more local and sustainable food sourcing. But while most can agree that the co-opting of the term by marketers in recent years is causing the true meaning of the word *artisan* to be diluted, the stereotype that has developed of the typical artisanal food maker is also one that these new producers either embrace or reject, and this further complicates the understood definition. I will venture to ask—must there be art in artisanal? Is skill enough? My goal is to begin to paint the landscape of the new artisanal producer today by way of four craft products: pickles, cheese, chocolate, and alcoholic spirits, looking at what *artisanal*, *craft*, and *small batch* really mean and how this new food revolution is reflecting the larger culture—and changing it along the way.

HISTORY FROM SETTLEMENT TO MID-1900s

When the first permanent settlers from Europe arrived in America in the early 1600s, they brought with them provisions including cheese, oatmeal, bread and butter, peas, onions, raisins, pork and beef, cider, beer, and some brandy. They quickly established working farms and learned to hunt and fish from Native Americans, replacing their disappearing stores with rye, maize, wheat, game, and seafood. Those who had livestock had access to milk and milk products, which, predating refrigeration, was often in the form of curds. In fact the preservation of milk in the form of curds and cheese—as well as other methods for preserving foods—was continually being developed at this time to provide nourishment beyond harvest times and for sailors making increasingly long journeys between and around the continents. [1]

In New England by the 1700s, major international trade routes had been established and exotic goods such as spices, sugar, coffee, and chocolate were widely available to supplement the standard boiled meats and vegetables that were popular among the growing colonies. Thus, these "exotics" became a standard part of the average eighteenth-century American diet, along with produce, meats, and dairy products available locally and seasonally. The working- and middle-class Puritans, mainly from England, were not used to much variety in their diet, although the newly wealthy merchant class was increasingly seeking out varied and extensive menus via their access to international trade, adding new selections of meats, sweets, and liquors to their diet. German immigrants came to the New World around this time as well, settling farther south in what is now Pennsylvania, bringing with them cast-iron cooking pots, new kinds of sausages, and vinegar, among other culinary influences. [2] Farther south, large plantations were established that grew mainly tobacco, corn, and grain, as well as other produce for subsistent consumption. Rum from the British West Indies in the Caribbean that was easily imported to the north was harder to come by in the south, and wine and beer was more difficult to keep in the southern heat, so distilled liquors, like corn whiskey, became a popular spirit in an area known for prodigious drinking. [3]

By the 1800s, large urban areas were being established in the north, creating low-income slums with little access to fresh produce. Farm animals, such as dairy cows, were still being kept within city limits, but the conditions were increasingly unsanitary—garbage and animal waste pickup was not yet a city function, and there was little ability to keep foods chilled, leading to spoilage and illness. Outside of prime harvest times, hearty vegetables like cabbage and foods preserved in salt or vinegar provided the main sustenance for urban dwellers.[4] Pickled and preserved produce, done in the home when possible, or available from many smaller local vendors, was the main source of produce beyond what made it to market during harvest. And while cities such as New York still had large working farms within city limits, these were quickly disappearing as the growing population pushed farther out into the Bronx and Brooklyn. In fact, the Bronx wasn't annexed to New York City until the 1890s and was until the early 1900s mainly suburban streets and working farms. Between 1900 and 1930, however, the population of the Bronx increased more than sixfold, and these farms were replaced by apartment buildings and retail stores.[5]

Outside of urban centers, small towns and cities were established as hubs for a mainly agricultural society. Game meat as a primary dietary staple had largely disappeared by this time, and crops such as corn and apples were found to do well from New England to the Virginias. A wide variety of pickling and preservation methods were used, developed by early settlers or brought over from Europe, such as the myriad pickled products important to the Germanic diet. In the south, the disparity of wealth continued to grow, with plantation owners using their growing coffers to expand their diet with goods imported from the north, the Caribbean, and around the world, while slaves and poor whites subsisted on corn, beans, salt pork, and some greens and vegetables grown in season.

Throughout the 1700s and early 1800s there had been continual migration from Europe and, forcibly, Africa, and it was beginning in earnest from Asia. With the advent of steamships, all immigration increased exponentially. And the greater numbers of people from many nationalities brought many new flavors, ingredients, dishes, and preservation techniques to be integrated within the evolving American culture.

Technological advances greatly affected foodways by the mid-1800s as well. The invention of the cast-iron stove meant that open fires were no longer required to cook, and the increasing availability of refrigeration—both in transportation methods and at home— meant that fresh foods could travel far from their place of origin and stay fresh longer for consumption. Meanwhile, with the introduction of Mason and Ball jars in 1858, home preserving finally became safer and more reliable. While pickling and preserving in honey had been used for millennia (and later a similar process was used with sugar), and vinegar and salt brines were common across cultures, the mid-1800s brought increased options for safe food preservation. New technology lowered the price of industrial canning and also expanded the options for home canners. These new methods allowed food to be preserved safely through heat processing that killed harmful (and even beneficial) bacteria, and eliminated contact with air, which also kept spoilage at bay. This development meant that foods didn't have to be overly salted, sugared, or soured to stay safely edible—but it also marked the first step toward safety and uniformity being prized over flavor.[6]

Interesting changes were introduced in recipes as well, with new preserves being made that combined traditional methods from the Old World with newly available ingredients, ethnic influences, and, of course, technology like home canning and refrigeration. Recipe books with directions on preparing various pickles (especially in the Pennsylvania Dutch area where German cuisine popularized many forms of pickling) and preserving seasonal fruits and vegetables greatly expanded the year-round culinary options for those with farms. The late 1800s also brought cheaper sugar to North American and the invention of "milk chocolate," which radically changed how chocolate was eaten, as it was packaged for easy consumption and sold at a price point that quickly made these bars ubiquitous in the diets of Americans from many cultural backgrounds.

These and other technological advances spurred cultural changes. Women in both urban and rural areas were now more likely to purchase staples like pickles, cheese, and canned goods at a store than to make them at home. Fewer homes had personal gardens, and more people were purchasing their beer, liquor, and wine from local distilleries, wineries, and breweries. Further, with the increased popularity of beer (influenced by German immigrants), consumption of liquor was decreasing in the late 1800s. Consumption of all alcoholic beverages dropped sharply during Prohibition, of course, ruining the remaining (legal) breweries and distilleries or driving them into other businesses.

The two World Wars and newly developed methods of food preservation also greatly influenced the movement toward convenience foods. New food safety laws were passed early in the twentieth century that made consumers more trusting of packaged and preserved food, increasing their popularity, and this growing food category coupled with more women in the workforce meant that less time was spent on food preparation. Further, electric household refrigeration became an accepted technology by the early-to-mid 1900s, with these new appliances outpacing sales of iceboxes for the first time in 1930.[7] This helped increase the popularity and accessibility of packaged foods like frozen TV dinners in the 1950s, and these new packaged foods were seen as the wave of the future: modern marvels to be embraced. Around the same time, fast food offerings grew, which made eating out easier and cheaper for more Americans.

The family farm, once an icon of American subsistence living in rural areas, began disappearing in the early 1900s. Many farmers went out of business due to the financial and environmentally hard times of the Great Depression, and increased mechanization allowed fewer people to work greater swaths of land in less time, starting a shift from numerous smaller family farms to fewer larger farms.[8] This trend also transformed farms from those that grew a variety of produce to large businesses that tended to specialize in the commodity markets of grain, corn, and soybeans. Government subsidies, created during the Great Depression to help struggling smaller farms, were now going to larger farms that had a financial interest in increasing the market for their products, which spurred research that led to the proliferation of soybean oil and corn syrup in so many mass-produced food items today. The agricultural trends toward monoculture, along with the rise of these mass produced foods, helped push culinary trends toward flavor homogenization. After the rationing of the World War II, which was successful in feeding many people food of uniform quality and safety, cultural shifts found these values to be the highest priority, rather than flavor.[9] Common household activities from a generation prior, such as canning, pickling, and fresh cheese making, were becoming increasingly rare in urban and suburban homes, and the versions of these products that could be most readily purchased were mass-produced, lacking many of the variations that had been brought over from the Old World or created in America through necessity in the previous century or more.

ARTISANAL FOOD NARRATIVES IN POSTWAR AMERICA

This is not to say that what we might now call "artisanal" pickles, cheese, and other products had completely disappeared from American culture after the vast cultural changes that occurred by mid-century. Rather, they were still present in small pockets, persisting mainly as family knowledge and ritual passed down through the generations. My own family was one that passed on such knowledge. On my father's side, my grandmother was brought up in Pennsylvania Dutch country on a family dairy farm. That farm, like so many, was sold to a larger competitor, and my grandmother married my grandfather, who worked in a lumber mill—his lack of a sense of smell kept him out of World War II. They eventually bought a few acres outside of a small town in western New York, and there they kept a large garden, which was intended to provide the bulk of the family's produce throughout the year. Thus, Grandma, with the help of her daughters, pickled, jellied, jammed, and preserved so that nothing was wasted from their harvest, which was necessary to feed her five children while my grandfather sought to start his own construction business. When my grandfather's company was finally a bit more financially stable, they could buy mayonnaise and Jell-O and lunch meat to supplement their many canned foods. By the time my father was a teen, canning had become more an expression of family culture—Pennsylvania Dutch, mixed with "modern" American convenience.

Today, my grandma and aunt continue to preserve bounty from the shrinking garden, sometimes buying produce from a neighbor to supplement what is needed for a favorite recipe. The number of jars each year has dwindled, and this Christmas I received a few for a present, indicating a shift in thinking about the role of canning in our family's diet toward a homemade symbol of love. My grandmother never taught me to can. She did eventually pass down her recipes, albeit annotated with tips and edits that could only be learned by canning *with* my grandma, and not attempting to decipher her jagged writing from five hundred miles away. Instead, I taught myself in the early 2000s, caught up like others in what would soon be coined the locavore movement. The recipes of hers that I possess include many variations of pickles, and some jams, sauces, and fruits that could be eaten alone in their syrup or made into pies, few of which I have actually made. It doesn't make sense for me to preserve quarts of peaches, halved and doused in sugar, when I know I will never eat them and I rarely bake. Canning, once a subsistence necessity, is now, perhaps as with my grandmother, a hobby. The preserves shelf in her basement is filled with jars marked simply with years, some going back a decade or more—the act of doing, of preserving the traditions as well as the food itself, has superseded its necessity.

My mother's Italian American family demonstrates a similar, but not identical, narrative—one of the newer immigrant, who experienced the tension between assimilation and cultural pride. My Nani was born in the United States but moved back to Italy when she was young. When she was six, the family returned to the States and settled in western New York, where she grew up in a tight-knit Italian American community in a small city on the shores of Lake Erie. From the time when my Nani was young through the decades when my mother was growing up, there were local butchers, *latterias*, bakers, and the like who made many of the artisanal foods that local women didn't make in the home. Nani's mother, and then Nani, made her own pickles and preserves, eventually employing my mother to help, being the only daughter. Fresh cheese, specialty salumi, and bread, among other items were bought from local Italian immigrant shopkeepers. These stores mostly disappeared as my mother grew older, and now none remain in the area where I also was raised. Despite the strong Italian American culture in which I grew up, I never had fresh mozzarella until I was an adult. My Nani didn't need to learn—or maybe she just didn't feel the desire—to make these Italian artisanal goods because a satisfactory alternative could be found at the grocery store. This convenience was part of the *abbondanza* of the New World. She did continue to can her own tomatoes and make a handful of other preserves, including fermented local peach "brandy"—most, but not all, of which had reasonable facsimiles at the local store. Maybe she did it as a yearly ritual that helped her stay close to her Italian culture, or maybe because she found certain flavors superior or preferable to the mass-produced version.

Whatever the reason, the knowledge ended with her generation, for while my mother helped her when she was young, the detailed recipes and methodology for preserving weren't passed down and died with her when I was in high school. Cans of tomatoes and mass-produced jars of Italian pickles and shrink-wrapped "dry"— not fresh in their own liquid—balls of mozzarella were the norm that I grew up with, although for a brief time when I was young, I do remember fresh "farmer's cheese" on the table every Sunday, and the occasional fluffy, salty ricotta, rather than the dense bland version, that was sometimes fed to me with a spoon. Did Nani make it, or maybe one of her older sisters, or was it purchased at one of the last Italian groceries in town? Those same fresh flavors jogged my memory as I tasted them again as an adult, as I taught myself to make fresh cheese. Like many new home cheese makers, I found it a surprisingly easy process that produced such a superior flavor. At first I wondered why Nani embraced the supermarket brands. And then I remembered how much she worked—as the office manager of the airport she and my grandfather opened after World War II, and the retail job she had on nights and weekends before the business was self-sustaining. Why would she take the time?

And I thought of the boxes of recipes that I sorted through when we cleaned out her house, long after Nani was gone. I was looking for the lost Italian-influenced recipes of my childhood, but instead found newspaper clippings of desserts made with pudding mix and Cool Whip and casseroles made with Campbell's soup or packages of seasonings. I didn't remember those dishes ever on our Sunday family dinner table, but, as my mother explained, these were the meals Nani thought she should be making to help her family become more American, meals that made occasional appearances for dinner when my mother was young. She refused to teach her children Italian, believing that assimilation was best for her children, would give them the best opportunities in the New World: this was the classic immigrant narrative. I later realized that perhaps I was seeking out these artisanal foods—these "authentic" versions of products I may never have tasted but thought certainly my Nani had when she was young—to connect to a woman who died when I was still a young teen. And I was not the only one who was reviving these crafts for similar reasons, as other second- and third-generation immigrants have given the same narrative of turning to the food of their heritage in part to reclaim their identity. [10]

Thus, a connection to subsistence living has kept some of these crafts alive for subsequent generations—whether directly or through a modern desire to revive the past. For others, a continuance or revival of methodologies for making ethnic or nostalgic foods was another way that this knowledge was passed along to the present generation, even if for personal—and not for commercial—consumption. But in using both sides of my family as brief, and admittedly not entirely representative, case studies, it is clear that not all knowledge was preserved, and the path for keeping these recipes alive is far from obvious. While I now know how to make mozzarella cheese—knowledge that was reintroduced to my family narrative and not passed down from previous generations—I still usually purchase it from the new "artisanal" purveyors in my neighborhood, both new to this business, but both inspired by the cheese-making heritage of their ancestors. Will making cheese be part of the next generation's food heritage? And will these artisans be here to stay when my infant son begins to source his own meals?

Certainly it was not just the spotty continuance of ethnic or "American" traditions or frugal necessity that helped pass long the knowledge of these food crafts for future generations. Food choices have had a long history in America of aligning with social consciousness. In the early 1900s, the new trend toward processed food was critiqued by the Progressives as indicative of the growing power of industry as well as the apparent gulf between the haves and have-nots, especially evident in the densely populated urban slums that were also expanding during this time of mass immigration and urbanization. In subsequent eras as well, a desire for more environmentally friendly food choices reflected the perceived destruction of the natural world through the use of nuclear weapons and destructive agents like napalm. Yet, beyond the obvious connection between political movements and food sourcing, food has also long been a springboard for consciousness raising. During tumultuous times, when change seemed hard to come by on systematic or political levels, food was seen as an arena where one could support a certain worldview three times a day. Thus choices that supported a nonindustrialized, nonconformist food system were soon a telltale sign of what has been dubbed the "counter-cuisine" movement of the 1960s and 1970s—brown rice and other "natural" dishes, as well as homegrown produce, meat, eggs, dairy, and other products were soon associated with "hippies" and their anti-establishment politics.[11]

At the same time, ethnic cuisine was also becoming more popular due to a new surge in immigration, increasingly accessible flights to various locales around the world, and the popularization of media, such as television and movies, that both informed about and romanticized the foods of certain other cultures. French food had long been seen as a sophisticated cuisine, edible symbols of class and worldliness. However, other cuisines, such as Italian food, considered in the early twentieth century to be odiferous and lower class, was suddenly thrust into the culinary limelight through newly popular Italian American foods like pizza and fettuccine Alfredo as well as the romantic idea of Rome presented in the movie *Roman Holiday*. With Pan Am's first flight from New York to Rome in 1958, Americans soon became interested in the fresh, seasonal, and traditionally made foods available in Italy—a story that was repeated with other ethnic foods that were becoming increasingly available and accepted.[12] But the Italian food narrative is particularly compelling, as many of their food traditions were particularly preserved within American culture well into the mid-twentieth century, and these traditions often focused on handcrafted, "artisanal" food that people of many backgrounds came to appreciate and that also influenced the counter-cuisine and modern artisanal food movements.[13]

FROM HIPPIES TO HIPSTERS

As might be evident by their moniker, the "hippies" of the counter-cuisine movement were considered the cool, sophisticated, fashionable, mostly younger generation—those who were setting the trends that influenced the larger culture. While the origin of the word "hip" is debated—some claim it came via slaves from Africa, others note its first arrival in English around the turn of the twentieth century[14]—it has been used in various generations to describe young, edgy trendsetters, starting with the "hipsters" or "hep cats" of the Beatnik era, the "hippies" of the 1960s and 1970s, and in current usage, the (neo) "hipsters" of modern day. It was during the hippy era that "hip" culture was also first strongly correlated with food preferences, specifically the counter-cuisine movement, as members saw food choices as a way to express their political and social leanings three times a day. And it stands to reason that some of these hippies would start businesses to cater to others who shared their values. Food scholar Warren Belasco dubbed these folks "hip entrepreneurs" and noted, "Historically bohemian businesses have performed vital functions as safe havens for industrious nonconformists and as advanced testing stations for larger-scale corporate involvement."[15] Essentially they created a bridge between the nonconformists and the establishment. Many of these businesses took the form of restaurants and food co-ops, with the sometimes conflicting dual roles of spreading their beliefs surrounding thoughtful food sourcing and consumption, and being a viable enterprise.[16] Artisanal food producers were not common among the hip businesses of this era. I believe this was in part because the movement's goal was to promote healthier eating and to make this counter-cuisine more accessible through low prices and by demonstrating that these crafts could be done by "anyone." Also the cost of making artisanal goods for retail would not produce a savory business model for consumers whose worldview involved opting out of a traditional capitalist economy.

This is not to say that there was not a strong interest in handcrafting food. Rather, the focus shifted to the process more than the end product. The counter-cuisine movement believed that "it was in their abuse of the process . . . that most manufacturers went astray," and that "the welfare of the migrant farmers, animals, slaughterhouse workers, and supermarket clerks mattered little" to mainstream America and the industries that were serving them.[17] This new craft movement created a resurgent interest in traditional methods of preservation and preparation. A trend toward "slowing down" to understand how foods were made, and utilizing traditional methods of doing so, was emphasized as a way to subvert the national trend toward fast convenience foods, while also being healthier, calmer, and closer to nature—a movement that was crystallized in the "Slow Food" movement that began in Italy in 1986 and eventually spread around the world.

In the 1980s, some of the trendsetting elements of the hippy movement that translated to larger cultural acceptance included the interest in "natural" and healthy foods, albeit less for apocalyptic fears and anticorporate reasons than for overall lifestyle preferences. As the hippy movement declined, the trends toward a "casually hip" lifestyle took its place—one that shared some "pastoral" and nostalgic values of the hippy generation, but embraced other more modern sensibilities in relationships, jobs, and technology.[18] However, not everyone went mainstream with their healthy food preferences.

There was still a more fringe demographic that began a resurgent interest in specialty cheeses, gardening, and small-farm production, which led to a "back-to-the-land" movement.[19] That movement produced some of the first rumblings of the small-farm and artisanal cheese fervor that continued to grow over the next few decades. International travel also hastened the shifting of cultural tastes, with sophisticated eaters returning from their trips interested in increasingly diversified flavors and more in touch with the traditional preparation and preservation methods that they encountered in countries like Italy and France, which had not moved as quickly toward mass production of popular foods as the United States. During this time, there was also a rise in demand for "organic" foods, which finally became more accepted and were noted by the FDA as being a viable, modern form of produce production—an about-face from earlier assessments.[20]

The larger cultural shift in the 1980s also saw an integration of some of the hippy values into the cultural mainstream. The remaining small, hip food businesses were being seen as rather quaint and even admirable, evidence that the counterculture could work with and within the mainstream.[21] Further, trend-watchers noted that "the press's sympathy for small business was the enduring value of 'small-town pastoralism'—and affection for craftsmanship, villages, and country traditions," nostalgia, "human-scale" productions, and a search for "control in a modern urban-industrial world."[22] However, these trends were seen more often in higher-income households. A 1975 study found that the wealthiest quartile of American households were concerned with buying "healthy" foods—a statistic that stayed consistent through the 1980s. Further, higher-income households were doing more canning in 1976 than in 1964, while the poor were doing less, suggesting a shift toward canning for reasons other than cost savings.[23]

It was, however, the search for cost savings that in some ways defined the food landscape of the 1980s and into the 1990s, despite consumers' seeming demand for "fresh" and "natural" options. Belasco quotes a taste researcher telling *Consumer Reports* in 1980 that "there is a movement afoot to return to simplicity in all aspects of life," while another food researcher asserts that the popularity of "natural" food products is a movement by consumers away from industrialization, and that "nostalgia" was a popular marketing strategy. [24] Rather than the food industry offering truly fresh foods, however, they began labeling and marketing relatively cheap processed foods as "natural" and "healthy." These mistruths in marketing happily fooled many consumers, who were thrilled to be able to buy seemingly healthy, tasty, and convenient prepackaged foods for a low price. And companies that were once classically artisanal were now in the forefront of products marketed as healthy, nostalgic, and natural—but in their mass-produced form. [25]

Yet, by the end of the 1980s, there were some rumblings of change. Mostly upper-income consumers didn't fall for these mass-marketed claims of health. They were more likely to eat a variety of produce (not just iceberg lettuce, the most commonly consumed green in a survey conducted in the 1980s) and even have personal vegetable gardens. Also, Belasco notes, there was wider availability and mainstream acceptance of once "hippy" foods like tofu, whole grains, and yogurt, as well as a growing interest in organic farming techniques and new university programs in "sustainable agriculture." [26]

As food culture moved toward the 1990s and imminently the turn of the millennium, predictions about the future of food were asserted by a broad swath of "experts" and others. Yet, despite the vision purported for this decade a generation earlier, the impending new millennium instigated revisiting predictions for the future of food. Meal "pills" and Jetson-esque food machines were not the reality, nor were they necessarily desired. Instead, aided in part by better education and more media coverage, there was a shift by the mid-1990s back toward (actual, not packaged versions of) nostalgic foods, fresh vegetables, small farms, and traditional cooking. After all, this decade saw the birth of the Food Network, created to inspire home cooks, and its popularity continues to rise. Further, the number of farmers markets began to grow. In fact, since the U.S. Department of Agriculture (USDA) began publishing the National Farmers Market Directory in 1994, the number of farmers markets have more than quadrupled nationally, with a steady trend upward since records were kept.[27] With these new markets came new customers interested in local produce and products made from ingredients—and by people—they felt they could trust. In addition, these markets provided a literal marketplace where small and start-up businesses could sell their products and start to gain customers relatively easily (with no need to deal with distributors or middlemen) and for a low cost. The beginnings of this new craft revolution were most apparent in the rise of craft brewing and the increasing availability of farmstead and artisanal cheeses being made in America.

But perhaps even more telling was the revamp of Disney World's Tomorrowland in the late 1990s. As head Disney imaginer Brian Ferren noted about these changes, "[the new] middle-class-American sensibilities [include] the house with a lawn, real plants a white picket fence, a recycling plant down the road, a house with cool moldings. Events like the explosion at Chernobyl and Three Mile Island diffused the sense of an ideal vision of the future as clockwork."[28] The new vision of food was a mix of nostalgia with skeptical modernism. As Belasco explained, there was a nod toward kitsch with many markers of "America's 'browning'—paving stones, planters of edible organic fruit, more Garden of Eden than Mission to Mars."[29] But, as Disney chairman Michael Eisner said, "We want to go back to the land, as long as the land is devoid of the kind of hardscrabble mongrels who used to live in the west. We want to be cable ready. We want good take-out. We want aroma-therapeutic herb gardens and a nearby trout stream where nothing ever dies."[30] The end of the 1990s and beginning of the 2000s saw a swing back toward this pastoral view of the past, embracing family traditions and heritage, and renegotiating a relationship with the land via farms and farmers markets.

This cultural shift was apparent in a small but influential portion of the population into the new millennium. The aughts also saw an increase in demand for unique, specialty foods in many areas, from cheese to charcuterie to sauces, with many finding an easy way to market their goods on the Internet and at the new farmers markets and specialty stores that arose to fill this demand. Culinary culture also saw rising popularization of the Italian Slow Food movement that made its way to the United States and over 150 counties around the world, calling for a return to traditional and sustainable food sourcing and preparation. Then, as unemployment rose and corporate jobs became vilified by some, small businesses focused on food rose as well. These businesses ran the gamut from food trucks serving mostly urban areas to smaller-scale organic farms to specialty foods like high-end cupcakes. Many of these businesses were envisioned to cater to the new "foodie" culture that, with more disposable income, sought increasingly unique or exotic products and dishes to satisfy their adventurous tastes.

As the first rumblings of the 2007 recession were being felt, the interest in family gardens, small-scale farming, preserving, and cheese making grew; farmers markets proliferated; and the term *locavore* was coined. By 2007 the term *locavore*—defined as one who sources food locally and sustainably—was the *Oxford American Dictionary* "word of the year," and the prevalence of farmers markets in the United States continued to grow exponentially. Add to this the recession that began around this time, when unemployment shot up. People looking to cut costs started to grow their own food—in fact sales of seeds spiked in 2007 and the National Gardening Association said that more than forty-three million households grew their own food in 2009, an increase of 19 percent from the year before.[31] Now, not only do we have more households who harvest their own produce and are, presumably, looking for ways to preserve their bounty, but also more people looking for work. In addition, there was an increase in food-based businesses starting up;[32] a greater cultural interest in homemade, local, and high-quality food products;[33] and more people trying traditional preserving and preparation methods in their home.

The focus on craft and the larger value system associated with this movement is being echoed today with the mostly twenty- and thirty-something modern hipsters—or neo-hipsters as they should more accurately be known—who began the new artisanal food movement with their renewed interest in canning, curing, distilling, gardening, fermenting, and the like. These new counter-cuisinists are seeking to reconnect with the past, take control of their own economic future, and do so with an edible (or potable) handicraft. Many of these new entrepreneurs see education as part of their mission, but also have their eye on financial success more than the previous generation. Perhaps more jaded than the original counter-cuisinists, these new artisans don't profess to be trying to change the world through their products, but rather just to make a difference, one handcrafted product at a time. While they are also concerned with environmental sustainability, healthfulness (more often by rejection of processed foods and embracing organic ingredients), and (often) worker's rights—and still consider the process of the utmost importance—the end product for this new generation of craftspeople is also greatly prized. What they produce must justify the high prices they are demanding and provide a living for the artisans themselves. Thus, they are not opting out of the present commercial landscape but seeking ways to integrate their values and the new counter-cuisine into the existing economy.

In particular, it is entrepreneurs who have gravitated toward these traditional methods of food and drink preparation and preservation and sought to return to the "small batch" or "artisanal" ethos of a century ago. This can be seen prominently in the recent rise of artisanal cheese, pickle, chocolate, and alcoholic spirits makers, among other products. The dominant narrative in each of these industries is a desire to reclaim what the makers believe is the original, traditional, or true essence of the product—and its endless variations—because of the vast dominance of mass production that each product had endured over the course of the twentieth and early twenty-first century. Few other products have retained their popularity yet also had their traditional character diluted so much as these four. And with few exceptions, no others have seen the resurgence in small businesses passionate about bringing back a product's original essence and moving forward in new and interesting ways. While seemingly disparate endeavors, the stories of the (mostly) new artisans focused on pickles, cheese, chocolate, and liquor share many values in common and help to define the new rise in artisanal food culture.

With this increase in interest in "local" foods came the inevitable adoption of romanticized narratives by food marketers. Labels with images of farmhouses or green fields graced junk food containers, and "local" farmers who provided raw ingredients for everything from potato chips to ice cream were now front and center in many advertising campaigns. Food had new storied identities; suddenly, it seemed, everyone wanted to know the farmer who grew their potatoes or wheat or soybeans (and of course, many of these farmers were in fact part of large companies, and not exactly the overall-wearing back-to-the-landers that the ad campaigns made them appear). And when local food began to be critiqued for its narrow focus on "food miles," for many this distinction was no longer good enough. Marketers began to notice that some of the "artisanal" pickles or jams from the farmers market were now selling in smaller grocery stores or some regional or specialty chains like Whole Foods—and for many times more than their mass-produced counterparts. During the recession that was caused, many believe, by greedy corporations, consumers preferred to give their money to small start-ups, craftspeople whose stories they also wanted to know, much like those of the farmers a few years prior. This growing food revolution was also catering to the new "foodie" culture— those who were inspired by the Food Network and wanted more complicated techniques, new and interesting flavor profiles, or food with a story—people for whom traditional fare was not adventurous enough, or did not reflect their own personality.

This renewed interest in traditional and "natural" foods and preparation and preservation methods mirrors in many ways the rise of the original counter-cuisine in the late 1960s and early 1970s, when "hippies" and "hip businesses" embraced foods that represented a worldview of living closer to the land and thoughtfully sourced raw ingredients, and farther from the mass-produced, industrial-owned, and chemical-laden foods that were so prevalent in the American diet. In part this was a reaction to the actual or perceived imminent threat of recession, but also to the more metaphoric causes or representations of the economic downturn: big business, which was controversially "bailed out," environmental concerns about greenhouse gases causing both floods and droughts and threatening food supplies around the world, as well as pesticides, natural resource mining, and other industrial efforts that were poisoning the soil and water.

A number of people—particularly educated, middle-class twenty- and thirty-somethings—similar to the demographic that embraced the hippy movement forty years earlier—found renewed interest in gardening, canning, pickling, cheese making, distilling, and other traditional activities. Yet many were unsatisfied with simply re-creating traditional foods and sought to revive even more obscure crafts, such as chocolate making, or to push these traditional methods and recipes to new and creative places, reflecting their more global, individualist, and often environmentally conscious worldview. These new hip entrepreneurs are not so interested in their parents' (or grandparents') cooperative business or living models, and a great number are choosing to stay in the city, versus moving off the grid (although there are those from this generation who do embrace communal living and working, and the number of young farmers working small farms is on the rise).

Thus many of the new food entrepreneurs are often called "hipsters," fond of facial hair and tattoos, who wear retro plaid shirts, pressed selvage denim or printed dresses that might be found on a particularly well-groomed member of the working class in the 1950s, and may or may not have a love of old-timey Americana music, hand-hewn furniture, and knitting, yet they are perhaps more worldly and business-minded than their hippy predecessors. Like the hippies before them, there are many who share some but not all of these sensibilities. Some are quintessentially modern hipster but bristle at the term, and others strive to embrace this neo-hipsterism but have a worldview that doesn't quite square with this appreciation of the old, except in a completely modern way. I'll admit that I don't quite consider myself a hipster, but by many accounts others might consider me one—I have an urban garden, occasionally make my own pickles, cheese, and preserves; I prefer a skinny, dark denim jean, and am married to a musician who plays the mandolin and banjo. My baby only eats organic food, most of which I make myself. I don't care much for labels, although it is hard to write about this new artisanal food revolution without recognizing the role of "modern hipsters" as a representative group, like the hippies were before them.

However, with the hipster lifestyle becoming more intertwined with the mainstream, the initial counterculture message becomes obscured. So while the hipster culture does appear to be the modern incarnation of the counter-cuisine movement, some are left asking: "What's a radical to eat?" As scholar Mark Engler notes, "Organic farming has been hijacked by big business. Local food can have a larger footprint than products shipped in from overseas. Fair trade doesn't address the real concern of farmers in the global south. . . . [T]he food movement has moved from the countercultural fringe to become a mainstream phenomenon."[34] Has the artisanal food movement gone mainstream?

DEFINING THE CULTURAL PHENOMENON OF ARTISANAL

There is no debate that *artisanal* has become the new marketing buzzword, supposedly denoting high quality, a personal connection to the maker, and a connection to a pastoral past. And, like similar terms before it, the use of *artisanal* is at times sincere and many other times misleading. However, while *local* has a very specific meaning (although it has grown to take on a host of other values, like sustainable and earth friendly), *artisanal* can be seen becoming diluted, the way that the term *natural* did decades ago. What makes a product artisanal? And, learning from some of the backlash from local, are there other values associated with *artisanal* beyond its literal definition?

Thus, as a sometime member of this neo-hipster crowd, I became well-versed enough in the new embracing of the term *artisanal* to describe this renewed interest in traditional food preservation and preparation methods, among other crafts. In the mid-aughts I was among those who had been using their grandmothers' canning and pickling recipes for years, while also striving to come up with new and adventurous takes on these classics. I wanted to learn how to make from scratch most of the foods I ate, and do so through the most sustainable practices possible. What drew me to this was a concern about the environment, yes, but more immediately a concern about what I was ingesting. I also was seeking to reconnect with my heritage, and found that I could do so while still being creative if I used food as a medium. I also loved *good* food—for example, the more styles of cheeses I learned about and tried, the more I became a discerning consumer. The same thing happened with chocolate and spirits and even pickles. I could learn to taste the nuances of quality and craft—which sometimes were more pronounced than nuanced. But I also learned that it was more than just flavor that drew me toward my favorites. It was the connection I had to the story behind the product—the artisan and technique and raw ingredients. And as the "artisanal" food industry grew, I saw more and more pickles at the farmers market or on the shelf at my local grocery. There were even more quality American cheeses to try, next to the many revered styles of well-crafted European offerings. I embraced local food and the larger philosophy behind locavorism and clearly saw the connection between that value system and these new artisanal food businesses. Some were acquaintances, and I knew of more than one that fit the clichéd beginning of a product made for friends and family in one's kitchen and got such rave reviews that the artisan decided to branch out to the farmers market, then the local grocery, with, perhaps, a growth trajectory from there.

Then a small-batch chocolate maker moved in up the street, and suddenly I was reimaging my own locavore propensities in a global context. And as more food businesses entered my radar I saw that many had even better products or smarter business plans or creative takes on an old favorite. And, almost without fail, there was some clear connection to the artisan as a person, to the methodology as integral to the product itself. No more did I—or many people like myself—eat *just* a pickle. Rather, the pickles I ate were ones either I made, or a friend made, or I bought from the person who made them, or at least I knew that the recipe was inspired by the craftsman's grandmother, or some other bit of personal trivia connecting me to what I was ingesting. My pickle now came with a story. And it was a good pickle—a better pickle than I had ever eaten perhaps, except for my grandmother's own. The people I met were increasingly committed to their craft, the process behind making their product, but also to where this product fits into the world they live in, both locally and globally. This was a worldview I had come to believe in and practice to the degree I could. But I also knew I was just seeing a small slice of this artisanal revolution from my home in Somerville, Massachusetts, and then a larger slice as the artisanal revolution grew and I moved to Brooklyn, which many claim is the revolution's epicenter.

And as a scholar of narrative—of storytelling—I wanted to see how these artisans' stories helped to identify them and this growing movement. The term *artisanal* was increasingly being used to describe everything from Tostitos to fast food hamburger buns; the sales of the former are so strong that the company plans on introducing more products to the line.[35] Why were these goods so popular, even to those outside of the core "hipster" market? And what was the definition of this term that seemed to have a clear meaning a few years ago but that has been diluted and co-opted by those seeking to have a nostalgic or (counter-) cultural "story" behind their product but little true tradition or quality. "Artisanal" goods (in the truest sense of the term) for sale in the United States have been on the rise, and appear to be poised to keep—and likely grow—a percentage of the market share. But what, exactly, does *artisanal* mean when it comes to food products? And when, if ever, does an artisanal product cease to be one, based upon ingredients, quantity produced, or production method? What are the definitions and implications of other, similar words, like *craft*, *small batch*, and *terroir*, that are used to indicate quality or history or tradition when applied to edible and potable goods in the United States?

From late 2012 to early 2014 I sought the stories of more than fifty mostly new artisans from the industries of cheese, chocolate, pickles, and alcoholic spirits, asking them to identify their business philosophy, how they define artisanal goods, and the larger narrative behind their influences and challenges. I found many similarities among these producers that help to paint the landscape of what is happening in these four industries today, as well as in general in this new food revolution. I told everyone that I am not a journalist, but rather a scholar and a storyteller. I was not interested in critiquing, but simply uncovering the nuances of these individual narratives, seeking to answer these questions while asking new ones, helping our rapidly changing marketplace gain a greater understanding of what "artisanal" is and who these artisans are, while trying to define the word in our modern context and starting to explain what is not just an industry, but rather a cultural phenomenon.

2

PICKLES

Artisans, Craftsmen, and Hip Entrepreneurs

I could smell the vinegar before I even walked into the combined store and production space of the Brooklyn Brine pickle company, located on an industrial block in the borough not far from the infamously toxic Gowanus Canal. The entire place was only about the width of a two-car garage and reached back perhaps another fifty feet. The retail area, only a few months old, consisted of a sliver of shelf and a refrigerator, with a rough-hewn wooden counter and a cash register. Behind the counter a blackboard listed offerings and prices, and a few wire racks held unlabeled jars full of various pickled produce. In the production space were a walk-in cooler; palettes of boxes packed, presumably, with pickles; a few kegs of beer (for a pickle collaboration with Dogfish Head Brewery, I was told); and a kitchen work area where I could see two rubber-gloved workers hand-packing jars with cucumbers not far from the machine that screwed on the jar lids one at a time.

Shamus Jones, the tattooed, fast-talking founder of Brooklyn Brine, explained how he had started a few years ago with little more than a dream, making use of the commercial kitchens of New York

City chef friends in the late-night hours after their restaurants closed. Brooklyn Brine had been growing exponentially, he explained. Yet, as I looked around, I felt very much in the space of an artisan—a commercial enterprise, but a small-batch purveyor nonetheless. Sure, Shamus wasn't still packing his own jars, but he explained to me that he and a few trusted employees were now free to spend time developing new products, and he pointed me toward the small refrigerator that held lacto-fermented pickles, super-small-batch creations sold only in this space, and made out of respect for the process, seasonal ingredients, and culinary daring. He just loved pickles, he explained. And he had found a great team that shared his love. They were making a go of it—a small pickle maker who could provide a living wage for himself and a few others just by practicing his craft. The space seemed quaint to me, a stepping-stone to something bigger perhaps, or maybe just the right size for a smallish but growing pickle purveyor like Brooklyn Brine. It certainly wasn't fancy, and though the neighborhood bordered post-hipster Park Slope, it was far from any promise of foot traffic. I was excited for Shamus, rooting for him and his pickles, which I had seen on the shelves of Whole Foods and in specialty stores in the New York and Boston areas.

And then Shamus told me that he was distributed around the United States and sold his pickles in five other countries. He had been growing at 40 percent a year since 2009 and was poised to keep expanding. He was a big boy in the world of small batch—a true success story. Was he still "artisanal"? When did small batch turn into big batch? I was amazed at what he could produce in such a small space, and by all accounts everything was done by hand. Maybe no longer Shamus's hand, but by the hands of a few employees that for the most part shared a penchant for tattoos and dark-framed glasses.

Shamus is in no way apologetic about his growth—and he notes that he retains full control over every aspect of his pickle production, from development to packing. He has stayed as true to his vision as possible, considering his exponential growth, and he has mutually beneficial relationships with farmers who supply him quality produce at a fair price. Thus, his story is representative of the new artisanal food start-up: Pickles have captured the imagination of both the craftspeople and the consumers as the quintessential small-batch food business. And Jones's is the very best success story, but also begs the question of what a food artisan or craftsman is, and when (if at all) does a small-batch food company cease being one.

BUT FIRST, WHAT ARE PICKLES?

While many people think of cucumbers swimming in a salty, acidic bath when they think of pickles, pickling is defined as a process that preserves food in an acidic medium, like vinegar or a brine (defined as a solution of salt and water that can encourage the growth of good bacteria). Pickled foods include various produce (which are most often preserved in a "brine" of their own liquid)—and even fish and meat. Pickling was developed independently across many cultures around the world; there is evidence of various brine and vinegar preservation techniques used in ancient Rome, Egypt, China, and Greece. Typically it is the dill spear or bread-and-butter chip that Americans think of—and generally buy—when considering pickles, but technically, foods from sauerkraut to kimchi to fermented vegetable slaws are considered pickled. Thus, the varieties of pickles made in America today are as numerous as the foodways from which they came.

These two variations of pickling—fermenting and brining—are not mutually exclusive, however. Vinegar itself is actually made through fermentation: a simple organic process of making an alcoholic brew from grapes, fruit, potatoes, or grains (think wine, vodka, beer, or liquor) and allowing the fermenting process to go unchecked, during which acetobacter transforms the alcohol into acetic acid and vinegar is produced. In fact the term *vinegar* comes from the French—*vin aiger*—or sour wine. This "living" vinegar produces a living symbiotic colony (scoby), unlike the distilled vinegar that is generally purchased at the supermarket, which creates a

Figure 2.1. Freshly packed jars at Brooklyn Brine. Photo by the author.

sterile environment that is so acidic that bacteria can't grow, thus prohibiting food from spoiling. Brine—or salted liquid, usually water—can also provide a hospitable environment, as vinegar does, either by promoting the growth of healthy bacteria or, depending on the pH, prohibiting the growth of all bacteria, good and bad. However, to achieve the same level of shelf-stable preservation without fermentation, the pickle would be so salty as to require first soaking it in water to make it edible. Before home canning and industrial methods of heat pasteurizing were invented, all non-fermented pickles were preserved in an environment that was highly acidic so that decomposition and sickness-inducing bacteria were held at bay. After home canning methods and refrigeration became available, however, making a highly acidic environment no longer necessary for food safety, techniques for preservation could move toward flavor enhancement.

Fermentation as a method for preserving food and enhancing flavor also has a long history of being developed across many cultures since ancient times. There are multiple processes that are considered fermentation, but regarding pickles, the more specific process of *lacto*-fermentation is supported by a brine most often made from the naturally occurring liquid from the produce itself, creating an environment that supports the growth of "good" lacto-bacteria that crowds out the bad bacteria and keeps the pickles safe, edible, and often quite delicious. Fermented pickling works in a similar way to vinegar-based pickling, only it is this naturally occurring acidification process (rather than the introduction of vinegar) that keeps illness and decay at bay through the nurturing of this good lacto-bacteria. Many foods that the average American encounters frequently have been lacto-fermented: aged cheeses, yogurt, sauerkraut, and some cured meats. Many of these shelf-stable fermented foods today have also been heat pasteurized, however—think canned or jarred sauerkraut or pasteurized yogurt with live cultures "added" rather than grown. Like yogurt, fermented pickled produce, which is the only form we will be discussing in detail here, also have beneficial cultures that can aid in digestion and promote gut health. However, lacto-fermented pickles have not yet been promoted widely as the "health" food that they were once considered to be. Fermentation is now most often used as a process to improve flavor or texture and not for preservation or health, although this is changing, especially on the West Coast. Some of the most common fermented pickles—such as kimchi and sauerkraut—while relatively widely available, are also still relegated to the realm of exotic or ethnic foods, and most are heat pasteurized to help make them shelf stable, which kills those naturally occurring cultures and stops the fermentation process.

However, it wasn't so long ago that many of the most commonly consumed pickles were fermented. That's what was happening in those big pickle barrels in the small-town grocery or sold as sours or half sours (indicating how long they had been fermented) along the sidewalk in New York City by the cuke: they were being preserved through these probiotic "live and active" cultures. Pickle barrels have all but disappeared, and the majority of modern pickle eaters consume fresh-packed or other heat-preserved pickles, rather than fermented, and often for nostalgic reasons or for taste. However, the healthfulness claims of pickles and the availability of "live" lacto-fermented pickles is increasing, along with the popularity of probi-otics, as a health food. These issues have made for a marked differ-ence among the influences and challenges of the fermented and non-fermented artisanal picklers today.

A (VERY) BRIEF HISTORY OF PICKLES IN AMERICA

Pickling made its way to America first in the 1500s via the earliest English settlers, who brought vinegar pickling of eggs, vegetables, nuts, fruits, and other foods, as a popular preservation method. Soon thereafter, the Dutch brought their passion for pickling to the New World, and by the late 1600s, Dutch immigrants started vast cucum-bers farms across what is now Brooklyn and established a concen-tration of commercial picklers in New York City. The common Dutch style of pickling was to ferment cucumbers in a barrel filled with brine, creating a classic "sour" pickle. These were sold, often individually, from small shops around New York City, and the method moved across the country as people migrated.

As immigrants from around the world moved to America, an equally diverse array of pickles came with them. German immi-grants, who populated much of Pennsylvania in the seventeenth and eighteenth centuries, brought with them a long culinary history of pickling both fruits and vegetables. As the sweet and sour flavor profiles were prominent in their native cuisine, so their pickling recipes took on a similar bent, with recipes becoming even sweeter when white sugar became cheaper and more readily available. And while a typical Pennsylvania Dutch household might make numerous pickles for daily and holiday consumption, the sweetened, vinegar-based bread-and-butter chip that later became so popular is perhaps the most prominent variety that can be seen as an adaptation of these popular sweet and sour pickles.[1]

In the mid-to-late 1800s, political unrest and persecution brought large numbers of Jewish immigrants to America, many of whom settled in the New York City area. Pickles had long been a vital part of the Jewish diet, and the growing number of pickle merchants and Jewish delis in New York City further popularized pickles as a healthy and easy-to-distribute snack in the late 1800s and early 1900s. The most common sour and half-sour styles of Jewish pickles were also generally made with plenty of garlic—and the "kosher" distinction in the common "kosher dill" variety refers to the addition of garlic, not to adherence to kosher law. These pickles were typically sold by the piece and were a favorite snack of the young immigrant children who filled the streets of the Lower East Side after school. Thus pickles were sometimes seen as a vice for immigrants and a barrier to their assimilation[2] by some American reformers and dieticians, like Bertha Wood.[3]

Around the same time, a new style of pickle—the fresh-pack variety—became more popular with the advent of home preserving, or canning. Up until the mid-1850s pickling for personal consumption was generally done in crocks, and most larger-scale pickling was done in barrels. Pickles hadn't made the transition to being preserved in tin cans in the early 1800s as did many other commonly eaten foods, mainly because the high acidity would corrode the metal.[4] When the Kilner and Mason jar was introduced in 1858, it was embraced by home picklers as a way to preserve foods in smaller portions and with more consistent results. This negated the need to use such a strong vinegar or salt brine in nonfermented pickling, enabling home cooks to focus on flavoring their brines and allowing them to make a milder pickle. It also lessened the need for fermentation as a preservation method. While many picklers continued to ferment their produce, they now often did so for flavor or to keep alive a family tradition, rather than out of necessity. One recipe from the 1700s describes the cucumber-pickling process as multiple vinegar-brine soakings and subsequent boiling, which was certain to produce a soft pickle, initially brined for preservation and then made edible from a final boil to remove much of the acid.[5] Thus, within a century when preservation technology improved, so were these recipes abandoned. And as the home "canning" methods—really heat preservation in jars—continued to improve, so preserving and pickling became increasingly accessible for the average housewife. Even as the home canning improvements developed at the same time as industrial production and preservation, home preserving was still quite popular, especially in rural areas.

While of course cost effective, the act of canning at harvest also took on increasing cultural importance as it became less necessary. Generations—often women—would can together on hot summer days, passing down recipes and perhaps, as in my family, sharing stories. The home canning experience of both of my grandmothers—one German and Dutch, the other Italian—are still very similar, even if the items they preserved were different. Together mother and sisters and daughters would divide the labor, one stirring, the other peeling, maybe the youngest—at one time it was my mother—being tasked with arranging the produce in the jar with her tiny hands.

Processes for preserving food in cans and jars on the industrial level continued to be refined throughout the 1800s, but the products available to the public were of varying quality. In 1906, the Pure Food and Drug Act passed, creating stricter quality control for mass-produced foods. This act was promoted by forward-thinking producers who realized that in order to have a successful commercial food business they had to have products that the public trusted, and this new law paved the way for greater acceptance by the general public for industrial canned, jarred, and bottled foods, including pickles.[6]

In the late 1800s and early 1900s the H. J. Heinz Company revolutionized mass pickling through various innovations in technology and marketing. In 1878, John Heinz, brother of H. J. Heinz, patented a pickle sorter, which removed the misshapen cucumbers and enabled jars to be stuffed with pickles of more consistent sizes. Soon thereafter, the company invented a method using the first industrialized boilers, which resulted in the ability to make a higher volume of pickles at a faster rate, but some argued that it compromised taste and texture. Heinz also took on a large-scale marketing campaign and was sensitive to attractive packaging. Thus he was poised to capture a larger market share of prepared and preserved goods, including condiments as well as pickles, as women spent less time in the kitchen and became more accepting of the convenience of mass-produced food. Surpassing the sidewalk pickle barrels in New York City and beyond, Heinz's marketing campaign truly made the pickle into a desirable cultural icon, even distributing the now-collectible Heinz pickle pins, initially given away at the 1893 World's Fair to promote their new product. At one time there was even a large light-up billboard—featuring a forty-three-foot-long pickle—standing where the Flatiron Building in Manhattan now reigns.[7]

Thus it was marketing that seemed to give pickles their new life as an "American" snack. The mass-produced varieties took on a more tame identity—fewer and milder flavors were now available in grocery stores, and pickles soon became known as a side to a deli sandwich or a topping on one of the new fast-food hamburgers. As women moved in greater numbers toward working outside of the home in the middle of the twentieth century, and thus pickling for family consumption continued to decline, Heinz's pickles became known more and more as the pickle standard.

Heinz, and a few decades later Mt. Olive, cemented their status as mass-produced pickle leaders, jarring pickles using the "fresh-pack" method. This method packs produce in a jar, often with some combination of vinegar and brine, and heat processes them to retain their freshness. A few varieties were fermented for a short time for flavor and then heat pasteurized, but "live" fermented pickles were rarely available commercially, except by a few small-scale or local picklers. Mass-produced pickle varieties also changed as public tastes veered toward sweet and away from sour, and Mt. Olive had the perhaps dubious distinction of being the first commercial pickler to use high-fructose corn syrup in place of sugar in 1969.[8] This industrialization of pickling happened at the same time that convenience foods were becoming more popular in America, with frozen dinners and packaged and processed foods quickly replacing the homemade versions on many American families' shelves.

While pickling—both fermenting and heat pasteurizing—did find some new fans among the counter-cuisinists of the 1960s and 1970s, it was the recession in the early 2000s that led to the aforementioned growth in people starting food-based businesses;[9] a greater cultural interest in homemade, local, and high-quality food products; and more people trying traditional preserving and pickling methods to continue to eat locally sourced food out of season, thereby reducing the need for imported produce. Although similar studies done in 1975 and 2000 noted that the percentage of home picklers dropped in that time period,[10] anecdotally, interest in these traditional food preservation methods has been on the rise. Thus, while statistics on home preserving are rarely compiled, the project director of the National Center for Home Food Preservation noted that the requests for information on home food preservation skyrocketed in 2009, and sales of canning equipment increased by 30 percent from 2008 to 2009.[11]

So why did pickles become the poster food for this "artisanal" or "craft" food explosion that started midway through the first decade of the new millennium? I assert that it was a combination of factors: pickles are relatively easy to make (although one might argue not as easy to make *well*), with a low barrier for practicing techniques and refining recipes. Unlike chocolate or coffee, ingredients can generally be sourced locally and cheaply, and there is no special equipment needed beyond what might be available in an average kitchen. Where wine or whiskey or many cheeses need to be aged for weeks or months or longer, many pickles can be tasted, tested, and sold in a relatively short amount of time. Further, unlike other foods that were typically preserved at home, the difference between the industrial version and homemade version was stark: Grandma's jar of jam is, perhaps, not *that* much different from a store-bought version, in part because the industrial and home methods of production are still very similar, only performed on different scales. Pickles, on the other hand, were made in a wide variety, influenced by many cultures and recipes; and the level of fermentation, the flavor from the pickle barrel, or the distinct taste of the pickler's seasoning mix could all add nuances to pickles' unique flavor.

However, I believe pickles regained popularity early in the new millennium for reasons beyond these. The narrative that pickles represent in our culture is one of being simultaneously indicative of an Old World heritage and yet distinctly American. While pickles came to the United States through myriad cultures—Eastern and Western—since around 1900, thanks to Heinz and other industrial picklers, they have become better known as a topping for hamburgers, a deli sandwich accompaniment, or a relish spooned onto hot dogs or potato salad. They were the initial jarred vegetable that could be found on the shelves of the new self-service grocery stores in the 1920s and beyond; visible cucumbers inside clear glass containers, they were a shelf-stable, healthy food that women could serve their families as they entered the workforce in increasing numbers and spent less time cooking and preparing food.

Thus, as artisans seek start-up food businesses, they have a lot of cultural references to piggyback upon—or upend. Many pickle companies seek to take on the mantle of pickles as a classic and beloved *American* food. Brooklyn Brine's name is an obvious reference to where the pickles are made. Jones notes that pickles are known as a beloved New York food, and the name also stakes claim to one of the areas of the country that has become known as an artisanal food incubator. In reference to their regional connection, their label features the classic pickle barrel, once ever-present on the streets of New York. Rick's Picks, another Brooklyn-based pickler, uses a classic serif font on their labels, as does Happy Girl Kitchen and numerous others, calling to mind labels from an earlier age. Picklopolis from Portland, Oregon, evokes the urban traditions of pickles—past and present—through both its name and picture of a man with a vintage (and now associated with hipster culture) handlebar moustache. Bubbies pickle jars feature a sepia-toned photo of Bubbie herself on the label. McClure's Pickles also evokes an urban connection through the image of a skyline on their label and puts their distinction of being from both Brooklyn and Detroit front and center. These are but a few examples of how labeling and positioning in the artisanal pickle world has embraced classic American pickle tropes—rural and urban—and is helping companies to align their products with a quintessential American snack, no matter what one's America looks like.

But many of these picklers are also working to modernize the concept of pickles, mainly by embracing classic techniques to pickle a wide variety of fruits and vegetables, using creative and exotic seasonings and flavor combinations. Such varieties of pickles have been finding their way to farmers markets and local grocers, has been such immense popularity of learning how to pickle, [12] and such widespread embracing of the creativity of the pickling process, that picklers have become the poster children for the new artisanal food movement, both for personal and retail consumption. The *Portlandia* skit "We Can Pickle That!" gives perhaps the most iconic version of the trend, with Fred and Carrie wearing the retro-hip uniform of apron, vintage dress, newsboy cap, and moustache, and claiming to be able to pickle anything, edible or non. A 2012 *New York Times* article on the artisanal food movement in Brooklyn was titled "Don't Mock the Artisanal Pickle Makers,"[13] though it was talking more broadly about the new craft economy as a whole. And while official figures have American pickle consumption holding steady at eight and a half pounds per year, anecdotally pickle consumption *must* be on the rise, especially among the more narrow demographic of artisanal food consumers. Pickles have been cited as a growing trend in food, and homemade pickles have been cropping up on many new restaurant menus. A recent *Slate* article was seeking to explain why people liked "sour" foods, and Katherine Alford, a vice president of the food-democratizing Food Network has noted the recent national preoccupation with pickles. [14]

So what came first? The artisanal pickler or the demand for these small-batch, high-end pickles? I would argue that pickling made a comeback first, and the commercialization of these increasingly skilled and creative efforts were a direct result of, to adapt Warren Belasco's term, this neo-counter-cuisine. I spoke with a dozen artisanal picklers about their influences, challenges, and perspective on the growing artisanal pickle industry, and have used these narratives to help illustrate this new pickle revolution.

WHO IS PICKLING?

Sam Addison of Pogue Mahone Pickles moved to Austin, Texas, a few years ago to go to culinary school, but also because of the reputation of the city as a funky, "weird," adventurous food town. Food trucks, farmers markets, and start-up artisanal businesses have long found a home here, prior to the seeming "explosion" in the last few years. So it made sense that Sam, when he wanted to get out of retail management and into food, decided to head south from Virginia to this liberal mecca. Sam has been making pickles for twelve years, documenting, tinkering with, and perfecting his lightly fermented, refrigerated method. Not long after moving to Austin, he began selling them at farmers markets and they consistently sold out; he only began selling in local specialty stores in 2013. But with a Good Food Awards—sort of the Grammys of artisanal food—nod under his belt, he's poised to keep growing. [15]

Sam wanted to start Pogue Mahone because he loved pickles, and wanted a job where he had more control over his day-to-day tasks and larger business trajectory. But he also was drawn to a job in food, returning to culinary school years after earning his undergraduate degree, because he wanted to work with his hands and make something tangible, creative, and delicious. "There has never been a jar of Pogue Mahone pickles made that I didn't have my hands on," he told me with pride, illustrating the importance of the handcraft work in artisanal foods. Yet this was about to change. I spoke to him days before he was moving his facility to ramp up production. He would soon be hiring help and recognized that he would no longer be the only one (with occasional help from his fiancée) cutting, packing, sealing, and labeling his jars. "And it will be bittersweet," he said about that change, "but I do look forward to that day."

Sam's narrative is typical of many new start-up food businesses, which grew in the first decade of the 2000s as a new wave of mostly younger urbanites were faced with job uncertainty or dissatisfaction and turned to artisanal edibles as a potential career. And many within that number chose pickling as their product of choice. Thus, a common narrative among pickle start-ups is the desire to work with food and to use pickling as a way to express oneself creatively. Like Sam, Shamus Jones of Brooklyn Brine and Michaela Hayes of Crock and Jar also came from a professional chef background and prized the creativity inherent in pickling. But within the context of a professional kitchen, both Michaela and Shamus were encouraged to use their creativity in developing ways to preserve a wide variety of produce, doing so in a way that keeps a menu diverse and interesting. Thus pickling represented to each of them a way to express their values regarding choices in food consumption.

Also common among some non-fermenting picklers with whom I spoke was the connection to family knowledge attained through pickling. Learning to pickle from a family member was the most popular form of home preserving education in both a 1975 and a 2001 survey—although one wonders if that has changed in the past decade-plus as pickling classes have proliferated. Travis Grillo of Grillo's Pickles, and Betsey Wilton of Our Favorite Foods, were among the picklers who noted that they used, at least initially, a family recipe to make pickles for personal consumption and gifts, but, for similar reasons, decided to turn their pickling passion into a business. Others, like Robert Schaefer of Divine Brine, said that his pickle recipe is his own but it was the ethos of his Italian American heritage—"the cuisine of my passion," that led him toward his pickle business. His initial recipe "wasn't [my mother's], but was definitely inspired by her." Schaefer—also a former chef, was saying that his inspiration was both his connection to his heritage as well as his desire to express himself in a unique way.

In many cases this creative food preparation was further inspired by health—personal and environmental. Shamus Jones is a vegetarian and committed to the lifestyle, while Michaela Hayes is dedicated to sourcing primarily organic and local produce and promoting seasonality, all for the end goal of sustainability in one's food sourcing. Fermenters Uri Laio of Brassica and Brine, Alex Hozven of Cultured Pickles, and Julie O'Brien and Richard Climenhage of Firefly Kitchens are also committed to the health aspect of their product for consumers and the environment. While those committed to lacto-fermented foods have long been on the fringe, these ideas of healthy eating are starting to become more mainstream, like the organic and the locavore movements of the past few decades. What is different, however, among all of these picklers—and across the various industries—is the increased integration of the new "hip entrepreneur" into the traditional food marketplace—which is different from the hippies and back-to-the-landers of the first counter-cuisine movement who were either content to stay on the fringe, never compromising their initial mission—or grew to a point where they were no longer representing the health foods and claims that first inspired them. It is interesting and new that most of today's food artisans are combining a true commitment to environmental and physical health, but are also increasingly savvy about their growth strategy.

Yet, whether the pickler was inspired by family, creativity, or personal or environmental health—or some combination of these—in each story pickling began as a hobby or culinary experiment, and grew to become a passion whose commercial viability was reinforced by the larger culture of artisanal goods growing at the time. Each of the picklers, whether a trained chef or a law school graduate, found they loved the pickling process—the act of creating something that was tangible, useful, had a story to it, and involved creativity. Robert Schaefer noted that "There's a real appreciation for someone putting in quality ingredients and energy." This is a sentiment shared by many picklers as well as the consumer base to which they are selling. Riding the wave of foodies interested in new flavors, and with growing social media making it easier to tell the

stories behind the products, the market for these artisanal pickles—
even at five, six, eight dollars a jar—grew. Or, as food scholar Amy
Trubek says, the American food scene is now beginning to appreciate edibles based upon quality, the narrative of its provenance, and
other reasons beyond "abundance and accessibility."[16]

Passion, creativity, desire to work with their hands—these are
the common qualities among the picklers with whom I spoke, and
also echo the traditional influences of artisans of nonedibles. This
return to handicrafts, especially by those who have earned degrees
or even worked careers in other professional fields, is not an anoma-
ly, and makes sense in the context of the recent recession. A rise in
useful, skilled work that results in products that are of general uniform quality and design while retaining their individuality through
their handmade provenance is, many believe, a response to the increasing digitization of the world around us—the lack of connection
to what is accomplished at the end of the workday. Matthew B.
Crawford, author of *Shop Class for Soul Craft*, spoke to the same
feeling. After earning his PhD and starting a job at a think tank, he
returned to motorcycle repair less than a year later. He cites the
same desire reconnect to the physicality and creativity of working
with his hands, creatively problem solving, and in the end, being his
own boss. He explained, "Many people are trying to recover a vision that is human in scale, and extricate themselves from the dependence on the obscure forces of a global economy."[17] This idea of
a desire to practice skilled crafts and the excitement and pride of
creating a useful product that they are proud of and consumers love
and appreciate was common among nearly all of the picklers with
whom I spoke.

It stands to reason that often the initial interest began with DIY
picklers fresh-packing and fermenting for their own consumption.
And, as noted, the interest in traditional preservation methods, as
well as the instinct to connect with heritage through food, has inspired home picklers to learn on their own or perhaps take one of the
many pickling classes being offered with increasing frequency, especially in urban centers. Michaela Hayes of Crock and Jar is both a
pickling instructor and owner of a retail pickle company, and she

explained that many people come to her classes because of a desire to connect with the land and seasonal and local produce, or to a family history of pickle making—similar reasons given by commercial picklers. When I asked Michaela if she was training people to make their own pickles and put her out of business, she emphasized that she did not see it that way. By "pass[ing] on the gift of knowledge" about the pickle-making process, she is helping people understand the work that goes into her products and the products of so many other professional picklers. This will lead, she believes, to a greater valuing of these artisanal, handmade products and to consumers who understand the cost and how it is reflected in its price. And while some of those who learn to pickle from Hayes will continue to make their own pickles and not buy from Crock and Jar or other artisanal makers, and maybe even a few will decide to go into business for themselves, for the most part many will seek out higher-quality, small-batch pickles to buy, with a new appreciation for the texture and flavor of an artisanal pickle made by an expert like Michaela.[18]

ARTISAN VERSUS CRAFT

Shamus Jones at Brooklyn Brine could be seen, arguably, as the quintessential urban artisanal pickler. Thirty-something and tattooed, wearing skinny jeans and frequently employing the f-word to emphasize his passion for his business, Jones's story shares similarity with many other artisanal food makers in business today. The story of his start in pickling was tied to his identity as a chef and vegetarian. Jones had been working in vegetarian restaurants and saw pickling as a way to use culinary creativity and add interest to his craft, truly falling in love with its possibilities when he turned to pickling to preserve food from a forager who often sold to the restaurant where he worked. He soon found that people responded well to "weird" pickled goods, which only increased his interest in the process. However, he grew tired of chef's hours and took on consulting in the mid-to-late aughts, noting the lack of opportunities for a vegetarian chef, even in New York City.

In 2009, Jones became another victim of the recession, losing his consulting job and forcing him to think creatively about making money. He started making pickles—a product that he believes can express "food as culinary artistry"—using the kitchens of chef friends overnight between dinner service and the next day's prep. He named his product Brooklyn Brine, adopting the borough's name as his moniker mainly because that was where they were being made, and before Brooklyn fully became synonymous with hipster and artisanal food associations. Jones's pickles were an instant hit. The look, quality, flavor—and perhaps Jones himself as front man—helped Brooklyn Brine to grow at an astounding rate for the first three years. He quickly hired four workers and stayed that way for a while, adapting their workload for the increasingly larger orders, without changing the basic method or adding mechanization.

As Jones grew, his philosophy in sourcing became clear. While he bought cucumbers locally when he could, with quality being of the upmost importance, it became clear that he couldn't source local to New York City year round. Michigan supplies 18 percent of the cucumbers for pickles nationwide,[19] so Jones works with a distributor to round out his needs when he cannot get quality produce locally. An upside of Jones's growth is that he can stay more competitive because of economy of scale and, in 2012, had a farmer in upstate New York planting exclusively for Brooklyn Brine, which is a benefit for both parties. His cucumbers are not organic, however. Jones is a proponent of organic produce, but also a businessman; he notes that the market cannot support the additional costs of organic produce at this point.

Brooklyn Brine's exponential growth started, as many artisanal food success stories have of late, with a regional purchase by Whole Foods. However, as his product has taken off—it is now sold nationally through Whole Foods and in a number of other smaller chains, as well as in five countries—Jones has been able to be even more creative, such as collaborating with Dogfish Head Brewery, including both beer-inspired pickles, available now, and a retail operation in the works.

Jones states that his goal is to change people's expectations of pickles. And, after spending a good deal of time in France in the past few years, he has started to see pickles as a food that conjures memories as well as tastes good. "New York City is the gateway to the U.S.," Jones says, and sees his pickles, in part, as a representative of American culinary traditions. He believes that the overall market share of pickles is growing, as is the artisanal pickle market share. Likewise, he welcomes newcomers to the pickling arena and believes that quality products will prevail.[20]

By most accounts Brooklyn Brine is an artisanal pickle producer, even as they have expanded. However, Jones sees the term *artisanal* as quickly going the way of *natural* and *organic*—a word that once meant something, but is quickly being diluted by marketing. When I

Figure 2.2.   Hand packing at Brooklyn Brine.

asked how he defined his business, he laughed, "It's pretty fucking obvious," he said. "You smell it, you see it. I don't need a label." Despite that, Jones would resist any moniker; in this new world of hip entrepreneurs and start-up food businesses, he represents the role of artist-craftsman, defined as a craftsman with "more ambitious goals and ideologies."[21] He recognizes the utility of his pickles—utility being seen as a classic definition of craftsmanship—but yet sees his product as doing more than simply filling a void. By collaborating with other like-minded artist-craftsmen from other industries—like Sam Calagione from Dogfish Head Brewery and the McKenzies from Finger Lakes Distilling—he is demonstrating his goal to change the expectations of pickle consumers through (re)writing the narrative of the modern artisanal pickle as one that is simultaneously about tradition and about the new definition of the pickle and its place in contemporary (foodie) culture. Being from Brooklyn is clearly part of his identity—and the identity of his pickles and his business philosophy and branding reflect this. And he is confident enough in the quality and distinctness of his product that he isn't deterred by the numerous faux-artisans who package lesser-quality pickles as if they were artisanal, occasionally even co-opting the urban pickler identity through naming and labeling. (Jones said that he received visitors one afternoon, who were asking a lot of questions about his business and taking notes. Not long afterward he saw a national brand with strikingly similar packaging.)

In this role he is also distinctive from the "craft" businesses of the past. The counter-cuisine and original hip entrepreneurs of the 1960s and 1970s had craftspeople interested in traditional methods of preparation and preservation and "whole" and natural foods as a symbol of resistance to the mass-produced foods so prevalent in the American diet by mid-century. While some may have been interested in the creativity inherent in these traditional methods, utility was emphasized rather than flavor. Thus, the overall narrative of the hip entrepreneurs of those decades was, in part, selling a connection to the past through healthy, whole, traditional foods. Some current entrepreneurs also characterize their business similarly. However,

Jones, I believe, represents the neo-hip entrepreneur—many of whom would also be considered hipsters by contemporary standards—who not only look back to tradition, but also desire to take their industries into the future, in terms of creativity, flavor, identity, cultural integration, and environmental concerns. His goal, and that of others like him, is to rewrite the modern narrative of pickles within American food culture, as can be seen through some of his collaborative efforts and by his adherence to making a product whose quality surpasses what might be made in the home and justifies its price tag and place in the specialty market.

PASTORAL VERSUS NEW ENVIRONMENTALIST

While Shamus Jones is all punk rock vegan edge, Jordan Champagne is the Earth Mama next door. Her retail space and café-kitchen in Central California is bright and sunny, with the sun's rays making a stained glass–like mosaic on the hardwood floor as they pass through the shelves of preserves lined up along the front window. Her café space features an open farmhouse kitchen, bright, with plenty of work space, and a wide variety of jams and pickles lined up along the walls or on a shelf that bisects the space. While Jones connected to pickling through his stint in urban kitchens, Champagne came to her business through a childhood spent among gardeners. The narrative of her business represents the organic growth—pun intended—of those who are pickling and making other artisanal goods as a way to connect to the land and support environmental ideologies. [22]

This space is a realization of a dream that started when Jordan was young. She grew up with close connections to a farm in the Midwest, and has long loved preserving and the "old ways" of making the harvest last for the long winter months. After spending a summer working on a farm in Norway, she returned to the states with her family and began farming on the central coast of California. The longer growing season means an even more abundant harvest, and she soon became known as the "abundance gal"—the person who would welcome any excess produce and find a way to preserve it. Pickling was an early method used to preserve this abundance, and she started a small line called Fearless Pickles. However, as her business grew both in scope and size, Jordan morphed her pickle business into the preserve-selling, educational-community café it is now. Happy Girl Kitchen now makes and sells both fresh-pack and fermented pickles, along with jams and many other kinds of preserved produce, all marked with a cute and kitschy label with lettering like an off-kilter typewriter. She is happy with her business having mainly a regional reach, with the exception of the few fans who special order from farther afield. After all, her business philosophy is relationship driven: she wants to help write the narrative for people as they make choices about what they eat. She believes that her products have a story—and she also wants to include the community within that story, whether it is through the personal relationships she has with her farmers, or through teaching her neighbors about the ways of preserving that she finds so fulfilling.

This philosophy, she admits, is not necessarily the best for expanding her preserving business. Embracing pastoralism as the antithesis of the neo-hip entrepreneur, she still buys what is available locally, and when it's gone, it's gone—often without satisfying customer demand. She sees a lot of growth in selling pickles and preserves, especially from her perspective in Central California. But she's happy with her balance of retail and teaching. Even her name and branding—colorful, retro, Happy Girl Kitchen, evoking a large farmhouse with an apron sink and plenty of room for boiling pots—brings to mind a personal garden rather than an urban warehouse. She is clearly connecting to customers through a mutual appreciation of connecting with the land and dedication to local, organic, and seasonal sourcing, and she doesn't profess to be an expert or an artisan. Rather, she's an "everywoman" with skills and knowledge that she wants to share. This, at first glance, appears to be the diametric opposite of Shamus, with his brand of urban, vaguely ethnic, artisan-produced pickles. Yet, in many ways their love of pickling comes from a similar desire to honor produce and traditional methods of preservation, and connect to others—personally or tangentially—through food, even if their business model appears drastically different. This return to craftsmanship—and Jordan, like Shamus, would likely eschew labels—is by her own words, more skills and utility based than Shamus's artisan-craftsman. Her mission is similar to the hip entrepreneurs of latter decades, but with the modern dire urgency that the contemporary environmental movement has necessitated. [23]

And then there is the story of Michaela Hayes's path to pickling, which marries the influences of Shamus in an urban kitchen with Jordan's dedication to organic, local, and seasonal sourcing and education to illustrate a new relationship with both the art and craft of pickle making. Michaela Hayes from Crock and Jar in New York also came to pickling and preserving as a way to use abundance, albeit first in the kitchen of Gramercy Tavern where she used to work as a chef. I met Michaela at a sunny café whose menu proudly notes the provenance of most ingredients—the Brooklyn version of Jordan's café, in a way. Equidistant from our Brooklyn homes (Michaela has since moved out of the city), we chatted at this café rather than her workspace because she only sublets the commercial kitchen she uses for production a few days a week, as needed.

That winter morning she was excited about a 2013 Good Food Award nomination (she was nominated again for the 2014 awards), and as I spoke with her, I was similarly thrilled for her, as her company was still small and included both retail and education. Yet while she admitted that her decision to diversify was in part a business one, it became clear that it was also made out of a true passion for the philosophy behind preserving. Like Jordan, whom she had the opportunity to work with a few years earlier, Michaela truly embraces pickling for its original purpose of wasting little and providing sustenance outside of the harvest. To teach these methods to others isn't fostering competition, she notes, but rather is practicing what she preaches.

However, even as an ardent locavore, Michaela is still a businesswoman first. To keep her business sustainable, there have been times when she has had to adjust her thinking. While Hayes buys most of her produce from the Eastern Pennsylvania and Hudson Valley area, she told me about how Hurricane Irene in 2011 caused her to adjust this philosophy a bit when the weather wreaked havoc on storage vegetables. She then sourced her cabbage through a farm cooperative in Pennsylvania, which got them in Florida from a farm whose methods they knew and trusted. She also noted that at times she has sourced ingredients from farms with Integrated Pest Management, which weren't strictly organic, but that she proudly knew each farmer and was familiar—and comfortable—with their farming methods. Michaela admitted—at this café of her choosing, which was serving mostly, but certainly not entirely local fare—that this thinking is what she is trying to teach others: to be conscious, but not militant, about one's food choices. And to do so, she needs to be a sustainable business as well as a conscientious one. As she grows she may make the decision to buy non-local ingredients again, but always with an eye toward the bigger picture. However, she did come to the realization since our first meeting that she did not need to be an urban pickler, and that, in fact, it made more sense—financially and personally—to move her business out of Brooklyn. This dual identity as both urban and rural does appear to be in line with her business identity—the crock might evoke the vessel that ethnic immigrants used to pickle on a small scale in their tiny urban spaces, while the jar brings up images of the rural farmhouse. Even in her lengthy business narrative, she used the phrase "worlds colliding" multiple times to represent where her urban-versus-rural sentiments come together in her business Crock and Jar.[24]

Michaela's story, I believe, demonstrates the tension between the urban and rural that can be seen among many of the new wave of food artisans. With more and more artisans and craftsmen coming to their food businesses with distinct values pertaining to environmental sustainability, and the strengthening of their connection to the land or seasonality, their critique of "industrial capitalism's wholesale exploitation of nature and culture . . . retains, while modifying, an opposition between city and country—and . . . hopes to offer a better way forward."[25] While none of these picklers are growing all of their own produce, or pickling cuke to jar, as it might be called, they are all, to varying degrees, intimately involved with the growth of their raw materials, seasonality, nurturing and not exploiting "nature's generative potential."[26] But, unlike the aptly named "back-to-the-landers" of generations past, these artisans are entrenched in their urban communities, often selling to other like-minded urbanites who want the culture and career benefits of the city, but are similarly concerned with environmental sustainability. Attention to sourcing was noted by nearly all of the small-batch picklers with whom I spoke, but it was of even more importance to Michaela, Jordan, and a few others who emphasize seasonality with their products. In fact, Michaela found the urban-rural tension too much—she decided to move out of the city not too long after we met, not only to keep production and living costs down, but to be even more in touch with the environment that she seeks to honor through her pickles.

THE BUSINESS SAVVY OF NEO-HIP ENTREPRENEURS

While some picklers came to their business as an expression of heritage or artistic vision, and others with a dedication to local and seasonal produce, all are savvy businesspeople. In his 1989 book *Appetite for Change*, Warren Belasco defines "hip enterprise" as "a bridge between the underground and the establishment."[27] He was referring to the hip(py) food entrepreneurs of the original counterculture movement, including restaurateurs such as Alice Waters and Molly Katzen, and owners of "natural" food markets among others, who mostly "claimed disinterested, non-profit motives" and operated to upend the status quo of mass-produced food items and corporate greed and to support more sustainable and environmentally healthy food systems.[28] Today many of the small-batch picklers, as well as artisans in other industries, are claiming similar goals for their business—but few among them are not unabashedly business minded, with an eye toward their own financial sustainability and the challenge of growing in a way that is still aligned with their mission. Thus, I am dubbing these new artisanal food businesses neo-hip entrepreneurs, seeking to integrate their counter-cuisine within the larger culture, with a goal to promoting change—and often innovating—while also making a profit.

One such neo-hip entrepreneur is Travis Grillo of Grillo's Pickles, who spent months pushing his pickles in downtown Boston, dressed like a cucumber.[29] It was 2007 and he was looking for his next career move; he had applied to countless jobs to no avail, but had a light bulb moment after friends praised his pickles, made from a family recipe. So Travis decided to put his energy into putting together a strong business plan and turning his pickling into his career. Initially, he was not only Grillo's primary pickler, but the company's salesman too. Investing in the pickle suit was a strategic decision. And it paid off. While Travis has since expanded his line of pickles—mainly of the refrigerated variety—he also has a small retail space and distributes them regionally as well. And his goal is growth, without compromising quality. While he does not explicitly espouse an environmentalist agenda, he is striving to change consumers' expectations about pickles by packaging them in plastic tubs in the refrigerator section. He offers a wide variety of lightly brined pickled produce, from spicy cucumbers to small cinnamon-laced whole apples, that all pack a satisfying crunch. And, like some of his pickle-making contemporaries, he has updated the traditional role of the pickle man, selling his unique product one spear at a time, to help Bostonians reimagine what a pickle could be and secure his place in Boston as their signature artisanal pickle maker.

Travis, Michaela, Shamus, and Sam—and most of the pickle makers with whom I spoke—noted their influences as being both a passion for the product and a keen eye for growing a sustainable business. None moved into the retail realm without a thought for how their personal pickling philosophy would meld with a viable business model. For picklers like Michaela and Jordan, this meant diversifying; they recognized that sustainably sourced produce could not keep their initial retail business afloat, so they each included education and a diversity of products to help them stay as sustainable a business as the produce they sourced. This decision to diversify was also out of a dedication to promoting their food sourcing values through teaching the process as well as selling their products. Even Shamus recognized the need to diversify, although he was doing so through collaborations with other non-pickle producers like Dogfish Head Brewery and his entry into food service with his new pickle and beer shack. Although he has professed to this being born from a creative impulse, these kinds of collaborations also have the benefit of exciting new and existing customers alike. These primarily non-fermenting picklers (although some do use fermentation in varying ways, for none is it their singular focus) share many qualities that help define them as artisans or craftsmen, most strikingly that they are building upon the counter-cuisine movement to find their balance as neo-hip entrepreneurs, striving to change consumers' perceptions and buying habits, one pickle at a time.

FERMENTED VERSUS FRESH-PACK CULTURE

While there are some commonalities in environmental values and their approach to business growth, consistently the main start-up impetus for picklers who only do lacto-fermenting was the health benefits of this type of pickle. For, while traditionally most pickles were fermented—like the sours and half-sours from the barrels of the New York City street stands—in the past half century, many fermented pickles were then heat pasteurized and sold in shelf-stable sealed jars, which retained their flavor, but killed the good bacteria that had fermented the food in the first place. However, the health benefits of fermented foods, once touted only in hippy zines, back-to-the-land cookbooks, and fringe health blogs, are becoming more widely acknowledged. "Live and active cultures" is a tag-line now commonly used to sell yogurt because the connection is being made about these cultures and "gut" health. Thus, while some vinegar and brine picklers, like Brooklyn Brine, are making only a small quantity of fermented pickles that preserve the live cultures (they heat seal the vast majority of their products), a few picklers who focus solely on fermented, refrigerated pickles have influences and narratives that are in some ways distinctly different from shelf-stable picklers.

Alex Hozven, with her Cultured Pickles shop, was an early proprietor of a variety of tasty, innovative, high-quality fermented foods for the Bay Area. I walked into a bustle of activity at Alex's small retail space and commercial kitchen, located on an industrial corner of Berkeley, California. A smiling twenty-something worker was earnestly slicing carrots, while a tattooed woman was lining up jars along the back bank of windows; another was getting ready to work the Berkeley farmers market later that day. Alex's husband greeted me warmly. Alex herself, however, was a bit more serious. She generously took time out of what appeared to be a busy day in the kitchen—although she said that it was always busy, or perhaps *efficient* is a better word—to give a quick tour of her many ferments. She offers ten varieties of krauts (or cabbage-based slaws) and a changing number of seasonal slaws from local produce like beets, various kinds of squash, carrots, green tomatoes, and many more, as well as various kombucha brews and other edibles—some still in their experimental phase. All the produce is organic, and all processes are overseen by Alex herself. She noted that some of her experiments are not yet cost effective, but she balances her business decisions with her passion for fermenting—and specifically the health benefits that fermented foods possess.

Alex Hozven's name had come up when I was speaking with Michaela Hayes in Brooklyn. Michaela had apprenticed with Alex years prior, after she had left her chef job at Gramercy Tavern and had decided to go into business for herself. Michaela had heard that Alex owned perhaps the most impressive and progressive fermented foods company in the country, although it was mostly unknown outside of the Bay Area. Jordan Champagne of Happy Girl Kitchen also spent some time working with Alex, and Uri Laio of Brassica and Brine professed to Alex being his idol. I got the sense that these apprentice fermenters had all worked with Alex for free, just for the chance to see up close her dozen or so different batches of kombucha lined up along the shelving or the various Japanese fermented

Figure 2.3. Ferments at Cultured Pickles.

pickles, called tsukemono (a Japanese style of ferment often facilitated with a bed of rice bran) that she is experimenting with—one of the only retail fermenters to be doing so in the country.[30]

Alex started her business in the late 1990s with her first brew of kombucha, and progressed to making krauts not long afterward. With her husband, Kevin, they have put long hours—twelve-hour days are the norm—into their business, eventually employing others to help chop, pack, and sell their products. Various kinds of kraut are their biggest sellers, and they currently go through two thousand to twenty-five hundred pounds of cabbage a week.[31] But they could be bigger. Demand for fermented foods is growing, and Cultured Pickle's products are largely unique and quite nuanced, both in flavor and packaging. These colorful slaws and krauts come packed in a heavy glass jar with a handwritten label, and the vibrancy of the squash or beets or carrots is obvious. But Alex believes that their roughly hundred-mile reach is enough. She has a great relationship with her growers, who supply her with enough organic produce to keep up with her current needs. She understands the complications of further growth—only one of which is that her products need to be refrigerated. Not to keep them from "spoiling" in the traditional sense of the term (fermented foods will only continue to ferment), but because she sells them when she believes their flavor, texture, and health benefit are at their peak. Refrigeration dramatically slows fermentation and sustains the peak qualities. Having control over the quality of her products once they leave her purview is another concern for growth. If the product warms, fermentation will continue, changing the flavor and texture.

Also Alex is, unsurprisingly, attuned to the environmental and social costs of shipping refrigerated jars across long distances, and as their website states, "We firmly believe in the value of buying food directly from the source," a credo that works for them as a seller and a buyer. Part of their responsible growth strategy is to keep that connection with their customers, selling out of their shop, a few local stores, and at the farmers market. This helps them ensure a connection with their customer, even at the expense of revenue streams. Even so, Alex believes that there is plenty of room to grow within the Bay Area, and is pleased at the increased interest in fermented foods, even though she is reluctant to become a vocal proponent of them. She believes her products should speak for themselves, saying, "I'm not here to convince people to eat fermented foods." But when pressed, she agrees that yes, of course, she believes that fermented foods are an important and often overlooked part of a healthy diet.

After my visit to Alex's sunny and busy kitchen, I traveled a few miles across town to the farmers market. Even in January, tables were stacked with produce, and local cheese makers', raw chocolatiers', and, yes, Cultured Pickles' products punctuated the neighboring booths with stacks of carrots and greens. To see Alex's goods among the other farmers market offerings was a reminder of their uniqueness: I had never before seen fermented slaw (or kraut), and jars of a few versions made from seasonal squash or carrots retained their vibrant orange. She also had available some of her tsukemono ferments and other offerings. I have heard that her products usually sell out. And it was easy to see why, even among the tables of food offered at one of the most progressive farmers markets in the country. Alex's slaws would be unrecognizable as "pickles" to most East Coast pickle eaters—heck, most pickle consumers in general. What Alex is making is still incredibly rare—although I believe similar products will be quickly making their way to farmers markets and specialty stores soon, albeit perhaps not at the same level of quality and creativity as Cultured Pickles' products.

Alex's status is due in part to her being one of the first—if not the initial—modern commercial fermented pickler in the Bay Area (and perhaps the country). It's a locale that has long been the start of food revolutions: nearby Alice Waters kicked off the seasonal and fresh "California Cuisine" trend in the 1970s, and the idea that a farm-to-table menu could be high end and adventurous, rather than limiting, only continued to grow. It was in San Francisco where the term *locavore* was coined, nearly a decade after Alex had committed herself to using only local produce for her pickles. The Berkeley farmers markets have been popular long before the numbers grew nationally in the 1990s and early 2000s. So it makes sense that Cultured Pickles has led the way as national consumers' awareness and appreciation of artisan pickles grew. Alex's interest in growing her business only within her hundred-mile radius or so is a sustainable goal because she is working from a place of such industry respect and expertise. Thus her challenges are not distribution—she appears happy with her current system of selling face-to-face at their small retail space and at farmers markets—but rather getting local customers to find her where she chooses to be. Her team is ready to adjust with demand. And her role as arguably the most successful and best-known commercial fermenter in the country has allowed her to stay true to her mission of serving only local customers. Whether this would be a sustainable model for a new business starting in this increasingly competitive market is debatable.

Thus, it can be said that Alex helped to write the narrative of the West Coast fermenter as someone who lives a lifestyle committed to the product, who is continually stretching the art of fermenting—for I do believe that she practices an art where others admit they are merely working on their craft—to create new and different products, for the sake of creativity and the challenge, and for healthfulness and flavor. One might look at Alex as representing the reluctant artist-craftsman. She is clearly a virtuoso, practicing ferments from many cultures and continually reinventing and expanding upon her repertoire. She also presents the face of someone who answers to no one—including her customers—in part because she doesn't have to. If she makes it, they will come—and buy. Not that she in any way delivers less than a high-quality product, or plenty of variety. Being at the top of her art has brought her many followers—that I met three of them in my relatively small sample of artisanal picklers should say a lot about the respect she has earned in the field. The only other person who has as high of a profile among fermenters is Sandor Katz, who has written books on the subject, but does not make ferments for commercial consumption—and fittingly a portrait of him and Alex and her team graces the wall of the retail area of their shop. Alex, a fore-mother of artisanal fermented pickling, is influenced most by her passion for promoting the availability of high-quality and delicious fermented foods as part of essential human nutrition. Yet she also has a business narrative that falls squarely in line with others in her industry. As she noted, she has organized her life around building and sustaining her business. There were a number of experiments—many flavors of kombucha, efforts at various forms of Japanese fermenting rarely practiced or sold in the United States—that were clearly done for the sake of her artistic fulfillment; and she is strongly committed to local, organic, and season ingredients. Further, like Shamus and numerous other picklers, although she has a team working with her, she is obviously the creative center.

THE MODERN CULTURE OF
FERMENTED PICKLES

Alex is not the only proponent of the health benefits of fermented foods. Uri Laio, founder of Brassica and Brine in Los Angeles, also came to fermented pickles because of a strong belief that fermented foods were necessary in our modern diet—and that our movement away from their gut-healthy bacteria was the source of some modern ailments. Uri has a unique perspective on the fermented pickle business. When I met him on a cool January morning in the Silver Lake neighborhood of Los Angeles—called by some the "Brooklyn of L.A."—he was dressed in a button-down shirt and sweater vest. I was happy not to have to wear my coat, and the folks around me, despite it being an unseasonably cold day for Southern California, were also in thin layers and sunglasses. Uri was around thirty years old, with the kind of thick beard I often saw on the Hasidic Jews in Brooklyn. And he was immediately forthcoming about his business story and his experiences as the founder and sole worker at Brassica and Brine, a fermented-only pickler.

Uri grew up in the suburbs of Los Angeles and didn't believe he would ever return. In truth, he reminded me of an un-ironic Brooklyn hipster, and was the most East Coast–looking person I had seen yet in my short time in southern California. Uri, in fact, had spent a lot of time on the East Coast, apprenticing as a pickle maker on a small farm in Connecticut with master fermenter Josh Rosenstein. He moved back west to the Bay Area to attend law school, but quickly figured out that the field wasn't for him. So he devised a plan: to open a pickle business.

While in the San Francisco area, Uri also interned with Alex Hozven of Cultured Pickles and noted that Northern California, while not saturated, did have a lot of fermenters. So he reluctantly moved back to L.A., where in November 2011 he started selling fermented kraut and a few other products. Within a year, he had grown out of his initial space (and is on pace to grow out of his current space as well) and was shipping his kraut around the country. As of winter 2013 Uri didn't work with a distributor and had no employees—just a few friends who helped out at especially busy times. He also noted that Los Angeles, with its strong interest in healthy food trends, had been particularly supportive of his product. Fermentation is noticeably more popular among West Coasters interested in natural health remedies. (He has his own success stories of fermented foods and health—he had viral warts on his hands for much of his adult life, which disappeared after a month of drinking just a shot of kombucha a day.) On the East Coast, fermentation is still a bit of a sleeper of a food category—recommended primarily by hippies and foodie first-wave adopters (although its visibility started to rise with a mention of it being a hot trend in 2013 in the *New York Times*). However, lack of competition combined with the closeness to tastemakers in the media that Uri's potential customers have helped give him stellar press in his first year of business. [32]

Uri is committed to making "artisanal" pickles, which he defines as a product made by an artisan according to a high standard. But he was also struggling with the challenge to expand responsibly while keeping the quality he is known for and adhering to his own business values. He told me that he discusses this a lot with his friend, chef Jessica Koslow from Sqirl in Los Angeles, who makes small-batch jam and has also been gaining a reputation for her artisanal goods. When we spoke, he knew he was on the cusp of having to make some big decisions regarding the growth of Brassica and Brine, and was not yet sure where he will go.

Uri was already feeling the tension that Michaela Hayes and others have illustrated, of staying true to ideological roots while also building a sustainable business. It was this tension that kept him in Los Angeles and also influenced a recent decision to be certified kosher and organic. Uri prided himself on establishing purchasing relationships with local farmers. In fact, he found his community among the farmers market vendors where he began selling his kraut. One in particular was a working farm within Los Angeles city limits. But when he decided to become certified organic, which he did to be more competitive on store shelves, he had to end that relationship, as they were not certified, even if their practices were in line with Uri's values. Uri knew, trusted, and supported this farmer's

Figure 2.4.   Kraut from Brassica and Brine.

practices, but, like many small farmers, this farmer had decided not
to be organic certified, in part because he sold primarily at farmers
markets where his clientele trusted his decisions and didn't need a
certification to ensure their foods' health and sustainability, in part
because of cost, and also quite likely to give himself some freedom
in farming practices. This represents an interesting compromise that
many artisans must make when growing their business—the organic
designation is an important one for consumers, who can't know the
workings of the farm where their produce is sourced, but yet it
disqualifies many smaller farmers from providing for these growing
numbers of artisans because of the barriers of being certified. Uri
regrets having to end that relationship, but believes his decision was
a good and necessary one in the long run. However, he anticipates
having to face similar challenges as he grows.

He has seen a huge interest in his product, particularly in Southern California, due to the increased customer interest in the health benefits of fermented foods, and fueled by his own health success story and his passion for fermentation as well. And Alex as well as Julie O'Brien and Richard Climenhage, who own Firefly Kitchens,[33] a fermented-only pickling operation in the Seattle area, and even Michaela Hayes, who suggested I reach out to Alex, all share this passion as a direct result of how they experienced lacto-fermented food positively affecting their health. However these fermenters may define themselves, the way that each of these artisans speaks about their business reflects a craftsperson's mentality, with a goal to make useful products for reasons beyond pure art or creativity. They are successful because they possess and practice a relatively "rare body of knowledge . . . which can be used to produce useful objects"[34]—or in this case, foods. A product that promotes health, rather than one that aesthetically improves one's life, is the ultimate goal, and I would argue that their business narratives, while demonstrating passion and business acumen, illustrate the distinction of being driven by craft. Yet whether these fermenters are artists or craftsmen, they are all neo-hip entrepreneurs—perhaps with the exception of Alex—who have a clear counter-cuisine mission for themselves but who also place business sustainability at the forefront. Perhaps this is the mentality of so many of these entrepreneurs because they founded their pickle companies in the face of—and often as a result of—the recession: They are all too aware that they must succeed financially to make a difference culturally—whether it is encouraging consumers to think more about the value of handmade products, the cost of environmentally sustainable practices, or the benefits inherent in preserving traditional methods of productions—in pickles or across artisanal food industries.

CHALLENGES OF THE ARTISANAL PICKLE MAKER

Where do I buy my pickles? As I started thinking about artisanal pickling, who was doing it, and why, I started to see pickles everywhere. A few years ago it might have been the farmers market, where I could meet the pickler myself, often standing in front of a table spread with hand-labeled mason jars. In my hometown in rural western New York, I still might. But increasingly, at the markets and shops of Brooklyn and Somerville, Massachusetts, picklers with an eye for retail were taking themselves much more seriously. The farmers market table offerings might also be found in a few local specialty shops. Labels often had a website, with online ordering instructions. Farm-to-table restaurants proudly announced—if they weren't pickling in-house—the local pickler who provided their brined or vinegared ingredients.

Increasingly, I buy my pickles from one of the small grocery stores popping up in areas with a high concentration of sometimes-locavores; they offer a curated selection of local preserves, eggs, cheeses, meats, and produce. Where I might imagine that the farmers market table represents the entirety of a pickler's inventory—whether or not that is true, the scope of their production seems about accurate—once products make their way to the store shelves—refrigerated or not—suddenly there is the perception of a force behind the jar—a team of people boiling brine or hand packing or slicing with gloved hand and sturdy knife. And with more and more competition in the pickle market, those who have chosen to enter the fray in the last few years have had to get smart, quickly, about production and growth. To be competitive today, picklers—and artisans across the industries—must keep the local connection with the main customer base—those who are paying to imagine the pickler stuffing jars in his production space the next neighborhood over, while also having the infrastructure to grow and reach those consumers who purchase for more aspirational reasons, perhaps to buy a piece of the local artisanal scene across the state, across the country, or maybe even internationally. Increasingly, businesses like Brooklyn Brine are seeking to cater to their local and far-flung customers by striving to retain their authenticity as a handmade product. Whether it's through offerings of special small-batch pickles at their retail shop, handwritten labels that consumers know are only available to those able to visit, or even the varying sizes of cucumbers in each jar, which helps the international consumer understand that the product had to be hand packed, even the smallest details on packaging work to create the narrative that can help—or hinder—the creation of the identity within the mind of the consumer. I know this careful brand building worked with me—I considered Brooklyn Brine my local pickle maker and was surprised at their volume—even after visiting their small production space.

This challenge of growing to a customer base outside of the region is one that Alex of Cultured Pickles and Jordan of Happy Girl Kitchen do not share, as part of their business mission is to establish and nurture a face-to-face community. And each, in her own way, has found a business model that is both sustainable and true to her vision. Yet that does not mean that growing locally is easy. The challenges of all of the artisanal pickle makers with whom I spoke were vastly similar: how to grow their business responsibly while adhering to their initial—or adapting—vision. All of these picklers (with the exception of Alex Hozven's Cultured Pickles) had been in business for about five years or fewer at the time that I had interviewed them, with most starting in the window between 2007 and 2010. Thus, their challenges regarding finding a customer base and plotting sustainable growth were all under the same cloud of the recession, but buoyed by both potential customers and outlets that might carry artisanal foods. There have certainly been successful pickle makers before 2007 who started out as small batch—Rick's Picks started in 2004 and McClure's Pickles in 2006, both capitalizing on a passion for pickles passed down from family members, and both still ensuring that each jar is hand packed. These two fresh-pack picklers also started in Brooklyn, selling to consumers known for being early adopters of the artisanal food movement, and both succeeded in gaining national distribution as this movement grew. But the newer artisanal pickle makers must work harder to create an identity—and a model for sustainable growth—in an increasingly crowded market.

THE VALUE OF THE ARTISANAL NARRATIVE

Who is buying these artisanal pickles? Those businesses that expanded beyond the farmers market spoke of customers who bought one jar at a time to help sustain them. In the newly appearing farmers markets, many of them in middle- to upper-middle-class urban neighborhoods, spending six dollars or more on a jar of pickles is an impulse decision, made amid a market stocked with five-dollar-a-pound heirloom tomatoes and six-dollar cartons of eggs. Put into that context, the price doesn't seem out of line. Plus the added value of, often, meeting the pickler or other artisan helps to cement the sale. You are supporting not just a craftsperson, but someone who shares your values—a person who supports local farmers and cares about the environment and is passionately preserving traditional skills (whether or not these things are true). The presence of the artisan can, perhaps, determine whether the pickles should be considered a "craft" or "artisanal" product. If someone other than the artisan is selling the product, it can feel like more of a commodity to the consumer. However, this can be mitigated by the story that the seller tells about the product and its provenance, as well as the narrative that the item itself tells. Are the cucumbers uniform or of varying sizes? Are the labels preprinted or handwritten? Is the pickled produce in season, indicating that it was made recently and has a connection to seasonality and, by extension, the land or farm? Are the flavor profiles or pickling or preservation technique classic or foreign or a modern version of traditional? On the other hand, a product that appears too amateur can appear to not have the mark of an artisan, and can affect the perception of quality or craftsmanship, and thus, the resulting value. Finding that balance between communicating both expertise and a unique customer experience is the tension that many artisans face as they strive to grow a sustainable business.

And this is where the counter-cuisine argument seems so apt. As Belasco argued, choosing a diet is an easy and obvious way to communicate and symbolize one's worldview. Thus a consumer who believes, like so many of these neo-hip entrepreneurs, that our food system is too dominated by unhealthy corporate business practices and that our larger culture would be improved by a return to more traditional methods of food preparation and preservation, then the purchase of a (delicious) jar of pickles is a reasonable way to both communicate and support those values. Yes, at first bite it may taste vaguely *like* a mass-produced pickle (although these artist-craftsmen are certainly working hard to offer products that could never be mistaken for commodity pickles), but it represents more than just an edible to both the consumer and the producer. This larger cultural value translates into higher prices, but a cost that both tacitly agree represents a fair market value that (potentially) takes into account a living wage for all who were involved in its production and the environmental costs of getting the pickles to market.

This willingness to place a higher monetary value upon an item based upon where the item is purchased can extend to the small local food shops or food co-ops that offer a curated selection of goods. A consumer may not obtain the added value of meeting the pickler or knowing exactly what worldview is presented in the jar, but the presence at such a market can help justify a higher price tag as the product is considered more virtuous and aligned with the consumer's values simply by being included among the product options. In this case, the products are, often, viewed as having been selected by someone with more knowledge about the industry than the average consumer, and can gain value by what is on the adjacent shelves. Thus, getting placement at competitive farmers markets, in well-curated food shops, and a regional Whole Foods (or another, smaller chain, like Bi-Rite on the West Coast) can help these companies capitalize on economy-of-scale growth to a point where they are sustainable, and even profitable enough to hire additional employees. Whole Foods, in fact, has been important in having regional positions whose job it is to seek out "local" artisanal products. While they are notoriously secretive about their selection process, I do know they are also serious about finding products that share their company philosophy of thoughtful sourcing and local artisanship. This careful attention to sourcing artisanal foods is beneficial to Whole Foods, which can retain a more personalized connection to their consumers, as well as to regional artisans, who can then expand their reach quickly through the chain.

This is what happened with Travis Grillo when his efforts in a pickle suit finally paid off—Whole Foods approached him about buying for their Northeast stores, and he found himself needing to expand—legally. This involved finding new, year-round sourcing beyond local farmers and finding a legal commercial kitchen in which to make his pickles. "Basically I discovered everything I was doing was illegal," Travis said, half-jokingly. He moved his operation to a commercial kitchen, and started churning out exponentially more pickles than previously needed for his downtown Boston pickle cart. That he was willing and able to expand so quickly was the key to his now thriving business that sells pickles across the Northeast.

Betsey Wilton of Our Favorite Foods in Portland, Oregon,[35] had a different approach to growth. Early on she hired a co-packer to pack and seal her fresh-pack pickles (which are only made seasonally from local produce). This enabled her to put out a larger quantity of pickles immediately and freed her to focus upon the more nuanced portion of the pickling process. She also did not go through the growing pains that many artisans who start food businesses out of their home face when they must find a commercial kitchen and obtain the proper paperwork and certifications in order to produce and sell edibles. The co-packing option was not flawless, however. In the first year the seals on some of her jars were faulty and she lost half of her stock. She—and her co-packer—learned from past mistakes, and she grew from 600 jars in 2009 to 16,000 jars in 2012, roughly doubling her output every year. This demand was driven, in part, from her distribution in a small local grocery chain, New Seasons Market, as well as a few other local markets, and online sales. As part of this growth, she has thus far stayed true to her commitment to use as much local produce as possible, and does all of her fresh packing for the year in a few hectic weeks at harvest. And from the beginning she chose to work with a packer, rather than process all of the jars herself, which some might argue is at odds with the artisanal ethos. But when I spoke with her she was at a point where to expand she would have to change her process—she was just unsure of how. Will she look farther afield for produce? Or start to make pickles year round? These questions of sourcing, sustainable growth, and identifying and staying true to one's mission are the issues that many start-ups struggle with. Yet the question of growth is one that can have impact on the larger distinction as being craft or artisanal.

What is interesting is that the idealized, often pastoral narrative of the passionate pickler, picking their own produce from a backyard garden, stirring pots, and wearing an apron, is one that is still beneficial to help gain sales and publicity—and it often is not completely inaccurate, at least initially. However, there is an interesting unwillingness for the average consumer to view the artisan or craftsperson as also being a savvy businessperson—a reluctance to be seen as moving toward a new post-pastoral narrative, perhaps because the (often urban) consumer believes that this negates the connection to the land and this higher ideal that they are vicariously buying into with their seven-dollar jar of pickles. Yet as more and more consumers are seeking "artisanal" goods, the values represented by these goods risk being diluted as the distinction becomes more marketing than a representation of actual counter-cuisine. For it can't be "counter" if the masses are buying into the same ideas. But yet, isn't this the goal of so many small-batch purveyors—not to be competing with "artisanal" versions of Vlasic and Frito-Lay products, but to raise the demand for—and value of—handcrafted goods sourced in an environmentally conscious way, and for a living wage for all involved?

Yet, despite the increasingly crowded pickle shelves, few of these artisans are making these decisions in a vacuum. Shamus Jones and Michaela Hayes both spoke of the openness of the Brooklyn artisanal pickle community. Jones noted that Rick Field of Rick's Picks and Bob McClure of McClure's Pickles both gave him invaluable advice on the business end, even sharing their distributor information. Likewise, Hayes said that she had reached out to Jones when she was first starting Crock and Jar and he was more than happy to advise her on balance sheets and other pickle business concerns. Hayes calls this helpful spirit, evident even among the seemingly competitive world of Brooklyn artisanal food producers, "coopetition." For, as Jones explained, he is open to more picklers. He believes the more that consumers are exposed to higher-quality (and more expensive) pickles—and other goods—the more they understand the difference and value of an artisanal food. As he explained, "No one wants to be the only restaurant on the block." Hayes is also exhibiting coopetition, as she offers many classes on pickling and fermenting. I asked if she was cutting into her own business with the classes she offers and she expressed a similar sentiment as Jones. Further, unlike Jones, whose business mission is more focused on a quality retail experience, Hayes also puts education—about the positive effects of local sourcing, about understanding where food products come from, and about the health benefits of fermented pickles—as part of her primary mission. She wants to sell pickles, yes, but she also wants to create a community around pickling and local sourcing, and sees diversity in her business mission as helping to accomplish this.

This diversity of mission has affected how Crock and Jar grows sustainably as well. Because supporting local and organic farms is a priority to her, Hayes is willing to pay a premium—and accept the uncertainty—of using only local produce. However, to keep her business sustainable, she has had, at times, to adjust her thinking, such as when she has chosen to source non-local or non-organic produce. However, she is not willing to alter this vision drastically, and has chosen to compensate for this uncertainty by diversifying—but staying with her passion of preserving produce and seasonality of eating. Similar to Jordan Champagne of Happy Girl Kitchen—who, in the spirit of coopetition, worked with Hayes before she returned to the East Coast to start Crock and Jar—Hayes has chosen to expand into teaching to help stay sustainable, by expanding her

potential customer base while also creating community and awareness about pickling and the locavore lifestyle.

SO WHAT IS AN ARTISANAL PICKLE?

A few weeks after Hurricane Sandy, I saw an ad for a Pickle Festival at Amsterdam Market in downtown Manhattan. The poster featured a bunch of pickles wearing aprons and fedoras, crowding
around tables to try cheese, bread, and yes, pickles, all under the
overpass of Lower Manhattan's New Amsterdam Market. To get to
the market, I walked past stores that had been flooded from the
hurricane, less than a month earlier, windows smudged with the silt
of the rising tide. Office buildings were clearly shuttered, with huge
dumpsters on the streets out front, ready to haul away floors of
debris. Much was different from the last time I had wandered
around the neighborhood, yet much was life as usual.

I turned a corner toward the water—a clear view of Brooklyn
was visible over the river—and there was a crowd, humans dressed
like the hip pickles in the festival poster, milling around a few dozen
tables of dill spears, kimchi, kraut, vegetables, and other preserves.
There were pickles from New York City companies that had been in
business for a century, and pickles from upstarts—including Brooklyn Brine, Crock and Jar, and even Grillo's from the Boston area.
There were fermented pickles and fresh-packed pickles. There was
pickled meat and pickled fruit and plenty of pickled cucumbers.
There were pickle makers who came from rural upstate New York
or Boston or Connecticut, and picklers who rented commercial
kitchen space in Brooklyn. I met an older gentleman who had been
in the business for decades and was currently in a fight over the
name of one of the oldest pickle companies in New York City. And
I met picklers in their twenties, who were equally passionate about
pickling—maybe more so.

As I walked around I tried so many pickles my stomach began to
ache from the acid. And I spoke with many pickle makers, asking
them about their business. Without fail, they were all very willing to

talk. This informal research reinforced much of what my longer interviews told me—that artisanal picklers were inspired by a passion for pickling, often through family or heritage, sometimes health benefits, but also through the creativity that pickling allows. I met, or at least tasted pickles from, many picklers who had been in business for a long time, Jewish or Polish or Russian, whose story relied upon the cultural history of pickles, both from their native country's cuisine and in the New World. There was little talk about sourcing or community, and clearly nostalgia and "authenticity" were these older picklers' selling points. Pickling was, and had long been, a method of preservation, a healthy snack, a food eaten off the street or on a holiday—fancy pickles and casual ones. Selling points were how long they had been in business, with images displayed of the original barrels filled with pickles, being sold street side.

The newer picklers, however, made claims to the farms they worked with, or the innovative flavors their pickles strove for, or the artisanship apparent in every jar. They spoke about how they started their business thoughtfully—they had what they believed was a quality product, and spent time to consider their business plan, how to become viable and sustainable, and what their philosophy might be, often spurred by their own changing place in the workforce or their desire to do something more tangible than sit in an office, or both. And their product was a result of an artisan or craftsman—as in they all are chopping and packing and boiling (when necessary) without the aid of large industrial machines. Their process is practiced and exact, and their recipes, often creative and nontraditional. These are handmade pickles done on a small scale, even when the scale is large.

So, what is a "craft" pickle or an "artisanal" one? Judging by these pickle purveyors' processes, they are hand packed; use high-quality, "natural," and fresh ingredients; and are made with high skill and practice. Common among the picklers is a dedication to sourcing high-quality produce, even if it isn't always local. And while many do express a preference for local produce, this is often—although not always—for business reasons rather than a commitment to the locavore philosophy. Rather, a preference for local has more to do with control over the freshness and quality and, when large enough, an ability to work directly with a farm to plant and harvest for a pickler exclusively. Community is important among most picklers as well, although in different ways. These relationships are highly valued by many picklers, and add to the dedication of the artisans or craftsmen themselves—for in every case it is an individual or partners who are the visionaries, founders, and decision makers for the company—to every aspect of the pickle's production.

The fermented picklers have their own influences, which very often are health-based; this, of course, is based upon traditional understandings of diet and eating for health, and combines classic whole-food and natural approach to eating with the modern interest in "health" food. Each pickle producer who focuses on fermented foods has a philosophy and mission that is more focused upon quality in sourcing, be it entirely or primarily organic, seasonal, and/or local. This interest in fermented pickles for health does appear to be more popular on the West Coast, where fermenting picklers already have a strong customer base without national reach. Fermenting on the East Coast, however, is still more often done to create "interesting" flavors—as with Shamus Jones at Brooklyn Brine—or is a part of the pickling process that is not necessarily highlighted or touted as being a selling point for health reasons, such as with Grillos or Pogue Mahone.

These regional disparities seem in line with consumer interests and regional identity as well; New York City, which has a long history with the pickle, from the many pickle barrel vendors associated with immigrants, to the pickle billboard in midtown when the pickle went mainstream thanks, in part, to Heinz. It stands to reason that many East Coasters see pickles through a more nostalgic lens, an edible reminder of cultural history, or a literal taste from the handful of pickle vendors who still sell fermented sours and half-sours by the pickle from barrels at small street-level store fronts, like their parents or grandparents might have done before them. Many of the West Coast picklers appear focused on pickling as a new and adventurous form of edible expression—one Portland, Oregon, pickle company is named Unbound Pickles and has a product titled Beatnik pickled beets—but there are, of course, outliers on each coast, with some West Coast picklers using iconic "old timey" imagery to sell their product, even if they aren't connected to a specific tradition within their city, and other East Coast picklers, like Real Pickles, touting the health benefits of lacto-fermented pickles. It seems, however, that pickling is on the verge of being more popularized, with fermenting getting the recent nod from the *New York Times* as the next food trend, and picklers from both coasts setting their sights on national distribution.

Yet, what distinguishes craft from artisanal? Alex Hozven seems to be the epitome of an artisan—fermenting for the challenge and the pleasure and the art of it. Taste is paramount, before considerations of whether a product is otherwise financially viable. One can't help but believe that she ferments for herself first and her customers second. And I can't help but see Shamus Jones as having the attitude of an artisan—striving to create new products and collaborations and finding value in the weird and interesting. But yet he is, arguably, the most successful of the picklers I spoke with, and is packing fewer and fewer jars himself, while delegating more and more of the daily duties of his business. When will his business no longer be that of an artisan? Is a "craft" pickler only focused on the skill and not being innovative with recipes and technique? While I do see shades of difference between these two terms, I also see much evidence for using these terms almost interchangeably—most especially because many of the artisans do.

Which brings about the issue of disparities seen among artisanal (or craft, if you prefer) pickle producers. When does a company grow so large they are no longer artisanal or craft? Shamus Jones, the largest pickler among those with whom I spoke, is by all accounts highly involved in the production of his pickles. Each pickle is hand packed, the recipes tested and refined, and the process closely watched by Shamus or an employee he trusts. Yet he also produces enough pickles to be distributed around the world. Unlike the process that Uri Laio or Sam Addison (until recently as least) claim, there are certainly jars that leave Shamus's cozy production space without him so much as gazing upon them. But will they taste the same as a jar that he has pickled and packed himself? I would venture to say *yes*. The traditional definition of a craftsperson is of one who practices his or her work with a high degree of skill, but for the consumption of others, and often under the tutelage or supervision of someone else. Thus, are Brooklyn Brine pickles craft, as they are made by the craftspeople that the artisan Shamus Jones taught and trained? One thing I could venture an accurate guess about is that Shamus Jones wouldn't care much on either distinction. He knows he makes a quality product, the semantics be damned.

So is craft just attention to detail or quality? Is artisanal about finding ways to move the craft forward? Most of these picklers noted that they were constantly refining their process and experimenting with new flavors, recipes, and techniques, which would create an argument for either moniker. Is it the pickler him- or herself that makes a pickle artisanal? I would say that quality is, of course, paramount, but that the answer to this question also lies with the story behind the product. We need both artisans to innovate and craftspeople to keep the industry strong—and often these people are one and the same. Many people will prefer one distinction over the other, or claim to be one or both. In the end, perhaps it is about the pickle and the story that gets the pickle to my plate. Thus the price of a jar of artisanal pickles buys one not only the tangy, thoughtfully sourced pickled produce inside, but also the knowledge that the purchase of this product helps to preserve and support the artisan—or craftsperson—behind the product as well.

3

CHEESE

The Power of the Post-Pastoral

I had to wake up before dawn in inland central California to make it to Marin County by our 9:00 a.m. meeting time. Driving through dark rural landscape to the sun coming up over the tangled highways of the greater San Francisco area, there was urban and suburban landscape as far as the eye could see—and I knew I was only getting closer to the coast. How could there be farms west of the city? I wondered. This East Coast girl was amazed that there could be some of the most fertile grazing land in the state this close to downtown. So as I skirted downtown, and the view from the highway quickly turned from urban to industrial to rural, I realized how unique Marin County is. Just northwest of San Francisco, Marin County juts out even further west into the ocean, its topography even more dramatic than the infamous hills of the city to the south. Mostly rural farmland and rugged parkland, even in winter the sun was shining bright and the temperature warm enough to leave my coat in the car. I drove up and over hills, watching the signal to my phone, acting as GPS, grow fainter in each valley and then stronger again as I headed back uphill. Only later did I learn that it is the topography of these hills and valleys that promotes such rich grasslands for livestock grazing.[1] Finally, I turned up the driveway toward Donna Pacheco's farm, where she makes Achadinha Cheese. It was only then that I realized that until this point, I had only met urban artisans—my GPS had found me distillers in back alleys and chocolate makers in unmarked industrial spaces. But I had yet to visit a rural artisan, let alone a farm. Only later did I consider what this meant about the artisanal food movement in America and so many industries that had their start in rural kitchens and now resided primarily in industrial spaces and rented commercial kitchens in urban centers. For now, I quickly changed into my rubber boots and opened the car door to the muddy dogs running to greet me.

Donna Pacheco was not far behind, and she was the most gracious tour guide, leading me through the immaculate cheese-making house—where I found just a large metal vat in the middle of an empty room, then moving on to the aging cave; there were dozens of perfectly round wheels towering above me from shelves that lined the walls. Then I had a taste of her small selection of goat's and cow's milk cheeses. But that was just the beginning of our tour.

Figure 3.1.   Pastures in Marin County, California.

I met her oldest son, now a twenty-ish young man who had grown up on the farm. He barreled up to the cheese-making building in his dirty pickup, en route to the outer reaches of the farm to do some maintenance. We visited a litter of piglets just a few weeks old, and then walked out to the milking area. It was what this northeasterner would describe as a perfect spring day—the shade was cool, but the sun was warm enough to shed another outer layer. And as Donna and I walked along her beautiful property, visiting her pigs and goats and chickens and cows, the cheese-making building and the milking room, I got the sense of how integrated her cheese-making craft is with her farming—and how much both of these efforts rely on her stewardship of the land around her and the unique climate of Marin County, not to mention the community of farmers and dairy-men and -women and cheese makers and consumers on whom she, in turn, relies.[2]

Donna Pacheco is passionate about her cheese making, but she is also representative of the subset of cheese makers who consider themselves farmers first. She said she began making cheese from her milk because "it made sense" financially. After the number of farms began to drop in Marin County—from more than three hundred at its peak to fewer than eighty today[3]—the Pachecos sought a way to keep the family farm alive. They found it in adding value to their milk—in making cheese. While it takes roughly ten pounds of milk to make one pound of cheese (plus both time and labor, of course), the price one can get for cheese is far more than ten times the price one can get for milk (which is generally less than twenty cents a pound), making cheese a smart venture for smaller farms looking for additional revenue streams. The Pacheco's dairy had been in the family since 1955, founded by Jim Pacheco's father, William. Jim and his wife, Donna, are now running the farm and dairy with their four children, whose pictures, often with either rounds of cheese or animals, adorn the website in almost equal number. But by all accounts, the Pachecos—and Donna in particular, as the point person for their cheese making—are dedicated to continually improving their product, which they have been making for more than a dozen years. The story of their cheese—how they

Figure 3.2.   The aging room at Achadinha Cheese Company in Marin
County.

present and market it to consumers—is similar to the narrative of many of the artisan cheese makers who tell their family story, the pastoral image of them working the land, and the terroir of their cheese, unique not just to California or Marin—or Wisconsin or Vermont—but to *them*.

Achadinha Cheese is very good. They offer two aged cheeses, one goat's milk and the other goat and cow, and fresh goat feta and flavored cheese curds (described on their website, somewhat jokingly but perhaps fittingly, as "counterculture"), sold at more than ninety farmers markets within a two-hour drive of their farm.[4] Donna, in speaking about her cheese making, does consider herself artisanal, noting that her process is "small, gentle, and by hand." Donna is exactly who I might have imagined a cheese maker to be. Loving with her family and the animals, generous with her time and energy as she showed me around her farm, and proud to be among the community of both farmers and cheese makers in and around Marin. The Achadinha Cheese actual *and* fashioned narrative is representative of one of the common modern stories of artisanal cheese in America.

More has been written about artisanal cheese than perhaps any other artisanal industry. To add to this research, I interviewed more than a dozen cheese makers in person, with almost a dozen more offering responses digitally. Integrating my research with other excellent writing about the industry today, I have come to see how artisanal cheese fits into the larger narrative of the new artisanal food revolution. While this industry is seemingly the most mature in the modern artisanal food movement, the contemporary narrative of modern artisanal cheese is still only a decade or so old. These cheese makers are family farmers and urban artisans, career changers, and those with ancestral dairy roots. Yet regardless, the relationship that producers have with their product and the narratives they represent have greatly influenced the new wave of artisanal food industries, providing a link between rural and urban artisanal traditions, and being on the forefront of using narrative to define the value that artisanal, small-batch or craft food provides beyond the product itself. That artisanal cheese has been available in the United

States on a more visible level than other industries causes it to feel more mature than others, yet the number of cheese makers has also grown exponentially in the past decade, and for reasons similar to other craft goods. And while pickle makers have often been defined as urban-based neo-hip entrepreneurs, cheese makers' place among artisanal food is, at first glance, that of the pastoral ideal, incorporating the influence of European traditions and American farming to create a product steeped in history—and not entirely revolutionary.

Yet, the true story of artisanal cheese today is moving beyond this pastoral image, and is just as likely to find its roots in American innovation as European traditions. There are examples of both those who consider themselves artisans and those who are focused on making a quality product to add value to their milk, who might shy away from the term *artisanal*. There are those inspired by the past—their heritage, their family dairy business, the long history of cheese makers domestically and around the world—but most are also seeking to do something new and unique. Influencing nearly all of the cheese makers is their connection to the land and the animals that live upon it—the terroir of their cheese—that also extends to how they work with the land, how they exercise their craft, the results of these aspects coming together, and how consumers interact with and perceive their product. And finally we see how the narratives surrounding cheese have helped to influence the artisanal food narrative as a whole—for cheese makers were among the first food artisans to find a foothold with the growing foodie population, and their post-pastoral story has influenced both urban and rural artisans in this new food revolution. Cheese represents living off the fat of the land, a connection not to just growing one's own food, but to animals as well, to fancy cheese courses and rustic snacks. The narrative of the contemporary cheese maker has helped inspire the new artisanal food revolution and represents an important story among them today. And while each industry relies upon the larger narrative of its artisans to shape the public perception of the product and sell it to consumers, none, perhaps, rely so heavily upon this than artisanal cheese.

WHAT IS CHEESE?

Cheese is a general term that encompasses many varieties of curdled milk or cream. Some believe that to be considered a "true" cheese (i.e., not a "fresh" cheese, like cream cheese or ricotta, which are curdled using acid *or* rennet) the milk must be curdled by *both* acid and rennet. First a culture is added to the milk (or with raw milk that culture is already present) that "ferments" the milk (using the basic process in lacto-fermented pickles), increasing the acidity. Then the rennet—originally an enzyme derived from the stomach of an un-weaned ruminant animal, like a lamb, kid, or calf, but increasingly made in a lab from both animal and vegetal origins—is added to break apart the milk caseins, separating the milk into curds (basically solids) and whey (liquid), often aided by heat. The curds (which are now, technically, cheese) can be cut apart to release more whey, or otherwise manipulated through molding or draining or aging to create various styles of cheese.

True to the nature of American artisanal cheese, there are no strict definitions of terms or categories. Various cheese authorities have asserted similar broad categories for classifying cheese, but I will defer to the American Cheese Society's distinctions: fresh, soft-ripened, semi-soft, and firm/hard. Fresh cheeses are those curdled using either acid or rennet, like fresh ricotta, chevre, and others. These can spoil quickly and when aged become a member of a different category. Soft-ripened cheeses are only briefly aged and ripen from the center. Their rind is edible and is sprayed with a special mold before the aging period begins. By U.S. law, cheeses aged less than sixty days—like fresh and soft-ripened—must be made from pasteurized milk. Soft-ripened cheeses include—and share characteristics with—brie and tripe crème, having milder flavor and an almost runny interior at room temperature.

Semi-soft cheeses have a firmer but still creamy interior, and may have a flavor that ranges from mild, like fontina-style cheese, to pungent, like blue cheeses. They may be made from either raw or pasteurized milk, depending on the aging times and preferences of the cheese maker, and have little or no rind.

Firm/hard cheeses are sometimes separated into different categories, and represent a wide array of styles. Their texture ranges from chewy to grateable, and their flavor can be mild or pungent or anywhere in between. The main characteristic of firm/hard cheeses is the aging process, which gives the cheese additional time for the moisture to evaporate. There is often an inedible rind, and the milk can be raw or pasteurized depending on the cheese maker's preference. Within these categories are natural rind cheeses, in which a rind develops naturally through the aging process, or washed rind cheese, in which a rind is created by surface-washing the cheese with any number of ingredients (like beer, wine, or some other mixture that encourages good bacteria growth).

Blue cheese is created when the added bacteria *penicillium roqueforti* is exposed to air, generally when the cheese maker punctures the exterior of the cheese to create "veins." Blue cheeses can be found in any of the aforementioned categories except fresh cheeses. Processed cheeses are cheese by-products made by combining any of the cheeses above with stabilizers, emulsifiers, flavor enhancers, or any other ingredient with the intention to make a shelf-stable product suitable for mass distribution, like cheese spreads and American cheese slices. There are, of course, a multitude of varieties of cheese within these broad categories, but these definitions are intended to give a brief overview of the industry standards.[5]

An understanding of the general styles of cheese is also useful when envisioning the cheese-making process. For example, fresh cheeses are the only styles that do not require any aging, which means they are the easiest styles to make for those with limited space, such as urban cheese makers. A longer aging process can be more influenced by the climate of the area and wash-rind cheeses can open the cheese maker up for a wide range of creative and technical variances. While the term *artisanal* is not regulated by the American Cheese Society or any other American governing body, they do note that the term "implies that a cheese is produced primarily by hand, in small batches, with particular attention paid to the tradition of the cheese maker's art, and thus using as little mechanization as possible in the production of the cheese." This is considered to be the accepted general definition within the industry.

BRIEF HISTORY OF CHEESE MAKING IN AMERICA

Like pickling, cultures around the world discovered similar techniques for cheese making and have been using these methods to preserve milk for millennia. The first goats and cows reportedly arrived in America with European settlers in the mid-1600s, and it stands to reason that their native cheese-making techniques came along as well. Thus cheese making was primarily a homestead activity until the technological advances of the 1800s saw a rise in the availability of refrigeration, transportation, and mechanization, and a subsequent interest in mass production of food. One such change was evident in New York State, once a hub of American cheese making. By the 1830s there were cheese "brokers" who bought and sold farmhouse cheese from rural areas to bring to urban retailers. They precipitated a growth of small cheese factories within the next few decades to collect local milk and make cheese on a larger scale, often by one cheese-making family. This promoted more uniformity in American cheese making and was an initial step toward mass production—including changing consumer tastes and instituting and broad safety measures.[6]

Also, while many think of Europe when considering long traditions of artisan cheese making, few give appropriate credit to the history of American cheese artisans. Wisconsin, in particular, found that their land was more inclined for dairy farming than growing crops, and small—and then larger—cheese-making facilities grew along with the ability to chill and transport these goods to other parts of the country. The styles from this initial hub of cheese making were influenced by the German and Swiss heritage of many Wisconsiners. These cheese makers were practicing artisanal production methods and often developing their own variations on European styles of cheese, but because they were viewed as laborers rather than artisans, this rich history is sometimes discounted. Further, the styles that are considered "everyday" cheeses—like limburger or swiss—are still being made by artisanal methods, but the craft intrinsic in their production is sometimes forgotten about in comparison to other cheese-making traditions, like those from France, Italy, and Spain, whose cheeses are considered "fancy" or special-occasion treats.

Inconsistencies in quality caused the American cheese industry to suffer in the mid to late 1800s, dropping off exports and damaging its reputation, and by the 1880s state commissions were established in various cheese-making regions to help ensure quality. Interestingly, pasteurization was initially seen as a cost-cutting measure that allowed raw milk to resist souring for longer, and pasteurized milk was seen as of lesser quality. This was not inaccurate, as before 1910 commercially pasteurized milk was often not heated to the temperature required to kill all dangerous pathogens, but because of the misconception about its safety, it was often handled more carelessly. The next ten years saw continued health issues with fluid milk as the industry standards worked to keep up with newly available technology and information on milk safety. By the 1920s, increased regulations—and the costs that came with them—helped to increased cheese production and consumption, as consumers saw it as a safer dairy option and small dairies were forced to sell to large cheese factories because of the increased cost of pasteurizing milk for fluid consumption, despite that this did not eradicate the risk of food-borne illness. However, it took another few decades to establish research on pasteurization standards to help eradicate rampant ailments like tuberculosis, and even after pasteurization standards were put into effect in 1933, as late as 1938, about 25 percent of all food- and water-borne illnesses could be traced to contaminated milk.[7] The result was eventually broad-based laws affecting the fluid milk and cheese industries, some of which were adopted with little critical analysis as new studies surfaced, such as the requirement that all raw milk cheeses be aged sixty days before they can be sold. While there is no doubt that laws requiring pasteurization and governing other aspects of food production have drastically improved public health, critics cite the one-size-fits-all mentality. Cheese makers, in particular, have noted multiple studies that indicate that pasteurization influenced "the microbial flora, extent of proteolysis, levels of D-lactate, some volatile fatty acids, and the sensory properties of the mature model cheese," thereby changing the flavor and chemical makeup of the end product[8]—statistics noted when arguing for changing the rules on raw milk cheese making.

Cheese-making trends in rural areas, following a correlation with dairy farms, saw the number of cheese makers decreasing but the amount of cheese being produced increasing into the mid-1900s. During this time, technological advances were also changing the way some cheese was being made by automating some processes and introducing new techniques for preservation—such as the invention of American cheese, really a shelf-stable processed cheese product introduced by Kraft in 1950. While the newly dubbed "American cheese" variety was becoming popular during this time, so were Italian varieties of cheese increasing in demand. The first *latterias*, or Italian cheese makers, opened in New York City around the turn of the twentieth century, offering fresh mozzarella and ricotta, initially from cows kept within city limits. It was in part the popularization of such immigrant food—most notably through American interest in Italian American foods like pizza and pasta—that further grew national interest in cheese. Many cheese makers, even in Wisconsin, where Swiss and German styles ruled, adapted to consumer demand and began making mozzarella, ricotta, and other newly popular Italian varieties, but they used mass-production methods that would allow the cheese to stay fresh longer than what was often made and sold out of urban and small-town *latterias*.

Similarly, the sales of the once-popular American style of dry jack, whose salty tanginess was often compared to Parmigiano-Reggiano, dropped when Kraft invented grated parmesan in 1945. Around this time many production facilities scaled up and automated, pushing smaller, artisanal factories out of business. Emblematic of this is the story of the cheese factories in Wisconsin's Green County, first established in 1868 and once considered the "Swiss

Cheese Capital of the United States." They boasted more than two hundred swiss-style factories by 1910, all making cheese by hand using artisanal methods. Yet by the 1950s the vast majority had upgraded to stainless steel and were molding swiss cheese in forty-pound blocks. Today only eleven of those factories remain.[9]

This industry movement toward mass production and consumer habits away from small grocers and specialty stores and toward larger supermarkets, paved the way for large-scale cheese production to overtake smaller artisanal makers. American consumption of cheese has been growing steadily since the mid-1900s, and has more than tripled—to thirty-one pounds per person—in the last forty years, with mozzarella making up more than a quarter of all cheese made in America.[10] These cheeses were increasingly mass produced with automated production methods; the prices were kept low in part by economy of scale—the number of cow dairy farms dropped by 88 percent between 1970 and 2006,[11] yet the sales of U.S. dairy products continues to rise.[12] This means that fewer farms are producing more milk, and the newer, larger farms can better compete against their smaller competitors. The artisanal cheese resurgence has happened in part because cheese making is one way for smaller dairy farms to add value to the milk they produce.

While there were certainly small cheese makers in America who continued to make handcrafted cheese throughout the 1900s—Ig Vella in California and Joe Widmer in Wisconsin for example—the overall trend was toward mass production and mechanization until the counterculture movement in the 1960s and back-to-the-land movement of the 1970s inspired other cheese makers like Laura Chenel, who was known as America's first commercial producer of goat cheese in 1979; Mary Keehn, who founded Cypress Grove in 1983; and Coach Farm, one of the first artisanal chevre producers in the Hudson Valley in 1985, to name a few. Suddenly fresh goat cheese was a popular salad topping or used in myriad appetizers and vegetable dishes, and more hip entrepreneurs were returning to the land to take up cheese making as a profession. Also, in 1983 the American Cheese Society was founded as a grassroots organization that supported artisanal cheese making, with thirty cheese makers entering the ACS's first competition in 1985. Throughout the 1980s more than a handful of people, angered by or bored with urban or corporate life, sought out a rural landscape in which to live their pastoral fantasies tending animals or growing vegetables. Some of these new farmers took up cheese making as well, as a way to exercise their creativity, be proud of their handiwork, or add value to their milk. These cheese makers were sometimes inspired by European traditions, other times with a goal to make something new—and slowly their numbers—and community—grew. Many of those entering this first wave of modern artisanal cheese making did so for "lifestyle" reasons—such as a desire to improve their everyday life through making a product they believe in or by working with their hands or the land. [13]

Yet what also grew during this time was the consumer demand for "fancy" cheese. Greater access to international travel introduced sophisticated travelers to classic cheeses from France, Italy, and Spain, and other European countries with prized food cultures. The European tradition of cheese plates became more popular at upscale restaurants, and while imports of European cheese increased, so did American efforts to make handcrafted cheese of similar quality. Further, with the number of farmers markets growing along with the artisanal mystique around these new places of commerce, cheese makers had more opportunities to sell their products directly to the public, and for a relatively high price point.

By 2003 the American Cheese Society had 776 members, which included cheese makers, retailers, home enthusiasts, and academics. This increased to more than 1,200 by 2009—and the number of entries in the annual competition to over 1,300—demonstrating the large increase in artisanal cheese making in the last decade. So while the narrative of the first wave of artisanal cheese makers was influenced by the desire for the pastoral, by and large the second wave artisanal cheese makers often speak of "building vital rural communities" [14] as a primary impetus, inclusive of economic reasons and larger cultural values. This new influx of artisanal cheese makers includes both urban ex-pats from the city as well as family farmers who had been in business for generations and were looking for ways to "add value" to their milk—as the Pachecos have with Achadinha Cheese. Noting the benefits of this growing industry, Vermont and Wisconsin—states with historically smaller herds than the relatively new dairy powerhouse state of California—both instituted programs to provide support to dairy farms seeking to expand into artisanal cheese making, with a goal to bolster small businesses and rural job creation.[15] These domestic educational efforts have influenced some new cheese makers, while others, more often those turning to cheese making as a career change, went to Europe to be inspired by centuries-old traditions, many times seeking out climates similar to theirs in the United States. Regardless of whether today's artisanal cheese makers started thirty years ago or within the last few years, or whether they were influenced by American traditions or European, the industry today is marked by the importance placed upon the treatment of the land and animals, the pastoral narrative of farming juxtaposed with innovation and originality in cheese-making styles and processes. Thus the new narrative of American artisanal cheese making melds the traditional and the modern to inspire consumers to value these handmade goods in a way that hasn't before been seen, and helps to bridge the gap between rural and urban artisanal food across all industries.

WHO IS MAKING CHEESE TODAY

The Vermont Cheese Trail takes you past, at my last count, forty-four cheese makers over almost three hundred miles of Vermont's varied terrain—highways that take you between mountains, country roads that connect small towns with one, or no, traffic lights, and the sometimes dirt paths that seem to be leading nowhere, until you end up exactly at the farm to which you were navigating. I spent a few days in Vermont in February 2013 traversing the state and meeting with a handful of craftspeople. In the time I spent in this rural landscape visiting artisans, I met a variety of people whose stories about how they came to make cheese and the meaning of *artisanal* represented the key narratives of Vermont—and even American—artisanal, mostly farmstead, cheese.

My first visit in Vermont was with George Miller from Jericho Hill Farm. I drove up to his farm in four-wheel drive, my small SUV navigating the deep, muddy ruts made by his pickup. He led me to his office—really a mostly empty room with a view of his cow pasture slightly downhill. While Marin County was hilly, its topography, with more rolling greenspaces, and, of course, considerably milder winters, is significantly more suitable for larger herds than Vermont's more dramatic, mountainous landscape. Looking out at George's pasture, sloping downhill, ringed by forest and covered in late-winter snow, this contrast was immediately obvious.

George is typical of the farmer who has turned to cheese making to add value to his milk, primarily as an effort to keep his farm economically viable. Jericho Hill Farm has been a working dairy for over a hundred years. "You'll eke out a living but you'll never get rich," George said—and it was, in fact, low dairy prices that got him into cheese making. It was more of a business decision than a creative one—George asserts, "I'm not an artist, I'm just a farmer." To learn his craft he worked with John Putnam at Thistle Hill Farm and took classes at the University of Vermont's Vermont Institute for Artisan Cheese (VIAC) and a workshop from Peter Dixon, a local cheese maker (and legend—most of the cheese makers with whom I spoke referenced Peter in some way). Rather than "artisanal," George calls his cheese "farmstead"—as in the American Cheese Society's definition of a cheese that was made on the farm where the herd resides and only from milk from that herd. He makes classic American varieties like Colby Cheddar and Jack, unabashedly everyday styles, made with care.

Jericho Hill Farm is a small cheese-making facility. George's primary source of income is selling milk, and his wife still works full-time at her non-farm job. In the late fall—they initially started making cheese in the summer, but he found that the milk was more suitable to cheese making later in the year—he brings about six cows a season to the barn and uses their thousand pounds or so of milk to make about a hundred pounds of cheese that he sells at small

markets and farmers markets in Vermont and New Hampshire. His
sister and nephew often help; it is truly a family affair, with the
larger familial interest in helping keep the farm afloat and in the
family. He's fine with the balance of selling milk and cheese at the
moment—the added revenue he gets from the cheese helps to sustain the farm. George finds the current regulations "doable." It was
the stricter regulations from thirty-odd years ago that forced out the
previous generation of cheese makers, he said. He is very safety
conscious and chose a longer-aged hard cheese to make, in part
because he believes there is less of a chance of any health or food-
safety problems than with fresh or soft cheeses. Now he is inspected
every three months and is happy about that. "I'd eat any of our
cheese—we don't risk it. People who do shouldn't be in the business," he said.[16]

Jericho Hill Farm's cheese is a semi-hard, aged style. George
doesn't use a natural rind, but ages in plastic, a feature more often
seen with commodity cheeses. George considers his cheeses "in the
middle"—farmstead and handcrafted, but not super high end. The
term *moderate-speed foods* has been coined recently[17]—as in not
fast-food-like processed cheese, and not slow, long-aged and high-
maintenance varieties that often go for twenty dollars or more a
pound. This middle ground of handcrafted, high-quality cheeses is
often forgotten in the overall narrative of artisanal foods, but it is an
important category to consider when painting the overall landscape
of handcrafted, small batch, and artisanal cheese today, especially as
more and more people are getting into artisanal cheese in Vermont.
George believes that "the recession had something to do with" it,
alluding, perhaps to the marked increase in the number of cheese
makers who started in the industry in the past decade or less. And
while George can understand most perspectives on the disagree-
ments around defining the term *artisanal*, when pressed, he says
that farmstead is an important element, because those who are producing the milk know the raw ingredients' characteristics[18]—something also inherent in many definitions of the approach of an artisan.
For him cheese making is primarily to diversify and create a new
revenue stream to make more money, perhaps more akin to the

cheese making laborers in Wisconsin, and he's happy making quality, everyday varieties. With sales that are "very word of mouth,"
George is pleased with the balance. And balance is something to
strive for when many narratives seem to support the assertion that
all handcrafted cheeses are expensive indulgences best suited for a
dinner party cheese plate. George and his Jericho Hill Farm cheese
remind us that artisanal goods need not be reserved for special occa-
sions or seen as high-end indulgences.

Like Donna Pacheco, George is typical of the artisanal cheese
maker who sees himself as a farmer first and foremost. However,
unlike Achadinha Cheese, whose public narrative focuses upon the
cheese itself, and whose offerings include both "everyday" cheese
curds and the most expensive aged varieties, Jericho Hill Farm's
story makes little mention of the product itself, but rather focuses on
the long history of the farm and the family. Their signature story, as
posted on their Vermont Cheese Council webpage, focuses on
Great-Grandpa George Nelson Miller buying the farm in 1907, us-

Figure 3.3.   The view from Jericho Hill Farm in Vermont.

ing money sewn into the lining of his jacket.[19] The accompanying photos further emphasize the pastoral life of the Miller family farm and creamery, featuring their iconic red barn in both summer and winter, as well as George with a cow and calf, a wheel of cheese, and his smiling family.

It is apparent that Jericho Hill Farm characterizes their cheese as representative of down-home goodness—an authentic farmer and farming family who value their animals and their land and their long farming legacy. The cheese is barely mentioned on the website—but of course it must be good: it comes from a fifth-generation farm run by an apple-cheeked family who love their cows and the cheese that comes from their milk. The narrative that Jericho Hill Farm cheese presents—from its small web presence to its point of sale, mainly at farmers markets—has helped to connect the consumer with the producer, and sets up that expectation for a "medium speed" but artisanal product. Consumers are willing to pay a few dollars more for George's Colby than for the block they can buy at the supermarket because of the relationship they have with him—as a neighbor, as a craftsman—and the trust they put in his stewardship of the land and his animals. While he may not explicitly package his cheese as "sustainable" or "local," by the sheer nature of his family's story, front and center, and the point of purchase at the farmers market—often meaning that George is selling to his neighbors—those values are implicit and help to raise the overall monetary value of his cheese.

If George Miller considers himself a dairy farmer who happens to make cheese, John Putnam might be better characterized as a cheese maker who has a farm. John grew up in Vermont, and then returned to the area more than fifteen years ago with his wife, Janine, leaving a successful career as a commercial litigator in Boston. At Thistle Hill Farm, John, Janine, and their children have a herd of Jersey cows—mostly Janine's purview—and raise them on organic feed. On the afternoon I visited, Janine was headed to the barn in her muck boots, clearly at home with her herd, while her husband was packing for a flight to Europe leaving later that evening. John showed me around his cozy cheese-making house, designed and built by him to meet his specific craft and business needs. We donned sanitary shoes and peeked in the main cheese-making room—a shiny copper vat its centerpiece. John explained that he had the vat custom made for him in a design more common in Europe and that the copper does impart flavor and encourages chemical reactions that enhance the taste of the cheese. He is clearly devoted to his single variety—Tarentaise—an aged, raw milk, semi-soft farmstead cheese made in the tradition of the Savoie region in the French Alps, but uniquely its own. John cites the terroir of North Pomfret, where he lives, as being integral to the cheese's uniqueness and success. And it has been highly praised: it has won eleven national and international awards since 2003 and has been written up in numerous national publications.

Tarentaise is a delicious, original cheese, even as it is influenced by French traditions. Creamy and nutty, very eatable but not so mild as to be forgettable, it is easy to see why it has garnered such praise and is enough for John and Janine to focus on a single variety. This is a noble addition to a cheese course, something to be savored on its own—slow food to George Miller's medium-speed cheeses. John, the primary cheese maker, is dedicated to his craft and process, and is as meticulous with Tarentaise's promotion and packaging, in the larger sense of the word, as he was with the building of his cheese house. The story of his cheese highlights the "local" connection, the handmade and artisanal nature of his cheese. (As his website states, "You know where it was made, by whom, when, and with what. This is a rare quality these days. We plant the seeds, mow and bale the hay, take care of and milk the cows, and make the cheese.")[20] But yet the cheese's public story also combines this pastoral imagery and local virtue with a connection to its European inspiration. The cheese is both local and not. It is unique, but influenced by a long tradition. It tastes of the romantic terroir of this corner of Vermont, but also uses scientific studies to speak to the cheese's healthfulness and purity. The Tarentaise narrative is a pastoral one, with a touch of European flair and a dose of the post-pastoral. John makes certain to touch upon all of the values impor-

tant to today's artisanal cheese consumers—and does so authentically.

Thus, unsurprisingly, considering the care that he has taken with
his space and cheese making, he believes that the term *artisanal*
does need to be defined and enforced, and agrees that it is getting
"diluted" with the current marketing efforts by big business seeking
to cash in on the efforts of cheese makers like him. The Vermont
artisanal cheese industry has been rapidly growing, with the Vermont Cheese Council around fifteen years old and the number of
cheese-making members growing from ten to over forty since its
inception, and John is already seeing the constraints of the land and
industry. Vermont farmers, with homesteads built on the state's
uneven terrain, can only keep so many cows, which means that only
so much milk and cheese can be produced. Thus John has been
particularly cautious to build Tarentaise as a brand in its own right,
crafting the narrative of his cheese—the story and influences of its
development, how it is influenced by the land and his family's herd
of cows, and the relationship he has with his environment, to expand
in ways that enable him to stay sustainable and still exercise his
creative muscle. He has licensed nearby Springberg Farm to make
Tarentaise, and plans to begin laying the groundwork to make charcuterie—what he believes will be a continually growing food trend.

John, who would define himself as a true artisan, is also a smart
businessman. He notes the need to be constantly promoting one's
product to get the press that is necessary to become successful beyond the local farmers markets. And John worked hard to reach the
level of success that he has seen, loading his first batch of cheese
into his trunk, and driving around the region to meet cheese buyers
and have them taste his product. Since he started making cheese in
2000, John can boast glowing national press and multiple awards.
As he has expanded his business to such success in the past decade,
he is thoughtful about how to continue that expansion into the future, understanding that one needs to keep quality high. He is a
cheese maker first, in the European tradition that inspired his unique
cheese during an information-gathering trip to Switzerland and
France more than a decade ago.[21] And as much as George Miller's

cheese reflects its humble beginnings, so does John's cheese reflect his worldview. Both are delicious, award-winning, handmade, and farmstead. Each presents itself via pastoral images of the cheese makers lovingly holding their product or caressing their livestock. And they consider each other friends and colleagues. But they also represent the opposite ends of the spectrum of artisanal cheese—at Jericho Hill Farm, cheese is a way to add additional value to their own milk to help keep their dairy farm economically viable; at Thistle Hill, cheese is a passion, an art, representative of the world-traveling cheese maker himself.

BEYOND PASTORAL

After visiting numerous, mostly farmstead, cheese makers in California and Vermont—as well as others in Massachusetts, New York, and Oregon—I have begun to see similar variations on the standard cheese-making narrative come alive at each location. The farmstead cheese makers often had the quintessential farm with a long driveway that led past grazing animals; the land and the sunny climate was often the focus in spacious California, which also featured newer buildings, while Vermont's typical turn-of-the-twentieth-century farmhouse and barn were more aligned with our pastoral vision of the area. The ground was muddy, the animals seemingly happily grazing unless being brought in for milking—which happens by machine, but with human facilitation. But then the cheese house, often a small outbuilding, was meticulously clean and modern. The steel—or in the case at Thistle Hill Farm, the copper—vat was gleaming, and muck boots and threadbare work shirts were swapped for hairnets and special shoes or booties. Cheese making is obviously science as well as craft; it's not a farm-hand delivering a sloshing bucket of milk to the farmer's wife standing at the stove, to turn it into curds and whey. It is here that the pastoral image—of the rolling green hills, the quaint old farmhouse and red barn, the farmer communing with the herd—meets the post-pastoral reality of farmer and cheese maker working *with* the land, where traditional meets modern, especially for the urban visitor like myself. And I can, after meeting cheese makers who have entered the industry for a variety of reasons, imagine how some combination of these dueling narratives is what has inspired some, often urban, career changers to (re)turn to the land, to cheese making. While some farmers have embraced this post-pastoral narrative as their own motivation to get into cheese making, largely it was a practical decision to add value to their milk, to express themselves with a new craft, or some combination of these. How they package and present their narrative to consumers, whether explicitly through their marketing materials or implicitly via their point of sale or other public face, also says much about their perspective on their place in the industry.

The media has certainly helped to romanticize the pastoral vision of the daily lives of some of these artisanal cheese makers, even if their own narrative has squarely reconciled with that of the modern process. But who wouldn't love the story of brothers Trystan and Max Sandvoss, who went to Harvard and then returned from promising careers in Hollywood to start First Light Farm and Creamery not far outside of Buffalo, New York? At first glance their story is pure pastoral. The press surrounding them always includes a photo of the smiling brothers with members of their herd, which have cute names like "Puzzle" and "Mayhem," and often shots of their goats grazing in the thick green grass of the western New York countryside. And as idyllic as this scene appears, it is largely accurate. These are brothers who are as handsome in person as in their press photos, and as charming.

I arrived mid-Sunday morning, during a sliver of time after most of the chores were done and before the brothers headed off to church. Trystan and Max showed me the cheese room and explained their process for making cheese from both their goats' milk as well as from local cow's milk that they purchase, and then detailed their plans (now realized) for making yogurt and bottling goat's milk for retail as well. The tour through the meticulously clean cheese-making room hearing of their process and plans was interesting, but not drastically different from the tours of other, similarly sized farms that I had visited. What was different was the time we spent in the barn, with the goats. The brothers, who had seemed conscious of time until this final stop on the tour, suddenly lost all hurry. They called each goat by name, stopping to pet or playfully tease one in the midst of answering a question. It was clear that they loved their herd and the products they produced from their milk.

But this classically bucolic scene is not the only one that Max and Trystan believe represents their business. "Our story" on their website quickly sets the scene of a modern milking operation:

> At 5:00 am on a Friday morning, most of the world is still asleep, but on 20 scrubby acres in pastoral Genesee County, a long hard day of work has already begun. The wash system for the milking lines is roaring, and its noise has awakened the herd, who are ready for breakfast and the morning milking. Nubian dairy goats are famously loud and . . . expressive. Luckily, there are no neighbors nearby who might complain. Trystan walks through the long, narrow, custom-built goat milking parlor, arms full of milking inflations. He slaps them into place, hooking the cups on a horizontal stainless steel bar, plugging the vacuum lines into ports underneath the waisthigh platform, and expertly inserting the milking lines into their own ports. "Alright, girls, we're ready for you!" A pulley is yanked, a sliding door opens, and suddenly a cluster of eager ruminants bursts into the parlor and quickly sort themselves into order, 12 at a time. . . .
>
> "We love cows too. We're milk people . . . milk nerds," Max laughs as he inspects a thermometer on one 5 ft x 5 ft x 6 ft stainless bulk tank (tiny, by industry standards) and opens the lids on another, inside of which is milk that has a rich, surprisingly yellow hue. It's 10:00 now. After a break for breakfast (coffee, toast, farm-fresh eggs, whey-fed bacon), the brothers have cleaned up, scrubbed in and started in on the second task of the day: transforming milk. "This is Jersey cow's milk—the good stuff!"
>
> First Light Farm produces both goat's milk and cow's milk dairy products. In four fast years that they've been here, their product line has expanded quickly and to great effect. "We started out with a fairly small supply of goat's milk, so we

reached out to our neighbor, who runs a Certified Organic Jersey Dairy, and started making blended milk cheeses," Trystan explains, flipping a switch above a tangle of plumbing lines marked, "Electrobrain." "Since then, our herd has multiplied and our supply has grown. So we have the ability to make lots of different kinds of cheeses, and we've moved beyond cheese too. We're at the scale where we can be flexible and make what people ask for."[22]

In true post-pastoral narrative style, the loving farmers also detail the work of an automatic milker; after a breakfast of fresh eggs and whey-fed bacon (when I visited them, neither lived with a partner, suggesting they also make their own three-course meals) they head to the cheese-making room, equipped with a sci-fi-sounding switch labeled "Electrobrain." While journalists and consumers may be drawn to First Light Farm and Creamery's classically handsome farmers and the story of young brothers returning to the land, the truth is Max and Trystan don't shy away from their use of technology, while still retaining their very personal and hands-on relationship with their animals and their cheese and dairy products, as is common with the new artisanal cheese maker today.

The story of Point Reyes Cheese similarly embraces this narrative that unabashedly combines the modern and the traditional to make quality cheese and preserve the family's dairy legacy. Not far from Donna Pacheco's farm in Marin County, I expected a similar tour from Jill Giacomini Basch, who had agreed to meet me and tell me more about their family business. While their website features pastoral images of their land, the cows, and the family—Jill and her sisters took over the family dairy business that their father had been running since 1959—it also had a slightly more polished sheen to it than that of some of the other, smaller cheese makers. But I was still surprised when I drove up a long driveway, past grazing cows, to a large new building that was part offices, part cheese-making area, part kitchen, and part public space, available for education purposes and events.[23]

Figure 3.4.   Goats from First Light Farm and Creamery in upstate New York.

Jill was extremely gracious as we sat down in lounge chairs around a coffee table and told me the story of her family's dairy—more than sixty years old—and cheese business, less than fifteen years old. Her father had grown up on a dairy farm and bought what is now called Point Reyes Farmstead with hopes of handing it down to his children. Then he had four daughters who weren't so interested in the dairy business. However, as their father neared retirement age, the daughters came up with a plan that would allow their father to (semi-)retire and still keep the farm viable and in the family. Like other dairies, they hit upon cheese making. However, unlike most of the other dairies I visited, they did not learn to make the cheese themselves, but rather hired a professional cheese maker to develop quality, unique products using the farm's milk, while the sisters took over the business and marketing. Point Reyes's first cheese was Original Blue, first made in August of 2000; they had chosen it partly because there were no other blue cheese makers in the region. Jill explained how they saw that first batch, which had to age six months before it was ready to be sold, as an experiment. They had no idea how it would be received. But Whole Foods became an early fan and proved that their gamble paid off. They have now gone on to make two blue cheeses, a semi-hard cheese called Toma, and fresh mozzarella that they sell mainly to nearby stores because of its short shelf life. Their cheeses have won numerous awards, and in fact my visit was a few days before the 2013 Good Food Awards were announced, and Jill shared that their newest cheese, Bay Blue, was to receive an award. Tasting the Bay Blue, it was not hard to see why. A blue cheese for those who don't like the style's pungency, it is also a blue for those who do. Perfectly balanced, a bit sweet and also sharp, with a texture that made it easy to eat on its own, it was truly one of the best cheeses I had ever tasted. After the cheese tasting, during which the cheese maker chatted for a few minutes and gave an overview of his rather scientific approach to developing his cheeses (while sneaking a few glances at Jill to ensure that he was staying on message), we went for a tour of the farm, which includes a closed herd of 330 animals that overlooks an inlet from the ocean.

I left Point Reyes Farmstead Cheese Company with a small logo-emblazoned cooler full of cheese samples, which I envisioned would make a fine happy hour spread a few hours later. But I also couldn't help but compare the polished packaging of Point Reyes with Achadinha Cheese just a few miles away. Besides the obvious differences in size, here was also a difference in cheese-making philosophy: the farmer/cheese maker versus the trained artisan. Both know their crafts well, but each came to this knowledge differently—and only one through the land on which they are working. Point Reyes is unabashedly post-pastoral—they embrace their family story and their modern comforts and their excellent cheeses. Their marketing and distribution is well honed, and their stated values are even aligned with those of the smaller cheese makers—local produce, land stewardship, humane treatment of livestock. The stated values are the same, the cheeses are still handmade, the milk

Figure 3.5.   Cheese Plate from Point Reyes Farmstead Cheese
Company.

used is farmstead—what is the difference between these two cheese makers? Does the answer lie only with their narrative—that Point Reyes Farmstead Cheese Company more fully embraces the role of the modern cheese maker using innovation and marketing to connect with consumers and stay viable?

Warren Belasco and Heather Paxson are but two food studies scholars who have noted how the modern narrative romanticizing farming (the pastoral lifestyle, the labor-intensive food production) influenced many artisans who are working today, as well as consumers' perception of these artisanal goods as imbued with similar values. And both have noted that it is the modernization of that pastoral narrative—the new post-pastoral vision of working *with* the land, rather than merely returning to it, of combining modern scientific understanding and traditional knowledge—that characterizes artisanal cheese makers, as well as artisans in other industries, today. The post-pastoral is characterized by the shiny vat in the cheese room, just a few dozen yards from the grazing animals themselves; it can be seen when the cheese maker tests the pH of the milk using a modern automated tool, but also relies on the feel of the curd to know when to remove it from the whey. The landscape is becoming a working landscape where modern scientific and technological advances meet traditions and intuitive knowledge passed down or relearned from generations past. The artisanal cheese makers of today are best characterized by this modern narrative, even as many still use classic pastoral imagery to characterize and sell their cheese, which comes to represent more than merely meal-time nourishment or a tasty addition to a cocktail party cheese plate. But yet even as most contemporary artisans do embrace this narrative, they are still sensitive to their product being perceived as a "vehicle for social and aesthetic value."[24] Thus many choose what narrative to highlight as they package and sell their cheeses, all with a goal to be a sustainable business.

Even as nearly all cheese makers willingly—and often necessarily—embrace the science and technology that enable them to milk more efficiently, better test their milk for safety, and sometimes even stir the cheese, there are some artisanal cheese makers who I believe are more openly embracing of their role as a contemporary artisan, helping to redefine the modern artisanal cheese maker. Neither First Light Farm and Creamery nor Point Reyes Farmstead Cheese Company is striving to be "authentically pastoral," and through this they are actually creating a modern sense of what is authentic.[25] While First Light Farm and Creamery demonstrates this through their detailed self-narrative, with Point Reyes the embracing of this identity was evident from the moment I pulled up to the beautiful modern building that housed their offices and event space. Yes, their cheese is technically farmstead, but it is not made by the same person who tends the animals or milks them; there is, in fact, a distinct separation between the two. But both sides of the same business are striving to do the best that they can—and the sisters who are (re)branding Point Reyes cheese are not pretending that it is anything other than what it is. They have built a well-designed multifunction space, and embrace the family narrative, but are also honest about the various needs of a sustainable business. They have the baby cows in the pen, they have the beautiful views, they have the fancy printed coolers to hand out cheese samples to visitors. And they are making delicious, award-winning cheese. Visiting the new office and cheese-making building, one doesn't get the sense that the sisters running Point Reyes Farmstead Cheese Company are in any way pretending to offer an "authentic" pastoral vision of ancient cheese-making practices. Cheese making is new for their dairy business, and they brought in an expert to do it well. What they offer is the quintessential modern view of the farmstead cheese company—sweeping vistas, comfortable seating, delicious cheese, a family story that consumers can get behind—but presented in a comfortable, uncompromisingly post-pastoral package.[26]

It is the acknowledgment that we must work with nature—that within nature we can find ways to improve our art, science, and technology—but it must be synchronous. Thus, cheese makers don't have to try and evoke a pastoral narrative—for themselves or their customers—but rather are helping to lead culture as a whole toward a place where urban recognizes and works with rural for overall sustainability. Urban also doesn't fetishize or romanticize rural, but sees it for what it is—an integral part of the overall ecosystem that provides food and nurtures all edible artisanal goods.

CONNECTION TO THE LAND

While many artisanal cheese narratives do present themselves as preserving traditional production methods, such as John Putnam's Tarentaise, most are also seeking to do something new and unique with flavor and variety. Influencing nearly all of the cheese makers is their connection to the land and the animals that live upon it—the terroir of their cheese—which also extends to how they work with the land, how they exercise their craft, the results of these aspects coming together, and how consumers interact with and perceive their product.

Take George Miller's acknowledgment that Jericho Hill Farm's cheese is best made from fall milk, indicating the difference that climate and pasture make upon the qualities of the milk. This direct connection between land and animal and milk is what most people think about when they consider terroir, a term most often used to express how the qualities of the land and climate are expressed when tasting wine. Yet terroir is increasingly being used to talk about other foods made with the expression of the raw ingredients in mind. I will discuss more of the scholarship being done on this topic in the next chapter, but in essence, more people are coming to embrace terroir—and a broader definition of the term—when talking about cheese as well, noting that cheese makers are "test-driving" using the language of terroir "as a vehicle for conveying the value of their craft practice and products."[27] Countries with more celebrated artisanal cheese traditions, like France, Italy, and Spain, have long used a similar idea of government-approved distinctions that indicate to consumers that the product has been produced in a specific region, using certain methods and raw ingredients, which have come to be synonymous with quality and higher prices among consumers. Yet American cheese makers bristle at such regulations and the governing oversight and lack of creativity implied with such distinctions. Rather American cheese makers tend to see terroir as scaled down to represent one farm, aging room, or small region. This exclusive notion of terroir has inspired innovation with cheese varieties and processes to help create products that are uniquely one region's, area's, or cheese maker's. One such example is Cowgirl Creamery's Red Hawk cheese, which was discovered when in an effort to rid certain bacteria that grew in their Point Reyes aging room during the summer, the brine wash instead promoted them, creating a uniquely flavored, well-balanced cheese that couldn't be replicated without the specific bacteria from the same specific climate. Thus a true American cheese innovation was born.[28]

But terroir has come to represent not just the flavor of the cheese, but also the values imbued through the cheese's production and the moral underpinnings of the cheese makers themselves. As scholars of terroir have argued,[29] how can one divorce the impact of human manipulation on the land, or the product itself? Further, cheese anthropologist Heather Paxson has said, "In calling attention to the material and effective relations between food-making and place-making, terroir might yet become an American model for the instrumental value of artisanal foods. Terroir's appeal lies precisely in its ideological flexibility; it can be translated to frame various relations between place and production."[30] And I will argue that cheese is on the forefront of the products that are redefining both the notion of terroir as well as the definition of artisanal food, in part because of its close relationship with both the land and the cheese maker, as well as its history—true and idealized—among American consumers.

It is these new cheese artisans who are forging a contemporary definition of American artisanal cheese in this country and beyond, and must do so in relation to European cheeses that come with their own inherent narrative of centuries-old traditions and pastoral vision of Heidi-like cheese makers toiling away on picturesque mountaintops. European cheeses have long been better known and more highly valued by upscale consumers, so it is not surprising that the smartest artisanal cheese makers understand that the industry has their work cut out for them as far as redefining American artisanal cheese. However, whether the cheese makers are large or small, located on the East Coast or West Coast, farmstead or urban, their stated values and public (and evident private) narrative are largely similar. Whether one chooses to embrace the pastoral or post-pastoral notion of farming or cheese making, in the end they are still selling a connection to the land, to the milk, and to the artisan, to make a product imbued with "added" value well beyond the milk itself.

HOW AMERICAN ARTISANAL CHEESE MAKERS HAVE INFLUENCED THE NEW ARTISANAL FOOD MOVEMENT

Driving past the rolling snow-covered pastures and leafless groves of trees—many with almost invisible sap lines crisscrossing them, feeding the local maple syrup business—the landscape looked no different here than in most other corners of the state. Vermont is decidedly rural—even Montpelier, its state capital, isn't much larger than a quaint small town with a couple of traffic lights. But I knew I was getting closer to the heart of sustainable agriculture and artisanal food in the region. Hardwick is home to the Vermont Food Venture Center, which provides resources and is an incubator for small, sustainable food businesses that help integrate and add value to Vermont's agriculture offerings. Their clients and producers make everything from hot sauces to baby food, with a mission to "build a regenerative, locally based, healthy food system" within Vermont and beyond.[31] While this wouldn't seem out of place in a "hip" urban center like Brooklyn or Portland, that this food business support system is smack in the middle of an area rife with family farms, many of which have been in business for generations, strikes one as particularly forward-thinking. But then again, the hip entrepreneur and counter-cuisine culture has long been alive in northern New England, home of Ben and Jerry's ice cream and Stonyfield Farm, two early businesses that were founded in 1978 and 1983 respectively, and whose missions were concerned with social and environmental sustainability well before these values became more mainstream.

Thus it is perhaps unsurprising that The Cellars at Jasper Hill in Greensboro, the next town over from Hardwick, is creating a new kind of American cheese entrepreneurial experience. While they do make their own farmstead cheese, they have also built state-of-the-art cheese caves to age their cheese—and the cheeses of other cheese makers that they co-brand—under the watchful eye of their skilled employees. No one is helping to write the modern narrative of artisanal cheese more than Jasper Hill. Not far past the quaint century-old farmhouses and barns of their neighbors, I turned onto Jasper Hill's property, and knew I was at the right place when I saw their iconic barn, so very Vermont hippy with its painted psychedelic imagery more than ten feet across, featuring a Bayley Hazen Blue cheese rising over the hills, referencing one of the first cheeses they became known for.

After driving past the painted barn, I pulled up to a small parking lot behind a nondescript building abutting a hill. Despite its unassuming exterior, I knew that there was an invisible hand of cheese caves reaching its fingers into the earth, and that these were modern, well-planned, and unique structures. As I entered the office, I met with Vince Razionale, my guide, who works in sales and marketing at Jasper Hill. He instructed me to don appropriate smocks, hairnets, and shoes, the latter of which I was expected to wash off between cheese caves to mitigate cross-contamination between aging rooms. After suiting up and receiving instructions, he took us beyond the office to the caves themselves. They are connected by the palm of the invisible hand—calling it a hallway would not communicate the vast football field–size of the space, or the tall ceilings that made it seem more spacious than it was in actuality. Some basic cheese-making work was done in this area, but it mostly was the connecting hallway among the caves.

The caves, known as "vaults," fanned out along this room, and some were larger than others, each with its own climate nuances—characteristics that continually changed and evolved, in part from the very cheeses that were being aged in the room and the terroir

Figure 3.6.   Barn at Jasper Hill Farm.

that they were imparting, but also from the *created* environment of symbiotic organisms manipulated by the cheese makers to maximize aging results. The first vault we visited had Jasper Hill's own bloomy rind cheeses aging. They had been made twelve days prior and were clearly labeled; a worker kept the detailed cheese calendar that identified when each cheese was to be wiped or moved.

A worker named Brian was in this vault and had rock music turned up loud, making me wonder, only half seriously, if that had any effect on the terroir. Racks of small rounds of cheese lined the vault's walls—the smell was unmistakably "stinky" cheese—ripe, pungent. We poked our head in the cave as Vince told me more about Jasper Hill's business model. They were co-opting a European tradition of separating the aging and cheese-making process, with a goal of "trying to help the scale of growth for the artisanal market."[32] Later I would consider this European model, and how it did make sense for a cheese culture whose products were based on tradition and consistency. Countries like France and Italy, who have designations for some of their products, like Parmigiano-Reggiano, which must be produced in a certain region and use specific processes and ingredients, have built brands upon these products and have reason to have workers who specialize in different processes of production. The end result is not intended to be unique from one maker to the other, and uniqueness would harm, rather than positively differentiate, the cheese maker. The result of the European model is consistently well-made, delicious, and high-quality products made with processes that have been passed down from generation to generation. This, combined with support from the government that is not given to artisanal producers in America, has also created a strong infrastructure for European cheese makers producing these classic varieties.

Some American cheese makers do point out, however, that despite the idealization of European cheese culture, many of their exported varieties are made using automated methods and in much larger batches than the consumer realizes. But for American cheese makers, uniqueness is most often prized. Rather than cultivating specific high-end American varieties, award-winning cheeses like Beehive Cheese's Barely Buzzed (a "new American Original" made with lavender and coffee)[33] and even Point Reyes's Bay Blue are striving to innovate on classic cheeses rather than merely create high-quality versions of standard varieties.

I was lucky to visit Jasper Hill's cheese caves and production complex. Known for their innovation in both cave design and business practices, they aren't open to the public and photos are prohibited. They are also the source of much debate—Jasper Hill makes their own (almost) farmstead cheese, using mostly milk from their herd of about forty-five cows, the rounds of which they age in their caves; they also have staff on hand to age other cheese makers' cheese in their caves, resulting in a co-branded final product. Amid the rumblings I heard from the various artisans I visited, some found this business practice good for artisanal cheese production: more cheese makers were able to expand to aged cheeses without having

to invest in their own aging facilities, at costs that were often daunt-
ing. However, others believed that this is harming the Vermont
artisanal cheese community by eliminating some of the variations
on aging of different cheeses, through Jasper Hill's various co-
branded or outright purchase agreements, which put numerous
brands under one, closely managed, roof. Others question the labeling of these cheeses as "artisanal" if they are now being touched by
numerous people, each with different—and sometimes autono-
mous—tasks in the process. It is an interesting question: must a
single cheese maker be the only one making the craft decisions with
an artisanal cheese? When does this kind of production model hurt
the idea of artisanal cheese versus helping some small artisans enter
the aged cheese market or other dairies add value to their milk to
help them survive?

The next vault we visited was number four, much larger than the
first and stacked to the ceiling with shelves of large rounds of clothbound Cabot cheddar. This was the cheese that helped the Cellars at
Jasper Hill actually happen, with its win of Best in Show in 2006
from the American Cheese Society. Cabot, a Vermont company
known best for its commodity cheeses and dairy products sold in
many area supermarkets and around the country, wanted to make a
high-end product and had approached Jasper Hill about working
together. They took the best of a single farm of Cabot milk to start
the process and the end result is considered "the centerpiece" of
what the Cellars at Jasper Hill does. This cheddar will be aged for
eleven to thirteen months, with the cloth—which helps to regulate
moisture levels—removed near the end of the process. Some local
artisanal cheese makers have reacted critically toward this partnership—the feeling being that partnering with Cabot, with its commodity cheese and large monetary resources, is akin to selling out or
diluting the definition of artisanal cheese. Regardless, Cabot cloth-
aged cheddar is about half of what Jasper Hill sells, and provides
steady income in an otherwise erratic market.

Before leaving the cheese caves, we also visited the vault of
Bayley Hazen Blue, perhaps their "signature" cheese. This cheese is
sold after eighty-five to ninety-five days of aging, and Vince noted

that every batch would be different—the opposite approach to Cabot's cheddar, which strives for continuity for its sixty wheels a quarter and has helped Jasper Hill get into larger-box stores and other venues where a small, artisanal cheese maker would not generally have the opportunity to sell. Thus one could say that Cabot's commodity dairy reputation helped their award-winning cheddar and Jasper Hill's blue cheese both become known to a wider audience. Cheddar is among the top five varieties of cheese sold in America, and a variety that has Cabot's name on it, but with the story of cloth binding and cave aging attached to its marketing, it is likely more palatable for consumers willing to pay for high-end, "artisanal" cheese. And with Jasper Hill's name attached, their Bayley Hazen Blue becomes a safe option for those new to artisanal cheese to try a new brand they might feel they can trust.

As we finished our tour of the caves, Vince also explained that part of his job was as one of their official "tasters" to help determine how much longer each batch might need to age and when they should be sold. Sometimes overlooked, tasting is integral to marketing because part of successful cheese branding and quality assurance is helping to communicate each cheese's shelf life to the seller. While blue cheese, for example, is safe to be eaten for a long window after it is aged, it will taste best when consumed during a certain time frame. Same with many bloomy rind cheeses. Helping stores understand this time frame and how it will be of advantage to both the makers and the retailers is an important aspect of his role at Jasper Hill. Vince and the tasting team also use their meticulous data to compare different batches of cheese on quality and trajectory, with a goal to creating a wealth of subjective and objective knowledge to help them continually improve.

Jasper Hill's approach and resources give them a leg up in the ever-tightening artisanal cheese market. They consider their relationship with their retailers of the utmost importance, especially as most are saying that they are packed to the gills with high-quality, local, artisanal cheeses. Vince noted that many of these cheese makers, in business now for a decade or longer, are getting continually better. Thus, one way to expand is to export artisanal American cheese to various global regions, including Europe. The new trend for European consumers is "something different" after the strict control of many of the various regions' cheeses—right in line with the American style of artisanal cheese making. This is facilitated by the larger profile that Jasper Hill has built compared to many of their neighbors who only sell locally—in no small part thanks to their collaboration with Cabot.

When I asked Vince if he considered Jasper Hill "artisanal"—and what his definition of the term is—he said that Jasper Hill is working to retain what it means to be called artisanal: quality control through human interaction at every step and focus on small batches of cheese—but they are doing it through specialization of labor. Jasper Hill has thirty-one employees at both the farm and cellars and they pride themselves on strong employee relations and support. Their goal is to continue to grow in the right way, to sustain the local landscape, despite not being able to compete with the economies of scale in the Midwest or California. "How much does it have to hurt to be called artisanal?" he asked. While the question of whether Jasper Hill is *truly* artisanal is asked by some of the smaller cheese makers in the region, the truth is that they are putting out some excellent cheese, made so primarily by the personal attention given to each cheese, whether a thirty-four-pound wheel of Cabot Clothbound, or a much smaller round of a cheese co-branded by a small local maker who can't afford an aging cave.

I was given a few hunks of cheese on my departure from the cellars, a welcome parting gift after seeing such gorgeous rounds in various stages of aging through the tour, and despite its controversy—for like many others, I love to root for an underdog, which Cabot was decidedly not—the clothbound cheddar was truly delicious. It had that aged complexity, a bit salty and crumbly, nothing even reminiscent of its commodity cheese counterpart—and despite its affiliation with one of the largest cheese makers in the northeast—I knew I would be looking for it again at the cheese counter. And, while it surpassed my expectations, I also questioned my own instinct to want to find fault in the large cheese maker's artisanal efforts. Was it because of the narrative behind the cheese? That there was no single small, struggling artisan toiling on the rounds from milking to deducing the moment to unwrap the cheese, to packaging the wedges for sale?

Which made me consider again why consumers—especially the most ardent supporters of artisanal foods—gravitate toward the narrative of struggle: the small farm barely scraping by, the pastoral vision of a single visionary nurturing their cheese like it was a small child.[34] Is this idealism, this prizing of the end product over all other aspects of the artisan's life, part of the counter-cuisine value system so closely tied to these consumers of artisanal goods? If so, it does make sense that the consumer who tends to support the counter-cuisine economy—small business, often environmentally sustainable practices—would be wary of the nuances of distinction among those who consider themselves artisanal producers.

Further, this new cheese-making model at Jasper Hill complicates the idea of terroir by equalizing the human element as well as the influence of the disparities among aging caves by bringing multiple cheese makers' cheeses to age in their various caves and by artificially regulating the environment. Some people see Jasper Hill as fighting the small artisanal cheese maker in Vermont—and there are claims that they have unintentionally put some smaller artisans out of business. Others, however, have lauded what Jasper Hill is doing—they are putting out really good cheese, and becoming better and better artisans in the process, while enabling other small cheese makers to be more creative about the cheeses they want to offer. They are clearly passionate about their work and meticulous about the slightest changes in each cave's climate. But whose artisanal work is this? What artisan owns the story? Does it matter that Brian, the rock and roll–blasting cheese tender, has no direct connection to the land or animals that helped create the cheeses he ends?

However, one can also see Jasper Hill as representing the future of artisanal cheese making. As Port Reyes Farmstead Cheese and others are helping to reimagine the "authentic," so is Jasper Hill rewriting the narrative of the art of cheese making in an increasingly competitive market. There seems to be little backlash when picklers use co-packers, or the distiller hires others to complete various aspects of their spirit making. So why is the cheese-making narrative so sacred? Is it that cheese is, more than many other artisanal products, so closely associated with the land and the animals that provide its raw materials? Is it that the cheese maker represents the pastoral notion of artisanal production in America versus the urban artisans in so many other industries who can't boast the farmhouse kitchen or red barn? Is it that cheese is more of an integral part of our modern American diet, and also more fragile and susceptible to contamination? Perhaps the idealized narrative of cheese making is the story we most closely associate with artisanal production—and is also, as it changes, representing the vision of the future. For every artisanal edible needs the rural farm to support its production, urban or not, and as the narrative of cheese making adapts to the modern world, perhaps there is fear that we are straying farther from where our food comes from—the very connection of which artisanal food is striving to reinforce.

What is changing, as well, from the consumers' perspective is the cultural cachet that *knowing* and maybe even participating in this narrative brings. The associated virtue that comes with supporting these artisans, most of whom also tout such values as environmental sustainability and humane treatment of animals, is part of the products' inherent value. Thus, as the narrative of artisanal cheese moves toward embracing modernity—or even as the line between artisanal and industrial becomes blurred—this added value can become blurred.

POWER OF NARRATIVE IN SELLING ARTISANAL FOOD

While driving over the high Grants Pass from Portland to San Francisco in January, the snow was swirling around the car and I was hoping that there was no black ice on the road. I had just left Portland—actually a small town just outside the city—where I had spent a few hours with cheese maker Liz Alvis. We met at the farmers market where her husband was handing out samples and exchanging cheese for money, and both were greeting most customers by name. A photo of some of the goats from which Liz's cheese was made was perched next to a tower of her product, emblazoned with the label of Portland Creamery—although the goats reside and the cheese is made in Mollala, Oregon, not far from Portland proper. Between sharing hugs and stories from customers of how well her cheese was received over the holidays, Liz explained that she wanted to tap into the artisanal food scene in Portland, and had a future goal of having the only creamery within city limits, but at the moment was working closely with a herd outside of the city. The connection to both was important for her—and her business identity. The urban identity helped to differentiate her as a newbie among the growing community of Oregon cheese makers, but her interaction with the goats themselves and the farm was also necessary for "authenticity." Liz was among the younger cheese makers with whom I spoke—in her thirties, fresh-scrubbed. She and her husband made a good-looking, hip, but still country-ish couple. She spoke to the health and happiness of the goats whose milk she works with, the healthfulness of her cheese, and her own cheese-making art—learned from and inspired by her mother, also a cheese maker, residing in Ohio.[35]

The farmers market was cool and damp that morning and Liz, her husband, and I all took turns warming our hands on her portable heater. But Liz's smile never left her face. This part of her job was as essential as making the cheese. Among these more small-town consumers, she was still convincing some to try chevre for the first time—a very different market than urban Portland, where her product would be easily identifiable as the city's local fresh goat cheese. She told me how so many had claimed they didn't like goat cheese. It was clear that the personal touch was integral to growing her business—that these reluctant consumers were convinced as much by the samples as by Liz herself. How could they not indulge the friendly cheese maker for just one taste? And her story was adaptable. For me and her customers in Portland, she plays up her desire to be an artisan in the city, but with a connection to that pastoral vision of goat farming. For her suburban and small-town customers, it is the goats she speaks of and her relationship with the neighboring farm and the land. Both are sincere. Both are necessary marketing strategies.[36]

This importance of narrative is also obvious in how urban versus rural cheese makers define themselves. Urban cheese makers often make fresh cheese, versus aged, partly because often there is a lack of space for an aging room and partly because having many potential customers within a smaller travel radius allows for the relative ease of selling larger quantities of fresh cheeses. Since fresh cheeses need refrigeration, this can be an issue with selling these products from more rural cheese-making locations. Some of the new or remaining Italian American fresh cheese makers, like Lourdes Smith from Fiore di Nonno and Albert Capone from Capone's, both in Somerville, Massachusetts, are typical of these urban cheese makers, producing not just a fine product but also one with a connection to their Italian heritage. Because authenticity cannot come from either working the land or milking the cows themselves, their narrative is the family connection to cheese making, both having watched family members make the same fresh Italian cheeses that they now offer. Thus it is connection to the past, to a tradition, that they are upholding—in both cases an urban tradition rather than one that connects the cheese maker to the land. While Liz may be straddling the urban and rural identity, she is also embracing the familial connection of her mother as cheese maker. And consumers of all of these cheeses are also buying a value-added product, but one infused with stories of heritage and familial knowledge, passed down through the generations.

So as I wound through the pass on that snowy afternoon, I was thinking of Liz and many of the other artisans whom I had met as I listened to an NPR story about a young contemporary visual artist. At the tender age of two, Marla Olmstead was given paints and began creating paintings. By the time she was four, she had attracted a great amount of media attention and was selling numerous works, many for thousands of dollars. Then a *60 Minutes* episode and a documentary on her suggested that she was coached by her father during her artistic process, and her work lost all value to most collectors.[37] The NPR piece I was listening to on that snowy drive was questioning the authenticity and value of art. The paintings themselves didn't change once it was questioned whether young Marla created them on her own or with her father, so why would their value? Which got me thinking about why the story of the artisan— the cheese maker and her goats, the pickler and his cucumbers— matter so much to consumers. Wouldn't a product's value be about taste alone? The answer to the question of the necessity of narrative to artisanal food cultural *and* economic value "depends on the successful communication of how one's social and moral values contribute to the crafting of a cheese and to the development of a business."[38] While the art buyers wanted a piece of Marla's prodigious work in order to be a party to her young success, as it were, by purchasing her work, so do consumers of artisanal food also want to support a food artisan whose larger values they believe in, and whose story they can live vicariously through in a few bites. These consumers connect to the animals and the land through the food created from it, and their purchase buys them not just something delicious, but a product that is a proxy for happy animals and being in the creamery with Liz.

So why does cheese, in particular, lend itself to narrative so well? I believe it does have to do with the pastoral notion of cheese making—and the post-pastoral understanding of how a cheese maker works the land. I also believe it has to do with the nature of cheese—because it is inherently connected to both the land and the animal from which the milk comes, a larger set of values are attached to *how* it is made, beyond "organic" or "sustainable," or even "humane treatment of animals." And cheese, being, arguably, the first and most developed artisanal industry in this new artisanal food movement, has had more time to develop a narrative. Thus a larger number of artisans work in the industry, selling to a broader consumer base, the former of whose stories all need to be told in new and interesting ways.

Is pickle-making a romantic notion? Do consumers *really* imagine Shamus Jones hand-packing jars in a tiny Brooklyn apartment kitchen somewhere? The urban pickle narrative had always been based upon pickles in a barrel, sold for sale on the street (a story that Brooklyn Brine nods to with the barrel on their label). Cheese, on the other hand, seems much more personal. Most people can imagine the basic cheese-making process. And often inaccurately, most of these narratives begin with the animal being milked by hand with a green pasture in the background. One can't imagine a more intimate connection between animal and cheese maker. The reality of cheese making is much less romantic. Milking is done primarily by machine, although most of these small dairies do require human assistance with the process. The cheese-making room more closely resembles a hospital or lab than a farmhouse kitchen due to the need for it to be sanitary. The cheese makers themselves must be clothed like hazmat workers, also to keep out any contaminants. Thus, while the pastoral nature of cheese making is often played up in marketing and in the story told at farmers markets and in-store tastings, the reality is much more about how the cheese makers work *with* the land to create a sustainable business within the modern confines of regulations, consumer interest, and available technology.

And finally we also see how the narratives surrounding cheese have helped to influence the artisanal food narrative as a whole—for cheese makers were among the first food artisans to find a foothold among the growing foodie population, and their modern story has influenced both urban and rural artisans in this new food revolution. Cheese represents living off the land, a connection not just to growing one's own food but also to animals and to one's heritage—as well as fancy cheese courses and rustic snacks. This wave of cheese makers has helped inspire the new artisanal food revolution, and they represent an important story in it today.

4

CHOCOLATE

The Localness of Exotics

It came as a complete surprise—a chocolate "factory" had opened along an industrial stretch of the small city of Somerville, Massachusetts, where I had just bought a house. Somerville had long been a working-class neighborhood, known more for its urban feel—it is the most densely populated city in New England—than its food scene, although with increasing real estate prices in and around Boston that had been changing in the previous decade. But more incongruous than the chocolate factory's mere existence was its chocolate, samples of which were becoming a fixture at the new weekly farmers market. I had never had anything like it—sold in rounds and not bars, matte, and not shiny, with a peculiar, almost crumbly mouth feel. And the taste itself—dark, earthy—was closer to my preference for dark chocolate, but I wasn't prepared for something so seemingly . . . unrefined.

Taza Chocolate is the brainchild of Alex Whitmore, a trained anthropologist who had his first bite of traditional stone-ground chocolate in Oaxaca, Mexico, in 2005. He understood the history of chocolate making. The Mayans had learned of the magic of cacao trees, which grew pods with beans and pulp inside that had to ferment and then be dried before it could be separated from its hard outer shell and ground with a stone. This powder was mixed into drinks, and then later turned into solids, the texture sandy and the taste bitter. This was the way Oaxacans had been making and preparing chocolate for more than a millennium. Alex was astounded by this new idea of a product he had been eating his entire life. And he knew he would not be the only person intrigued by this traditional approach to an almost universally loved product. But he also understood the greater purpose of bringing this traditional approach to chocolate to the American consumer: He could teach the true history of the product, help to counter the many wrongs that the Mexican cacao growers and eventually others around the world had faced since European explorers first "discovered" this chocolate, and also help preserve a nearly lost tradition. [1]

Plus Alex had a head for business. Responsibility in food sourcing and production was starting to become a selling point for consumers who were increasingly socially aware and more willing to spend a little extra for sustainable, traditional, or environmentally conscious products. In the first decade of the new millennium other industries, like coffee, had begun offering fair-trade and single-origin options, with great success. Perhaps he could offer the same, but with chocolate. And Somerville, Massachusetts, with its proximity to Boston and Cambridge—all easily accessed on the subway line— and its growing profile as a still-affordable haven for the young and hip who were being priced out of these neighboring cities but still wanted access to arts and shopping and other creative types, was a great match. So Alex rented a space and created a chocolate factory, employing Oaxacans in Mexico to harvest, ferment, and dry the cacao to be ground using a traditional stone that Alex helped design.

Alex was among the first in America to start offering a more interesting and socially responsible alternative to cheap, mass-produced chocolate, and he is still relatively unique with his approach to grinding and his product's texture. But he has been joined in the past few years by a number of chocolate makers with similar goals, although most have kept their product focused on more tempered— shiny and smooth—chocolate products. What is unique about Taza Chocolate and other new bean-to-bar chocolate makers is the clear values that each company espouses that are so in line with those of some of the most outspoken proponents of sustainable—and even local—eating, including liberal stances on raw ingredient sourcing, worker pay, and environmental impact. And they are doing so with a product that is firmly an "exotic," or a product that cannot be made in the United States (although more than one chocolate maker is working on that)—which means that there will be shipping costs, yes, and relatively limited control over the land itself. Yet, it is exactly the land, and the work and processes that take place on-site primarily by people who are natives, that these new makers espouse as integral to the quality of their chocolate. Thus, these new bean-to-bar chocolate makers are helping consumers reconsider what it means to support "local" products, as well as how this idea of the characteristics of the land and these traditional and "authentic" processes are evoked in a product in the evolving notion of "terroir."

As I toured Taza's production facility and heard about their chocolate-making philosophy, and then met other chocolate makers and learned about their process and product, I was told again and again that it was the land itself and the climate in which the beans grow that help give cacao unique flavor profiles. Earthy, bright, fruity, mineral—these words I was more used to hearing when talking about wine, with the same idea behind how similar grape varietals could produce such different-tasting wine—the thinking, of course, was that when working with quality raw materials, minimal processing is needed (or desired) to create the final product. In wine, the manifestation of the earth and climate is called terroir, and I couldn't help reflecting that this is the same idea that many bean-to-bar chocolate makers were also talking about, and that is essential to their influences and identity as bean-to-bar chocolate makers. Further, the preservation and highlighting of terroir is also a key goal of these new makers, expanding the idea of the term while also relating an embattled exotic to similar values of those who seek local, seasonal, and sustainable goods.

Taza Chocolate roasts their own beans—as do most small-batch chocolate makers today—at their Somerville factory, and uses traditional Oaxacan stone mills to grind their cacao nibs with the granite millstones Alex carved. These stones process the cacao minimally, compared to the typical modern product, creating a matte, textured, gritty chocolate. The flavors are less subtle, more bright and interesting. Alex is proud of their unique approach to chocolate making; he came to this business with the appreciation of traditional methods from his anthropological background, the desire to preserve these recipes and give a fair wage to his workers, and a businessman's mind to do so in a way that could be financially sustainable as well. People love chocolate, he knew, and the trend toward thoughtful sourcing was just starting to gain steam when he and cofounder (and now wife) Kathleen Fulton started Taza in 2006. Taza's specific style of chocolate is still mostly unique among American chocolate makers, but they were not the only ones who decided to turn consumer desire for quality, sustainable chocolate into a new business. A handful of smaller chocolate makers around the United States began around the same time with a similar desire to make a quality, environment- and worker-friendly product, most with a similar desire to teach consumers about the origins of chocolate through a return to (more) traditional methods of chocolate making, and the use of high-quality cacao, often single-origin and fair-trade sourced. In the process they would help introduce needed changes in an industry rife with human rights abuses, so often overlooked by the millions of Americans who like their chocolate cheap and easily accessible. So, as bean-to-bar chocolate has grown to become an, arguably, new "American" artisanal product, it is interesting to look at the way producers relate to a product that is both foreign and quintessentially American, and the way the land, tradition, and artisanal practices play into craft chocolate identity.

WHAT IS TERROIR?

Wine swirling in a long-stemmed glass, the smacking of tongue on palate, the intake of breath to fully taste the liquid—these are the clichés of wine tasting. Fruit forward, mineral, earthy, long finish are declared, with some credit being given to the winemaker, the artisan who helped bring out these qualities in the grapes themselves. The grapes were on a south-facing hill, we might learn, or the rainfall was particularly heavy that year. Or maybe there was a smoldering forest fire in the vicinity. All could be tasted in the grapes, the wine. That is its terroir, we are told.

Terroir is a French word, meaning literally "land" or "earth," but there isn't quite a direct translation in English for its larger idea. It is generally used to describe the way that the land and climate manifests itself in food and drink, most often wine. But various scholars are noting that the understanding of terroir is larger than that. In 2012 an article in the *International Journal of Wine Business Research* noted, "*Terroir* . . . is much more than the taste of place. *Terroir* defines the particular attributes of place embodied in cuisine and narrated through words, actions, and objects." The term itself originated in France in the mid-nineteenth century, and has been used as an ideal to determine *appellation d'origine controlées* (AOCs) which are legally defined agricultural products that are produced in a certain place and through specific methods within France—the terroir of which is integral to their assumed quality. Thus it is understood to connote not just the influence of the land upon a product, but the human craftsmanship upon that land, and even the "artisanal quality of a product."[2]

In America too, the idea of terroir is being expanded. "Place alone, however, fails to translate the deeper associations that *terroir* projects about identity," says Bernard L. Herman,[3] who was speaking about Southern cuisine, specifically. He goes on to emphasize the point that it is the larger narrative around place that is included when one speaks of terroir. Thus, terroir is the story of the product as situated in place—what it means to the producers and consumers and how it has been valued by the larger culture as a reflection of where it is from. And with artisanal chocolate, the narrative of where cacao is grown, how it is harvested and traditionally processed, and *then* where it is turned into its final form, often in an urban facility in the United States—all this is integral to the story of the bar and how both the chocolate makers and the buyers relate to and value the end product. Terroir, therefore, is integral to the way bean-to-bar chocolate is situated in our modern artisanal culture.

Food scholars and appreciators are embracing a larger definition of *terroir*, noting that the term is being used to represent a broader set of values beyond the product's quality, including environmental and social concerns, that help set artisanal products apart from their mass-produced counterparts.[4] Environmental stewardship, paying workers a living wage, and other responsible business practices with regard to land and workers are integral to the story surrounding bean-to-bar craft chocolate in America, and part of the narrative that makes it so valued by consumers. Recent studies have supported the assertion that the notion of terroir also includes human attributes, the values of the producers, the narrative of the place or method of production, the inherent connection of the product to the consumers themselves, as well as the presentation and relative place of the product in the marketplace.[5] And it's not just academics—or producers—who are redefining terroir. One study looked at the consumer's interpretation of terroir in regard to wine and found that consumers' understanding of terroir was dependent on the product itself, their own knowledge about the product category, and the packaging and communication from the company. In addition, even those industries that promote terroir as integral to appreciating the product acknowledge that it must often be taught to be tasted.[6]

But besides the variances in the understanding of terroir, cultural theorists such as Certeau and Barthes argue that place cannot be separated from the people that inhabit it or the inherent narratives they embody; thus the idea of terroir cannot be separated from the stories behind the products and the language we use to talk about it. Even France's terroir as relating to their AOCs, while referring literally to the land and human production factors, implies the human history behind the products and methodology and the relationship between humans and place.[7] And in relation to chocolate, cultural scholar Tomasik asserts, "not only the concept of terroir is rooted in the localization of a particular place, but also that it acquires the cumulative history of human practices associated with it."[8] Thus, as we look at the idea of terroir in chocolate—a relatively new way that these bean-to-bar makers are thinking about, sourcing, creating, and packaging chocolate—it can be argued that the idea of terroir is integral to this industry, even as the products are made with beans almost always sourced from land very far away from the factory itself.

We see terroir evoked in bean-to-bar chocolate most literally when makers note that their bars are made from single-origin beans, or even give the distinguishing batch numbers. Yet labels often also highlight where in the United States the bars themselves are produced. To further expand the notion of terroir to these larger characteristics, this idea is also invoked through the education process from maker to consumer: a focus on how the chocolate is grown and processed at the source, the values associated with the treatment of the workers and the land, and then how the maker later manipulates it in the factory. It is more than the mere soil from which the cacao grows; it also is the ancient techniques used to make chocolate, the social history of the food, and the way that these new bean-to-bar makers are bringing these products to the modern consumer. But first, it is important to understand the techniques, traditions, and history behind chocolate.

HOW CHOCOLATE IS MADE

It all starts with the theobrama cacao tree that grows long pods that house what will become the edible beans. The criollo variety was the dominant cacao species until less than a century ago, but due to its relatively low yield and low resistance to disease, it has become rare, although it is considered to produce the best-tasting beans. Today the most popular species of cacao trees is the more heavily fruited, hearty forestaro variety, although there have been efforts to combine the more nuanced taste of the criollo with the best qualities of the forestaro, resulting in the cross-breed trinitario. The cacao tree is tropical, and can only be grown within twenty degrees latitude of the equator in specific conditions; thus the first stages of chocolate production are limited to Africa, South America, the Caribbean, and a few areas of Asia, with some entrepreneurs pushing the limits of cacao growth in Hawaii as well.

The first steps of cacao harvesting and chocolate making are very similar today to what they were centuries ago. The large pods are picked from trees—a process that must be done by hand because they ripen at different times—and then they are split open and the beans and pulp are fermented from two to eight days. The fermented beans are then spread in a single layer and left to dry completely, often by the sun. The fermenting and drying process are integral to the flavor of the chocolate, and are most often done very near where the beans are harvested by native workers. Once the beans are completely dry, they are bagged and shipped to the processing plant, where they are roasted. The length of time and temperature are dependent on the relative moisture of the beans and their type.

Next the beans are winnowed—that is, their outer shell is removed, leaving the nib, composed of cocoa butter and cocoa solids. The nibs are then ground into a paste known as chocolate liquor.

Figure 4.1.   Chocolate making at Woodblock Chocolate.

The liquor is then pressed to remove the cocoa butter—which, when ground is basically unsweetened powder (although quite unlike the Dutch processed cocoa powder one might buy in the store). The next step depends on the intended end product, and the cocoa is combined with other ingredients on its way to consumption. If it is to be a low-quality commodity chocolate, the pure cocoa will be mixed with fats, sugar, and perhaps other flavoring. Higher-quality chocolate is re-combined with cocoa butter, sugar, and perhaps milk or other or ingredients before it is "conched." Conching is a process—originally a machine that was so named because the kneading elements resembled seashells—that kneads the chocolate to improve flavor and texture. This can take hours or days, depending on the desired end product. Finally the chocolate is tempered—cooled to specific temperatures through constant movement—in a process that also helps determine the texture and shininess of the end product. Then it is poured into molds for sale and consumption.

A BRIEF HISTORY OF CHOCOLATE

Even though the average American eats more than eleven and a half pounds of chocolate a year (which still ranks as only the eleventh-highest consumption in the world),[9] few know much about the product's origins or methods of production. Even at specialty stores, high-end chocolate selections were once dominated by brands like Ghirardelli and Lindt (who are now owned by the same international company). These companies offered a higher-priced and higher-quality alternative to Mars and Hershey products, but cocoa solid percentage or country of origin were rarely noted. Further, the U.S. government's attempt in 2000 to bring the severe human rights issues of the vast majority of chocolate workers to public consciousness was thwarted by industry heavyweights, who watered down efforts to ensure that workers were treated—and paid—fairly.

It is perhaps hard to imagine that the Western world's favorite indulgence has been rife with controversy since Cortes first tasted the chocolate beverage offered to him in the early 1500s (as most sources believe) when he landed in one of the chief cacao-producing regions of Mexico. There, in the previous centuries, Aztecs and Mayans held cacao in such high regard that the beans were used as currency and their consumption—generally as a bitter drink revered for its health benefits—was often used in religious ceremonies. This "food of the gods" became a sought-after luxury good in Europe by the end of the 1500s—and the pressure for the New World to produce more beans intensified. Fertile land from central Mexico through Central America was commissioned to grow cacao, and this insatiable appetite was fed by what would amount to slave labor. As Spanish colonists took over large swaths of land, a medieval system known as *encomienda* gave these colonists the right to demand that local workers toil these lands, creating a seeming return to the antiquated feudal system of the Middle Ages.

Cacao wasn't the only product prized from the New World. Spices and especially sugar were also sought after, with aboriginal people forced to work on plantations in horrific conditions for little or no pay to satisfy the desires of the upper- and middle-class Europeans. While it is hard to estimate the true death rate in the Americas during this time, some scholars note that by the 1600s as much as 90 percent of the native population died from introduced diseases and overworking.[10] Soon, Europeans were importing slave labor from Africa to make up for the labor shortage in the New World, with African slave labor being well established on Caribbean plantations by 1600.

In Europe, demand for chocolate was growing, with a slow acceptance in France and a quicker adoption by the Medicis in Italy, in addition to Spain's initial embrace. Cocoa made its way to Britain by the 1700s, alongside coffee and tea, and, sweetened with sugar from the New World, became the drink of choice of scholars and great thinkers in cafes that featured these new delicacies. Initially chocolate was introduced to the Old World in the sixteenth century as medicinal, and physicians were challenged to keep chocolate identified as treating ailments as opposed to being consumed for purely gastronomic pleasure. Ultimately, by the end of the seventeenth century, pleasure won out, in part because of controversy among the medical community concerning a unified stance on chocolate's medical powers.[11] Thus, the European demand for chocolate grew so steadily that new plantations were soon planted in South American countries like Brazil and Venezuela, as well as the West Indies and Jamaica—creating new varieties of the bean that could survive and thrive in these increasingly disparate areas. Meanwhile, cocoa and chocolate were increasingly available to the American colonists in the New World, especially as trade routes were established and wealth was increasing.

In the early 1800s, cocoa was still often bought in pharmacies, to be prepared as a gritty, bitter, high-fat drink that promoted general health and well-being. However, with the growing popularity of drinks like coffee and tea—both of which were relatively easier to prepare and more pleasing to the European palate—cocoa was starting to lose favor. With the rise of manufacturing, that began to change. A number of entrepreneurs were experimenting with ways to simplify the cocoa-making process and make it more palatable to Europeans. Chocolate was being transformed by the industrial revolution. Hydraulic presses could simplify and mechanize the process of grinding the cocoa beans into a paste, and also could be used to de-fat the cocoa—with the Dutchman Coenraad Van Houten eventually creating "Dutch" cocoa powder in the 1820s, which began to transform the chocolate industry. Now the average household could easily add Dutch cocoa to liquids, and sweeten as desired; Van Houten's cocoa powder became a hit across Europe and eventually the United States.

Meanwhile, other entrepreneurial folks were tackling the problem of what to do with the by-product of Van Houten's cocoa powder: the remaining cocoa butter. A Quaker doctor from England, Joseph Fry, began combining the cocoa butter with cocoa solids, sugar, and other flavors and shaping them with molds. While Spanish monks and French sweet shops had both experimented with solid chocolate, Fry created the first sweet, meltable treat that could be mass-produced in a manner that made it affordable to the average consumer. In essence, he invented the first modern chocolate bar.

With the advent of an inexpensive and easily mass-produced chocolate treat, chocolate consumption grew exponentially in Europe and the United States, inspiring new businesses, increasing the demand for cheap cocoa, and greatly altering public perception of the flavor and texture of "chocolate." Now very different from what the Mayans considered *kakaw*[12] back in the ninth century, "chocolate" in the 1800s had much lower cocoa content, was much sweeter, and had additives like milk that affected its flavor and texture. No longer was it the earthy beverage drunk by rulers or the bitter, gritty nugget that kept Mayans satiated for days while hunting or farming.

Those who capitalized on this quickly growing market for chocolate did so by investing in industrialization and marketing—and by streamlining and consolidating the process between bean and bar. By the mid-1800s the British tea dealer John Cadbury had realized the potential for chocolate among consumers and was responsible for the next big innovation in the commercial chocolate industry: marketing. He packaged sweet chocolate in pretty boxes of bite-sized bonbons with clever wrapping and was the first to make chocolate a symbol of romance, by selling Valentine's Day–themed products. Soon thereafter, he created the first chocolate Easter egg. By the late 1800s, chocolate was no longer consumed for health benefits, but for pleasure and celebration. Of course, other entrepreneurs followed suit.[13]

Even before Cadbury's marketing genius greatly expanded the market for chocolate, cacao crops from the Caribbean and Central and South America were becoming depleted and diseased. Having discovered that cacao could grow anywhere within twenty kilometers of the equator, European cacao traders decided to import cacao stock to their country's colonies in Africa, ironically bringing the crop back to the continent from which they had exported so many slaves during the previous centuries. By the end of the 1800s, reports of maltreatment and enslavement of cocoa workers in the Portuguese colonies of Sao Tome and Principe, off the coast of present-day Cameroon, were as horrifying as what had been happening in the New World earlier in the century. While a British lawsuit was eventually brought against Cadbury in the early 1900s for human rights abuses, slavery and abusive worker treatment in these colonies and elsewhere in Africa were only slowed, or operations were moved to different locations to keep up with the demand for cheap cocoa in Europe and North America.

Meanwhile, the United States was breeding its own chocolate magnate in the mid to late 1800s. Milton Hershey chanced into a job with a candy maker and, intrigued by his employer's method of making caramels with milk instead of paraffin, tinkered with his own recipe, eventually striking out on his own and realizing great success. By 1890, Hershey was wealthy enough to retire at the age of thirty-three. However, he became enamored of Europe's growing chocolate culture—through the 1800s, chocolate was still consumed mainly as a beverage, and as late as 1872 was noted as such in a dessert cookbook by "A Boston Lady."[14] Hershey again borrowed ideas from another confectioner, taking elements of the Swiss chemist Henri Nestle's recently developed method of making "milk chocolate," and set about to create his own Americanized milk chocolate bar that he could mass produce and sell for a nickel. Soon bars—milky and sweet, with perhaps only 11 percent cocoa content—bearing that iconic name were being shipped around the country. Initially attempting to avoid the controversy that surrounded Cadbury's use of African slave labor, Hershey sourced his cocoa primarily from plantations in the Caribbean. However, by the 1930s, disease had wiped out much of these crops, and Hershey looked to Africa for his cocoa as well.[15]

By the 1930s, many farmers' cooperatives had been established in Africa, which became the main source of cocoa for the world, resulting in both cocoa brokers and farmers feeling relatively stable for a few decades—particularly in the newly independent country of Ghana. Then a price-fixing scandal in the 1960 and 1970s weakened the industry, and farmers cleared rainforest to plant more cocoa to make up for their losses. The result was that the change in the landscape made severe drought more common, and fires decimated Ghana's cocoa crop in the early 1980s. Chocolate companies around the world merely looked for the next place that could provide them with their cheap source of cocoa. That place was Côte d'Ivoire.

The newly independent country of Côte d'Ivoire was already on its way to becoming a key producer of cocoa when the fires devastated Ghana's crop. For a while during the 1980s, the dictator, Houphouet-Boigny, saw the opportunity for his country to become the dominant producer, and he subsidized the fluctuation of the cocoa commodities prices while Côte d'Ivoire edged its way to becoming the number one cocoa producer in the world. This eventually came to an end in 1987, however, when the country was thrust into bankruptcy. Cacao farmers attempted to eke out as much production as possible to make up for the losses, but this only lowered the price of cocoa, especially since production was increasing in other parts of the world, namely Asia. By the end of the century, the government of Côte d'Ivoire—and the farmers—were in deep financial trouble. And even as Côte d'Ivoire retained its distinction as the number one producer of cacao in the world—as of 2009 they exported more than 37 percent of the total crop—there also have been numerous accounts of a return to slavery to do so.[16]

Since about the turn of the century, there have been a number of agencies and activists who have been calling attention to the issue of adult working conditions and pay and child slavery at cacao farms in Côte d'Ivoire, Ghana (which exports about 19 percent of the world's cacao), and elsewhere. In 2005 a class action suit was making its way through the U.S. court system on behalf of "Former Child Slave Plaintiffs"[17] and between 2006 and 2012 numerous books, articles, and documentaries were produced to publicize this issue. Much like Cadbury had a century earlier, faced with public backlash, companies like Ferrero and Nestlé are currently promising to make a plan to change their sourcing. However, much of these efforts are voluntary and progress is slow.

Meanwhile, by the late 1970s, Hershey was eager to source their cacao closer to home and encouraged the formation of cacao plantations in Belize, suggesting that if farmers took out large loans to plant the crops Hershey wanted, they would be on the receiving end of the current high prices being paid for cacao in the wake of the unrest in the African cacao market. The Mayan Indians, in particular, were excited at this opportunity and went deep into debt to start these new plantations. However, by the time the crop was ready for harvest in the early 1990s, prices had dropped and Hershey would offer the farmers less money than it was worth to harvest. The Mayans—centuries after their ancestors used cacao beans for currency—left the crop to rot in the fields.[18]

In the late 1980s British entrepreneur Craig Sams recognized a fast-growing sector of packaged food: organics. He had been traveling the world looking for opportunities and came across a small number of Belizean farmers who still cultivated the native Criollo cacao trees beneath the cover of rainforest canopy in the ancient method—which was, by definition, organic. Convinced that consumers would be willing to pay a premium for this unique product, he made a few notes for further consideration. Back in England, Sams's wife, Josephine Fairley, was convinced that an organic chocolate product would be popular among the growing consumers of other organic goods—and especially women. With her support, Green & Black's was born. The first bars of organic 70 percent cocoa—they were among the first to note these percentages on their packaging—sold in 1991 to instant success. They were primarily sourced from the African nation of Togo; however, with a quickly growing business and African politics becoming increasingly volatile, Green & Black soon had to seek alternate sourcing for their cacao. Sams remembered his trip to Belize a few years earlier, and soon the Mayans, abandoned by Hershey, had replaced their theobrama trees with criollo and were cultivating cacao again. By 1994 "Maya Gold" chocolate bars were being sold around the world—the first with a fair trade distinction. This recent development grew out of increasing consumer consciousness in Europe and North America, which called for more products that ensure that organic practices are used and workers are treated well and paid fairly, with a premium going back to the growers to help establish schools, water systems, or other needed infrastructure. By the early 2000s, Sams had more than proven that consumers were willing to pay more—

often many times more—for a bar of fair trade chocolate, inspiring other bean-to-bar chocolate makers to enter this market as well.

Today's craft bean-to-bar chocolate makers may not be as prevalent as craft cheese or pickle purveyors, but the number of artisans entering the marketplace is surprisingly high considering the barriers: chocolate was never something one produced in the American home, thus the method of production was almost certainly not passed down as family knowledge as so many artisanal industries are informed, and the raw materials and machinery needed to make chocolate are expensive and relatively difficult to procure. So why are these artisans choosing this form edible expression? The reasons are perhaps surprisingly similar to those who are making pickles and cheese and spirits: to create a high-quality product that is closer to the traditional, pre-mass-produced form, from raw materials sourced responsibly.

WOODBLOCK CHOCOLATE AND TERROIR

Charley Wheelock of Woodblock Chocolate is an example of the quintessential chocolate artisan, even if, like the other bean-to-bar makers with whom I spoke, he has only been in the industry for a few years. He and his wife and business partner, Jessica, became interested in making bean-to-bar chocolate after they moved to Portland, Oregon, and realized that Charley's handcrafted furniture business was not financially sustainable. So Charley and Jessica brainstormed about a business they could start that was creative and food oriented. They hit upon chocolate making—Charley noted, "It's unbelievable how much ground there is still to be covered with chocolate." They did some research and fell in love with the process, invested $3,000 for a bag of beans, and never looked back. Charley may have only been making chocolate since 2010 but he and Jessica are diligent students. "It gets more interesting and cooler every day. It's the best. The best," he said about his new industry. He loves the creative problem-solving aspect of chocolate making, and trying to "figure out how to do it in the coolest way possible," an indication, I believe, that he is not only attempting to perfect his craft, but is striving to move his product, and the industry, ahead in interesting and creative ways. [19]

When I visited Charley's chocolate "factory" in an up-and-coming neighborhood in southeast Portland, Oregon, he still had the original sign from the former letterpress that once occupied the space. Walking in, the sweet and earthy smell of roasting beans and the loud hum of the tempering machine distracted from our initial introductions. Sacks of beans were stacked near the front door, waiting to be transformed into their signature single-serving-sized bars of smooth chocolate. Charley is nothing if not passionate about chocolate making, and we soon moved beyond formalities and into tasting his exceptionally nuanced chocolate, from nibs to bars. Despite his late entry into chocolate making, he has clearly immersed himself into all aspects of the process—learning about the authentic flavors one gets from making chocolate simply and well, forging relationships with cacao brokers and growers across the world, and perfecting his handcrafted technique. In short, despite the exotic nature of chocolate, he is as dedicated to learning the trade and improving his craft as other artisans who were inspired by family recipes or childhood memories. Yet what inspires him is the farthest thing from a typical family farm in the Pacific Northwest. Rather, he is inspired by the product of a land thousands of miles away, and the possibilities of transforming a bean that has been picked, fermented, and dried by strangers who may never have even tasted a square of chocolate. While this may seem anachronistic compared to the close relationships that many other modern artisanal and sustainable industries espouse with their suppliers, often due to their physical closeness, what Charley, Alex, and others like them are doing, is redefining terroir and the values it encompasses.

Further, despite the seeming simplicity of this new artisanal chocolate, many of these bean-to-bar makers cite the creativity—in production and overall problem solving—as what drives them as artisans, and not just businessmen. Many of these entrepreneurs saw chocolate as a new frontier with which to experiment with taste and technique. Attention to—and working with—the terroir of the

Figure 4.2.   Woodblock Chocolate factory.

beans, the fermenting process, and the roasting technique are just some of the ways that the flavor of chocolate can be altered to create different flavor profiles. These entrepreneurs are moving chocolate culture in America beyond milk and dark.

Some are comparing the new chocolate revolution to that of "gourmet" coffee's rise a few decades ago. Chocolate makers are striving to educate consumers not just on the broad strokes of cacao growing and chocolate making, but also on the unique characteristics of beans from specific geographic areas and even heirloom varieties of cacao. Just as consumers became educated about single-origin coffee beans or careful small-batch roasting—and began accepting that these higher-quality beans were worth paying two to three times (or more) for—so do these new American chocolate makers see a similar education as necessary to get consumers to pay for their more labor-intensive, socially responsible, better-tasting chocolate. To do this, some are highlighting the nuanced flavors of single-origins beans—using words like "citrus" or "smoke" or "brightness" to help encourage consumers to slow down and really experience what chocolate can taste like—and how the single-origin beans and the climate and land from which they come, influence these flavors.

It goes without saying that dark chocolate, with relatively little added sugar or flavorings, makes up most of the new offerings. Typical dark chocolate bars are 65–77 percent or more cacao, which means that is the percentage of the bar that is cocoa solids and cocoa butter—the remaining percentage is generally sugar or sometimes minor (as in less than 1 percent) flavorings like vanillin, although these craft chocolate makers tend to pride themselves on simple recipes, maybe using salt or almonds to increase flavoring options. Few offer the sugary milk chocolate that has been the default chocolate for so long, which is often as low as 10 percent cacao solids, the rest being sugar, milk powder, and other additives. Woodblock Chocolate, for example, offers all 70 percent dark chocolate, with some bars flavored by salt or nibs, and others featuring single-origin beans. They also note the batch number on each bar, and Charley strives to keep detailed notes, continually assessing roasting technique and bean quality to work toward improving his technique while also acknowledging—and celebrating—that each batch will be different, as it should, he believes. Like all of these industries, consistency is a goal, but acknowledgment of both human and biological variations is part of what makes artisanal foods attractive to so many.

REDEFINING "AUTHENTIC" AMERICAN CHOCOLATE

When I first spoke on the phone with Nat Bletter, who cofounded Madre Chocolate with David Elliott, he was walking from his house in Hawaii to the cacao farm that he is helping to establish, with the goal of making a completely American bean-to-bar chocolate. From my chilly urban apartment, I imagined him in shorts and a T-shirt, walking down an unpaved path lined with lush greenery. Judging by the photos Madre posts online, this wasn't far from the truth. Nat, who grew up in New York City, commented on how it took him moving a third of the way across the world to truly appreciate how the seemingly ubiquitous American food—chocolate—is made. Nat's path to chocolate making is similar to Taza's Alex Whitmore's—both of whom came to this industry through an academic fascination with the ancient culture of growing and consuming cacao. Nat is similarly passionate about his chocolate's bean origin and is committed to creating American cacao groves in Hawaii (Guittard is another company producing Hawaiian chocolate), the only state close enough to the equator to enable this. He earned his PhD in ethnobotany from the City University of New York, where he studied, among other topics, medicinal and stimulant plants of Central and South America and Mali, including cacao, which spurred him to start a traditional-ingredient chocolate company. Thus, while Alex's academic and personal interests focused on the cultural aspects of chocolate, Nat's interests lie more in the botanical characteristics of the plants themselves, and how cacao—and its traditional flavorings—were a part of native diets. He has studied various species of cacao plants and chocolate making around the world, but has founded Madre Chocolate in Hawaii in part to bring chocolate making to the United States as a means of educating consumers about traditional cacao farming. Through this farm, and others he sources from in Central America, Bletter is focusing on direct trade with cacao farmers, quality beans, and also close attention to the fermenting process done at the farms themselves, which is integral to the final flavor of the chocolate.[20]

To help differentiate themselves from the growing number of bean-to-bar chocolate makers, Madre blends cultural tradition and ecological appreciation of cacao with the selling point of offering truly "American" chocolate, and highlighting its antioxidant benefits. The use of spices and flavorings native to where the beans are grown, which traditionally were often used to flavor chocolate, highlights the cultural aspect and strives for a deeper sense of connection with the past and the land. The health benefit angle has been largely ignored by the craft producers of chocolate, even as multiple studies have come out that note the positive health attributes of dark and minimally processed cacao. It is perhaps surprising that not many craft chocolate makers highlight these studies that link moderate dark chocolate consumption with lowered rates of heart disease, stroke, and depression—especially considering the long history of chocolate being prescribed for medicinal purposes.

It makes sense that the ethnobotanist would be the chocolate maker who has come to his business in part inspired by the "traditional ingredients of the Aztec, Maya, and Olmec tribes that invented chocolate, to both preserve their cultural heritage and give you that original taste."[21] Madre must still create an easily digestible narrative, however, that both helps to differentiate their approach to chocolate while also representing values that are similar to the identity of other bean-to-bar chocolate makers. In this case, the end product is a distinctly American, expressly modern product— whether their cacao is from Hawaii or another source. Shiny bars of "chocolate" were not how the Mayans and Aztec consumed their cacao, and the cacao coming from Hawaii, while "local" to the United States, is still coming from a very different terroir than that grown centuries ago in Central and South America. While I see this as a distillation of a larger narrative into bite-sized pieces that consumers can savor, this re-storying of terroir does represent the trend of the "reassertion of local, culturally constituted identities, places, work practices and commodities as a source of distinction and authenticity . . . precisely because they can be commoditized and sold as such."[22] While I do not believe that any of the craft chocolate makers with whom I spoke are abusing or taking advantage of the long cultural history and deep story of terroir of traditional chocolate, it is important to remember that they are re-creating it for a modern consumer and producing a product that is distinctly current with only a tangential connection to the long traditions that are inherent to these bean-to-bar makers' identity.

Thus for all the socially responsible concerns for chocolate's traditional and cultural identity, creating a more environmentally and socially conscious product, and honoring of those working with a product beloved by the artisan, many of these new chocolate makers also acknowledge that there was, after all, a business angle to their decision to start a chocolate company. Small-batch chocolate was still relatively rare when the first of the most recent wave of chocolate makers began, and many acknowledged that chocolate was a food category where artisanal potential was not yet realized compared to other food businesses, which was an attractive reason to focus on chocolate as a product. The relative rarity is in part due to the fact that chocolate is an exotic product and cultural knowledge of its traditional production and preparation was not passed down through family knowledge in the United States, even though it was a food integral to American culture. And while more producers have entered the American-made craft market in the last half decade or so, following a similar trajectory as other food industries, the number of American chocolate makers who have dedicated themselves to being small, independent, and supportive of traditional chocolate making are few. The Craft Chocolate Makers of America (CCMA), founded in 2008, has fewer than twenty members as of early 2014, although there are also a handful of chocolate makers with a similar mission who are making craft chocolate in America or other countries and are not a part of this group. (Of those I interviewed, four are members of the CCMA, and one is not.) The CCMA cites their association as helping to preserve traditional methods of production and "honesty and transparency" in the production, marketing, and selling of their products, which extends to many socially conscious business practices, but does not explicitly spell them out. Further, they coordinate on sourcing and technical issues to "promote and protect American craft chocolate making," in essence acknowledging this new artisanal form as being distinct, while most products' packaging also notes its influence upon tradition. [23]

CHOCOLATE AND ITS AMERICAN TERROIR

While the narrative of connection to tradition and place is the method so many craft chocolate makers use to sell their product, Mast

Brothers does much of their storytelling with their packaging—and very few words. Mast Brothers Chocolate bars are recognizable from twenty paces—the wrappers are simple, colorful wallpaper-inspired prints on matte paper, with little copy. "The chocolate sells itself," longtime employee Derek Herbster says, referring both to its eye-catching packaging (that says so much about the business's aesthetic and niche in the marketplace) and to its high quality and unique flavor. "We don't have a marketing team, we have an education team," he notes. Mast Brothers exemplifies perhaps one of the most stylized versions of craft chocolate. They embrace the "artisanal" moniker and have been bolstered by the family aspect of artisanal business in and around the Williamsburg neighborhood of Brooklyn, where their factory has stood since early 2008.[24]

Mast Brothers was first conceived in Brooklyn in 2006, the brainchild of siblings Rick and Mike Mast, who, along with a contingent of others at the same time in Williamsburg, were trying their hand at craft food projects from pickling to home brewing, among many others. It was at the start of what Herbster referred to as the "food revolution"—and countless articles, as well as many interviews here, have supported this claim of a collective consciousness arising at the same time in this one place. One day the brothers came up with the idea of making chocolate—so many people liked it, yet it was industrialized and not yet easily available in a more pure form; they saw it as the next untapped food category. So they bought basic machinery and some beans, and tried their hand at making chocolate themselves. Being in Brooklyn among these distillers and farm-to-table restaurateurs and pickle makers gave them a strong community to inspire and support them in their initial chocolate-making efforts—and they wanted to represent the place that inspired their product. At first they sold bars wrapped in newspaper and sold them at the local "Artist and Flea" market a few blocks from the Williamsburg waterfront. But soon they moved on to wrapping their bars in reproductions of vintage wallpaper they had found in a shop in downtown Manhattan, after working with a local designer to hit upon their now-iconic packaging. This thoughtful, beautiful packaging certainly said a lot about the makers' aesthetic, and it helped consumers feel that when they bought a Mast Brothers bar of chocolate, it not only tasted like, but looked like, a work of art. Something worthy of a birthday or housewarming gift—worth its price of many times a bar of commodity chocolate, back when craft bars were less ubiquitous.

The goal of Mast Brothers from the beginning was to take the same idea that many wine makers and farmers had believed in—the taste of terroir, or the flavor of the land itself—and apply it to chocolate. Thus their emphasis on education, apparent in the education board in their storefront in Brooklyn and on their website, shows their customers how chocolate is made and discusses the different environments where the beans are grown, as well as their distinct characteristics. "We need to teach people why it's worth it to buy a $7 bar of chocolate," says Derek. This education also led to various activities, like the sailing of beans from the Caribbean to New York, in part to demonstrate that this once common form of environmentally friendly raw ingredient transport was still possible. Their thinking was that this low-impact mode of transportation used to be the norm for this trade route—and with so many unused docks near their home base in Brooklyn, perhaps it was time just to see to what extent they could minimize their carbon footprint and return to the pre-industrialized methods of transportation and production.

Mast Brothers are, arguably, the most stylized bar of the new American chocolate revolution, as more than one maker has dubbed this influx of bean-to-bar makers in the last decade. They are available in Whole Foods and many high-end grocery and specialty stores across the country—as well as many food co-ops and other stores that support sustainably sourced products. All of their chocolate is currently produced in Brooklyn, but their goal is to continually push toward more efficient and green practices, perhaps resulting in regional chocolate-producing factories around the country.

Focused on quality ingredients from the beginning, Mast Brothers has not had to compromise their ingredient sourcing as they grew. "In fact we are able to be even more thoughtful about it," says Herbster, which echoes the experiences of other chocolate makers: Because of the nature of sourcing cacao, once a business's demand

Figure 4.3. Mast Brothers chocolate bars. Photo by the author.

for raw ingredients increases, so does their buying power with the local farmers. The beans are all purchased straight from the farmers in various parts of the world—who are also brought samples of

Mast Brothers' end products during twice-yearly trips to visit these plantations. They also strive to source as many remaining components to their business as possible from small producers in the United States.

While the Craft Chocolate Makers of America have embraced the term *craft*, Mast Brothers (which is not a CCMA member) uses the term *artisanal*, and sees their birth from the artisanal movement that started in Brooklyn in the mid-aughts. They define *artisanal* in its literal sense—made by an artisan who knows and performs a craft well. They see themselves very much as a part of the birth of the artisanal movement in Brooklyn, and, like other artisans who were working on their craft in the mid-aughts, they bartered their goods for beer and food and other craft items, and claimed inspiration from the original food production going on around them in their neighborhood of Williamsburg. A number of other successful businesses were born from this community and are still thriving, and this group of artisans linked by neighborhood has proven to be helpful across the industries. The real inspiration for these artisanal food businesses is a desire to understand the craft behind the products that people enjoy consuming—and a return to original and high-quality ingredients that are often kinder to the environment and workers.

Yet, whether they call it artisanal or craft, Mast Brothers is certainly cultivating the image of an artist; their eye-catching bars are also offered in three-packs that highlight various single-origin and custom-blended bars from around the world (in a belly band with the title "Origin") including a "Brooklyn Blend." Another pack called "Artisan" features chocolate pairings with other artisanal producers like Stumptown Coffee and Maine Sea Salt. Thus, while many other craft chocolate makers do embrace their hometown as part of the larger terroir—Woodblock Chocolate has Portland, Oregon, proudly printed on the front of its wrapper—none connote the importance of the sense of place in their end product as does Mast Brothers chocolate. "Brooklyn Blend" implies that the particular roasting and blending of beans was intimately inspired by the borough in which it was made, and could not exist elsewhere. And by pairing that bar with other single-origin bars they elevate Brooklyn terroir to that of Belize or Papua New Guinea. This pride in Brooklyn and wanting to market themselves as being from a place that nurtured this new food movement is not unique to Mast Brothers. Brooklyn Brewery is a few blocks away from Mast Brothers' factory and King's County Distillery is the next neighborhood over. The Breuckelen Distilling and Brooklyn Brine pickles, among others, also tap into the Brooklyn cachet. While many food businesses have come out of Brooklyn, and Williamsburg in particular, Mast Brothers is among the earliest that helped foster a creative and supportive food community during the birth of the "food revolution" in artisanal products in the last decade. Yet all of these producers are instrumental in helping Brooklyn create its own sense of terroir—through the establishment of a community, traditions, and values inherent among these local producers.

At first glance, Dandelion Chocolate in San Francisco is a bean-to-bar chocolate maker with a similar product and mission as Woodblock Chocolate or Madre. The quality and sourcing of their beans is highlighted through single-origin bars, educational material is presented around their new retail space, and they are committed to traditional production techniques. Started by Todd Masonis and Cameron Ring, who sold their tech start-up in 2008—which helped generate the money and help with connections to raise additional capital—they opened their first production facility in 2010. When I visited their new facility in the Mission in early 2013, it had just opened and seamlessly combined retail and factory space like Taza, Mast Brothers, and Woodblock. Dandelion also has a mission to source quality, often single-origin beans sustainably and for a fair wage. And they are also committed to making the chocolate by hand as much as possible—on the day I visited I watched two employees in the cordoned-off bean room hand sort the beans to be roasted from those that were damaged and wouldn't be used. Heavy bags of beans still to be winnowed lay stacked against the wall behind them. Cam showed me the production floor—their team numbered perhaps a half dozen or so that day, from winnowing to tempering to bar shaping and wrapping, with much done by hand, or through lightly mechanized processes—and told me about the company's history and mission. Further, they relish their identity as a San Francisco chocolate maker—also implying that their concept of terroir includes the artisanal refinement that happens in their urban production space as well as the land and traditional harvesting, fermenting, and drying processes at the cacao plantations.[25]

Despite the obvious money behind this endeavor—they've been in business as long as Woodblock, but through investments they have been able to grow much faster—their story sounded very much

Figure 4.4.   Hand winnowing at Dandelion Chocolate.

the same as the other chocolate makers with whom I had spoken. Many of their challenges are similar to both Madre and Woodblock, who started around the same time: they are working to increase distribution, tweak their product recipes and offerings, and further solidify their niche within this growing marketplace for craft chocolate. Cam spoke to his and Todd's methodical approach to trying new beans or tweaking their production techniques—still creative problem solving, as Charley Wheelock had explained, but the language they used made it sound more like troubleshooting a computer bug—appropriate, perhaps, for chocolate makers coming from the culture of nearby Silicon Valley. Yet, tasting their chocolate—smooth, earthy, nuanced flavors—I would be hard pressed to taste any "coding" mentality in it. It was just good, quality chocolate.

Thus, the solution to the challenge of how to differentiate each company's chocolate in an increasingly crowded market lies, in part, with the distinction of "local" identity, in addition to the origins of its raw ingredients. Chocolate is relatively cheap to ship and easy to display (unlike the weight of pickles, refrigeration needed for fermented goods and most cheeses, or the regulations to be dealt with when selling alcohol), but consumers are perhaps most resistant to price. Commodity chocolate has been extremely inexpensive for a very long time—less than a dollar for a bar at today's prices means that a small indulgence could be had for the same price as a bottle of water—and is often consumed quickly for a sugar rush. Not only do these new chocolate makers have to overcome pricing their chocolate at many times the price of commodity bars, but also they have to educate consumers about the culture around chocolate consumption—a much harder task. The idea is to get consumers thinking about chocolate less as a quick snack and more as a luxury food or part of one's local and sustainable diet. It is an arguably easier sell for other industries to simply educate consumers on the immediate benefits of higher-quality wine or alcoholic spirits they can slowly drink, or pickles or cheese that can be shared among friends or eaten over the course of a few days, just as they would have their cheaper, mass-produced counterparts. But breaking apart a single bar into squares and savoring them is not how Americans have been accustomed to eating their chocolate, and it is harder to convince consumers to change these habits, although the luxury chocolate makers are certainly making progress.

In fact, the dark chocolate and "artisan" market share of chocolate is growing, with "expensive chocolate being seen as an affordable luxury," says Marcia Mogolonsky, a global food analyst. While the 2012 UK study "The Chocolate of Tomorrow" study does not differentiate between "artisan" brands and other luxury chocolate, it does name higher-end chocolate makers like Godiva and Lindt and offers them up in opposition to other mass-produced behemoths like Hershey and Cadbury. They noted consumers' increasing demand for darker chocolate and brands with a story, citing Godiva sales almost doubling in the last decade as further evidence. The study went on to note, "Larger brands are keen to get a bite out of this burgeoning sector, but without the personal story required to buy such products, they can struggle."[26] The solution offered is for these large conglomerates to purchase smaller brands with an artisanal identity—like Hershey's purchase of originally San Francisco–based Scharffen Berger—and continue to market them as if they were still independent. "Consumers like artisan companies because they are high quality and unique," said food analyst Mary Nanfelt, yet many are smart enough to know when their uniqueness has been compromised by affiliation with a larger conglomerate.

Dandelion's online biography slyly notes the hole that Scharffen Berger left "now that they moved east to join Hershey"—a possible knock for losing their independent and perhaps even craft status—and they added that they are "excited to bring artisanal bean-to-bar chocolate back to the bay area."[27] Thus the narrative that Dandelion has embraced that helps them in the luxury chocolate market is their identity as both a socially conscious producer in touch with the issues surrounding sourcing from far-flung locations, as well as a business that is essentially San Franciscan. They are "local," even if their product is exotic, and their affiliation with the city is an integral part of their identity. As terroir scholar Terrio writes, by "locating food" in a place in which the consumer is invested and familiar, it helps to make it theirs and can train consumers to appreciate it in

new ways.[28] Thus, San Franciscans—or Somervillians or Brookly-
nites or Portlanders—can connect to their "local" bean-to-bar chocolate in part because of its identity as "locally made"—even if the
raw ingredients and initial production (the fermenting and drying)
are exotically sourced. The open concept production facility and the
stylish packaging all also work to provide a narrative of place and
sensibility that speaks to consumers who relate because they are
members of this group—the hipsters of Brooklyn, the DIY-ers of
Portland—or aspire to possess and taste a few bites of sweet earthi-
ness that are representative of the artisanal food scene from these
locales.

THE CHALLENGES OF CHOCOLATE AS A MODERN ARTISANAL PRODUCT

Beyond the narrative of the chocolate's main production location,
the other aspect of terroir that is essential to craft chocolate is that of
the sourcing of raw materials. The idea of "fair trade" began in the
1940s as an effort to help third world craftspeople sell their handicrafts to more affluent markets to help them combat poverty in their
home countries. The concept has been extended to other goods,
namely exotics like coffee, tea, bananas, and chocolate, to name a
few, and Fair Trade USA noted that sales of certified products grew
75 percent in 2011.[29] All of the bean-to-bar chocolate makers with
whom I spoke, and all members of the Craft Chocolate Makers of
America, are committed to the ideal of socially and environmentally
conscious sourcing of their raw materials, although some have their
own philosophies that often go beyond the assurances of Fair Trade
USA. However, the visibility and consumer interest in fair trade or
similar product distinctions has helped bring awareness—and
sales—to artisanal chocolate, adding to the story of the products'
production, from the farmers who grow and ferment the beans to the
chocolate makers who produce the bars by hand in their factories
and store fronts around the country. It further aligns the farmers and
workers in the far-flung countries of origin of the cacao as "part-

ners" in the production process, helping to add authenticity to the narrative of chocolate as an exotic of ancient foreign traditions and production methods, even as it is also a "local" product from mostly urban factories around the United States.

This notion that terroir can extend beyond the land from which the product's raw material grew is supported by the new global debate on GI—or geographical indications—which is based on the French AOC labeling as a model for a discussion on terroir. France believes that artisanal knowledge on the craft of making certain products is collectively owned, while the United States sees a more global position on GI as infringing on individual ownership and "intellectual property right." I argue that since GI distinctions are "relinking production to the social, cultural and environmental aspects of particular places" that the producer does not need to be present in that place to make these connections. In fact, especially when dealing with some remote and international producers, it can be difficult or nearly impossible to complete the circle, as it were, of bean-to-bar at the place of origin. Further, Barham, Paxson, and others make the point that terroir can be beneficial to these rural, and in the case of chocolate, third world communities, helping farmers—appropriately called "partners" by Taza Chocolate—gain the compensation and respect their traditional methodology and care for the land deserves.[30] Thus, as the idea of "local" is an important distinction among artisanal producers and consumers, the underlying value system in sourcing local—to be stewards of the environment, to help farmers earn a living wage, sometimes to preserve authenticity in terroir—is still intact with these craft chocolate makers who are so connected with place, even if their primary place of chocolate production is many thousands of miles away.[31]

And, since American craft chocolate is, by these definitions, a new product, it has a new identity, and new association with terroir. Unlike other artisanal goods that are learning from past traditions often passed down from one person to another, bean-to-bar chocolate is creating a new tradition where the makers must learn to make the end product from directions published on the Internet or from another craftsperson who taught themselves from various non-human resources, in essence creating resources and a new industry that will be the standard for future craft chocolate makers. Further, some steps of the chocolate-making process are mechanized—the smooth texture and shiny exterior couldn't happen without it. And this is one of the reasons that Taza's chocolate—and other stone-ground styles—are so different, as they have continued to perform some, but not all, steps by hand that other craft makers now do by machine. This manner of creating craft supports the assertion that this is an ancient product re-made for the modern consumer.

But this is not to say that what the bean-to-bar makers are doing is exploitative or inauthentic. None are making claims that are untrue, and in the end what is striking is the extent to which all members do seem committed to social consciousness as integral to their commercial mission. In the end, it is about honoring the raw ingredients and the farmers who work the land (perhaps more consistently so than any other industry across the board, as it is almost a definition of bean-to-bar chocolate to be stewards of cacao and its workers). Still, the very nature of craft chocolate in America is that it is made for the modern consumer, expressing a sense of both the original traditions of chocolate, as well as the terroir of the urban landscape from which it now comes.

For all its American identity, craft chocolate still depends on the ability to source raw materials that are high quality and adhere to the values that these small chocolate makers are striving for. Although Nat Bletter of Madre Chocolate and Guittard Chocolate in the Bay Area are striving to grow beans in Hawaii—and cacao is available in Mexico and parts of the Caribbean, geographically closer to the States than Hawaii—the "exotic" nature of chocolate is its largest challenge. Initially, the answer for Charley Wheelock and other DIY-ers and start-ups lay with John the Alchemist, who has been a key sourcer for smaller batches of quality cacao beans in the United States, and can arguably be credited with helping to shape this new American artisanal industry.

In the story of Charley and Jessica Wheelock's initial efforts at chocolate making, they invested $3,000 for a bag of fermented but unroasted beans from John, and, because he lives not far from Portland, Charley asked if he could visit and learn about the chocolate-making process. When they met, John gave some instruction on how to roast them in a coffee roaster—John taught himself from written directions and through trial and error—and Charley eventually bought his own, a used, gleaming drum that sits in the corner of his shop. John was described as a true hippy, who roasts his own coffee, makes his own chocolate, and brews his own beer—an artisanal food guru in the woods of Oregon. And he had an integral role in helping to start this chocolate revolution after having broken down some of the barriers to obtaining smaller quantities of quality beans and demystifying the chocolate-making process for so many. This was born for him out of his efforts roasting his own coffee beans—again, a process that once seemed beyond the average artisan's realm, both for lack of start-up resources, as well as the fact that as an exotic product, knowledge was unavailable and one had to find ways to learn the craft independently. When he next had his mind set on chocolate, John was tenacious and finally was able to source a 135-pound bag of cacao beans from Ghana in 2004, with the broker joking that he had just made the smallest purchase of cacao on modern record—most sales were for a minimum of 2,000 pounds, but often for many times more than that. This knowledge, however, that so few others were making small-batch chocolate, only inspired John to continue to find better-quality beans to make his own chocolate and to help others do the same. [32]

Inspired and mentored by John, Charley and Jessica's Woodblock Chocolate has been slowly growing, starting with a bag of beans and a few local stores who agreed to carry their blue and white, often single-origin bars. John has helped Charley source higher-quality and more rare beans since their initial meeting a few years ago—in fact Charley declared it a historic day when I visited his factory in January of 2013, as he offered me a taste of the first chocolate made in America from grand cru beans from Trinidad. Inspired in part through John's tutelage and the raw ingredients he helped them source—Charley has since been fostering connections with farmers and bean brokers in the Caribbean—Woodblock is finding their own niche among the growing craft chocolate industry.

Figure 4.5.   Bags of cacao beans at Mast Brothers' factory. Photo by the author.

Their growth is typical of most artisanal food start-ups—a slow move from creating at home to a commercial space, retail accounts found by the owners pounding the pavement and acting as their own salesperson, hand-wrapped bars in tow. Or working with local chefs or bakers who choose to use and promote the products of local artisans, as is often found in Charley's hometown of Portland, and in numerous restaurants around New York City, or a few other places where there is a community of support for local food artisans as well.

But, like most food start-ups, the issue of money and sustainable growth will loom overhead long after their customers think they've "made it." This is made somewhat more complex with the necessary outlay of costs for beans from less certain provenance—Charley mentioned early on obtaining an order of what he had thought were higher-quality beans but turned out to be mostly replaced by lower-quality commodity cacao. When working with small, international brokers, there isn't much recourse for such a discovery. In his characteristic optimism, he noted that he didn't exactly blame the international brokers for their mistrust of American chocolate makers, given the history of chocolate making in the past few decades. Although Charley does note that with the increased demand for these higher-quality beans, and the improving reputation of American chocolate makers, helped very much by these socially and environmentally conscious craft bean-to-bar makers, he has every reason to believe that these transactions will continue to become easier and more trustworthy in the future.

WHAT IS ARTISANAL CHOCOLATE?

I could describe the taste—maybe textured like Taza Chocolate, or with nuanced notes of brightness or underlying berry like Woodblock. Or the smell: the rich, green, sweet smell of cocoa being tempered before being made into bars or rounds, wafting down the block from Mast Brothers, near the Brooklyn waterfront. Or maybe the experience of watching an entire team take on nearly every task of chocolate making before my eyes in Dandelion's large, consumer-friendly retail and production space. Or what I could only imagine as the pride Nat Bletter has in the foliage of his nascent cacao grove in Hawaii. And certainly, it is the story behind each of these chocolate makers that helps to make them unique, just as each has their own connections to cacao growers around the world, modern production techniques, and city-based factory.

I believe the comparisons to both wine and coffee are apt. Like coffee, chocolate is an exotic, coming from farmers whose work and beans were once wildly exploited. And now, with the focus on quality production and fair trade, the consumer knows more about the product and can make better decisions based upon personal preferences and values. Terroir can be tasted, too, if the products' beans are treated with care, and consumers have already come to understand the variations possible among chocolate and the value of a good product. Just as the rise in "designer" coffee beans and coffee cuppings increased the amount one could charge for good coffee, paying many times more for a quality bar of chocolate will be de rigueur. And like wine, the nuances from the beans themselves can, very much, lend themselves to tastings and talk of the nuances of bean origin. Heritage varieties are being preserved in a live grove in the Caribbean, and increasingly consumers are aware of certain small nooks around the globe from whence their fancy chocolate comes.

Yet for all of the talk of individual stories selling these surprisingly unique variances on what I once thought of as a standardized product, their influences, challenges, and approaches to their businesses are surprisingly similar. Artisanal chocolate implies a concern with the welfare of cacao farmers and workers, attention paid to the nuances of growth of the beans themselves, and dedication to traditional, handmade methods of making chocolate—plus the general acceptance of tempering to achieve (with a few exceptions) the glossy look and smooth mouth feel of modern chocolate. These are all values that have come to be an essential part of the American bean-to-bar chocolate narrative.

Perhaps even more so than most other artisans discussed in this book, artisanal chocolate makers are in touch with the long history of their product, and see education as part of their mission. Artisanal or craft chocolate must be concerned with the provenance of their raw ingredients, specifically cacao, and the method in which it is cultivated, harvested, and processed. Further, spoken or not, these artisans recognize the history of wrongs that have been committed, mainly by Europeans and Americans, to keep so many plied with cheap chocolate. Fortunes have been made in chocolate, while slaves or maltreated workers were doing the dirty work. And promises were made that weren't kept, leaving craft chocolate makers to have to work that much harder to regain trust from those with whom they are trying to build a mutually beneficial business.

This commitment to ancient techniques and quality, often single-origin beans is also inspired by the desire to provide a living wage to cacao farmers and workers who had been taken advantage of for so long by the industry. Yet part of the challenge of this is to convince consumers that higher-quality chocolate made from these artisans, many of whom are also fair trade or "whole trade" certified, is worth many times more than the Hershey bars of their youth. One way some are convincing them of this is through chocolate tastings and education, which are aiming to teach consumers to identify the nuances in the beans grown in various regions around the world, or roasting in specific ways. And by many accounts this is working. Craft chocolate consumption is on the rise and is displayed prominently in food co-ops and grocers who focus on selling "local" or sustainably sourced food.

And with the common narrative of attention to sourcing, social consciousness, and return to using at least some ancient methods (the first steps of chocolate harvesting and production—the harvesting, fermenting, and drying—have continued to be done by hand), other producers are moving back toward hand winnowing, or more hands-on versions of tempering or shaping or wrapping chocolate, for example. Yet all employ certain modernized steps unapologetically, although all artisans with whom I spoke had strict human quality control at every juncture. This combination of the modern and the traditional can also have implications for defining the term *artisanal* across industries—perhaps reconciling why one industrywide definition would allow some mechanization and others eschew it. This all adds up to a modern story of chocolate—a newly interpreted terroir that helps set craft chocolate apart from other versions of the same, ubiquitous treat.

How does the contemporary chocolate artisan see him- or herself within the larger context of chocolate making throughout time? These new bean-to-bar makers seem to want to tell a common story of being modern Western caretakers of both knowledge of ancient processes and the anthropological and botanical history of chocolate, while also seeking to put their artistic fingerprint on their product through their own nuances of production, more "authentic" or rare—to the modern Western market—bean sourcing, and the way that they combine these ancient processes with modern packaging and presentation and even flavorings for a contemporary consumer.

Thus they are combining new and old production techniques with a contemporary presentation to give added value to their end product while still giving the consumer something both classic and contemporary, both nostalgic and in line with more modern palate preferences. They are creating a new artisanal product, rather than simply reviving the old.

The craft chocolate industry has been instrumental in preserving traditional cacao production methods, heritage variety trees, and even ancient tools that were in danger of being lost forever. It is entrepreneurs like Alex Whitmore and Charley Wheelock, Nat Bletter and brothers Rick and Michael Mast who not only want to make a quality product that honors the long tradition of cacao growing and chocolate making, but also take the industry of craft chocolate making into the future, sustainably, creatively, and deliciously—creating a new sense of terroir along the way.

5

SPIRITS

Looking to the Past
to Create the Future

Stories of heritage and tradition matter. Ask a cocktail drinker how they came to love their favorite spirit and the answer will likely have more substance than "it tastes good." Drinking cocktails is often a social activity, one that inspires community and evokes a sense of time and place—and the choice of cocktail can say a lot about the drinker. One makes as many assumptions about the person who orders a Cosmopolitan as one whose drink of choice is "whiskey, straight." Are you Carrie Bradshaw or Clark Gable? It's the cocktail or the spirit's narrative that imbues itself into the drinker with every sip. Bourbon, perhaps, has one of the grandest stories—the quintessential American spirit, which by definition is made from at least 51 percent corn and is aged in new, charred oak barrels, among other specifications, including the internationally agreed requirement that it is made in the United States. To drink bourbon is to share a moment with Southern dandies of the 1800s as well as bootleggers of the early 1900s; its embodied story is of backcountry distillers and modern cocktail mavens. It is a classy, but also rugged spirit. It can be dressed up in a julep or dressed down, on the rocks. It is an American original.

Bourbon might be the first spirit one thinks of when considering American booze, but the narrative surrounding artisanal spirits in America today is much more varied. The number of small-batch distillers, generally defined in the industry as producing less than twenty barrels of a single bottling of a spirit (which is about 1,000 gallons) is growing exponentially, with some equating the rise of craft distilling with that of the craft brewing industry in the 1980s and 1990s. Yet artisanal distilling in America has its own story. Many of the new distillers have been influenced by the trajectory of American history itself: the westward migration of those looking to start a new life, or at least live their current one by their own rules; the cocktail culture of the cities in the northeast; the creative uses of the excess crops of any given region; the national tale of Prohibition, but the very regional way that the laws were followed—or not—by its residents, and then the way that each state reacted to the end of Prohibition by defining their own laws on making and selling alcohol. These narratives of the past are integral to how modern distillers define themselves and their products, and are an inherent element of what makes an artisanal distiller today. While cheese makers are actively redefining their traditional pastoral narrative to incorporate the modern, artisanal distillers are often doing the opposite—looking to the past to help create their modern story.

This is a tale of two cities. Or really, two states. In one state we have regulations, which initially hampered progress and creativity. In this state, little happened in artisanal alcoholic spirits distilling for a long time. But when these regulations were eased, entrepreneurs and creative types were inspired to work within their confines to create quality and at times innovative products. Those who did get into distilling were passionate about it, willing to challenge bureaucracy for the sake of their potable art. And fighting and adapting and flourishing is what has happened in this state in the past decade, and it is poised to continue to nurture its own distilling niche, developed by necessity because of the more onerous regulations and laws. Perhaps surprisingly, this state is New York.

In the other state, distilling was legally easier, and it did flourish, eventually, for many of the same reasons that like-minded distillers sought to change the laws in other states around the country. Its distillers are also more diverse, due in part to the relatively lax regulations compared to its counterpart on the country's other coast. There are still exciting things happening in distilling in this state, but the identities of these distillers are spread across a broader spectrum. And what is happening there, in Oregon, is helping to evolve the very definition of craft distilling. But the story of how these two states came to have such different distilling identities begins where many other stories of American foodways begin—on the boat with the first settlers coming over from England.

HISTORY

It's easy to look at the history of alcoholic spirits in the United States as bifurcated by Prohibition. But, while Prohibition did have a profound effect on the culture of drinking spirits in this country, it did not alter the landscape inextricably. From colonization through the mid-1800s settlers brewed their own beer and distilled their own spirits, using ingredients like hops, wheat, corn, and fruit that could be grown locally. Some farmers saw distilling and fermenting to be a way to add value to their excess crops, and they would sell or trade their goods for others they couldn't grow themselves. Primarily, however, whiskey and fruit brandies and ciders were made for personal consumption or to trade or sell to one's neighbors, often without much in the way of consistency or quality control. Also, until the mid-1800s or so, rum was also a popular spirit, made in various localities from sugar cane or its by-products imported from the Caribbean. The northeast in particular became a hub of rum production, with large distilleries in Boston, New York City, and Rhode Island, areas conveniently located on the coast for easy access of raw materials that weren't natively grown, with more also imported from the Caribbean. Rum was such an established part of drinking culture that even President George Washington requested rum at his inauguration. However, it was also associated with the Triangle Trade that brought slaves over from Africa, and rum fell out of favor as politics changed and whiskey became more popular.

Whiskey distillation was also brought over with the settlers, but by the early 1800s distillers (very often farmers who also grew the grains that went into the spirit) were becoming larger and their product more refined. Perhaps unsurprisingly, many of the first distillers were Irish and Scottish, building stills both from scratch as well as importing stills from Europe. Other stills were erected on the recommendation of President George Washington, who owned his own prolific distillery[1] and suggested that others be built around the country.[2] Whiskey also grew in popularity in part because imported spirits were beginning to be taxed at a higher rate and whiskey was seen as a relative bargain. In addition, perhaps this was the first triumph of local over global—whiskey was made from local grain or corn by distillers the consumers often knew personally. It's not hard to imagine the perceived value added to the product when the buyer had a personal connection to the craftsman and raw materials.

Throughout the 1800s, however, there was also a strong temperance movement, with evangelical Protestants leading the call for moderation—and even abstinence—regarding the consumption of intoxicating potables. Those at the forefront saw the eroding of morality, health, and even economic prosperity as being a major factor in the push for making alcohol illegal. There were some successful efforts by temperance advocates throughout the nineteenth century, including short-lived laws that outlawed the manufacture or sale of "spirituous or intoxicating liquors" or other similar legislation, but all were repealed within a few years. However, the temperance movement was gaining popularity, as represented by the creation of the Anti-Saloon League in 1893, and it became a strong political force for decades.[3] Once the Anti-Saloon League gained political power, they focused on influencing politics on a local scale, and succeeded in passing versions of Prohibition in nine states and numerous communities before 1913. This patchwork of state laws set the stage for some federal regulation of intoxicants, including the Webb-Kenyon Act of 1913 that made it illegal to transport liquor into states with Prohibition laws.

Prohibition seems like a quaint decade or so of our national history—with speakeasies and bootleggers retaining the charm of their colorful lore even today and more than a few new artisanal spirits being named after these historic relics. But really, when you stop to think about it, the fact that the United States—the land of the free—outlawed the manufacture and sale of alcoholic potables is rather unbelievable. By the early 1800s, Protestant reformers led the way for various local communities and even states to ban all alcohol, or more often just spirits, well before national Prohibition in the 1920s. The Prohibition movement gained steam, however, in part evidenced by the passage of the Webb-Kenyon Act, and by the late 1910s thirteen states had instituted Prohibition laws that banned all alcoholic beverages; an equal number had banned only higher-proof potables. This emboldened the "Drys" as they were known, to push for not just a federal law prohibiting alcohol, but a constitutional amendment.

In 1917, the Senate approved an amendment that prohibited the manufacture, sale, transportation, import, or export of intoxicating liquors, and by January 1919, the Eighteenth Amendment had been fully ratified by all states of the union by wide margins. The strict enforcement of this amendment was outlined in the Volstead Act, which defined procedures for enforcement and—controversially— defined intoxicating liquors as any that had over .5 percent alcohol. Until this act was passed, many had assumed that only distilled liquors would be affected, as some areas allowed the manufacture of beer and wine. Thus the beer and wine industries and the spirit distillers did not band together to fight these regulations, creating a separation that is still somewhat apparent today. Despite the wide margin of victory in Congress, a number of states, including Oregon, made legal movements against Prohibition, although none succeeded. However, intoxicating potables hardly disappeared in the United States. Rather, bootlegging—or the illegal sale, transportation, and distribution of liquor, so named in the 1600s for the practice of squirreling away a bottle in one's boot—proliferated, with hundreds of thousands of gallons coming in from places like Canada and the Bahamas and more being produced by moonshiners who operated illegal stills.[4]

Once in effect, some in the liquor industry adapted, changing their business to make other products, while others simply went out of business. But Prohibition affected other industries as well—in New York state, for example, once known as one of the largest grain producers in the country, the agricultural identity changed drastically during Prohibition when the demand for grains for distilling decreased. Many of these farmers replaced their wheat crops with apples or other crops, which required different demands from the land and the farmers and changed the landscape markedly.

By the mid-1920s, public opinion began to turn against Prohibition; in New York State, for example, one 1925 survey asked if residents were "satisfied" with the present condition, and 68 percent said no. However, while there was a strong "wet" contingent, not all discontents were calling for total repeal—some were upset at lax enforcement, while others wanted just beer and wine to be legalized. Eventually the argument to end Prohibition was secured in part because some believed that underfunded and lax enforcement threatened the overall integrity of adherence to all laws. Also, some argued that the government was missing out on a large amount of taxes from bootlegged alcohol. In 1933 the Twenty-first Amendment legalizing the manufacture and sale of alcohol was passed and soon thereafter states adopted their own laws governing everything from saloon licenses to regulations on the creation of breweries and distilleries. Some states, like Oregon, created a statewide agency that became, in essence, the only distributer of alcoholic beverages in the state, and strictly controlled who could sell alcohol. Others, like New York, took an even stricter stance, allowing the consumption of alcoholic beverages but making the in-state fermentation and distillation of potent potables difficult to do legally. It would take almost seventy years for these laws to be significantly loosened.

NEW YORK DISTILLING HISTORY

In the late 1700s and early 1800s New York State was among the leaders in wheat production in the country. However, after the completion of the Erie Canal in 1825, this distinction changed, as cheaper wheat could be shipped in on barges from the Midwest. Thus farmers began diversifying their crops to include barley, rye, corn, hops, and other items to provide for the growing dairy, brewing, and distilling industries.[5] From the 1840s to the 1880s, New York State also produced more hops than any other state, supporting one of America's largest brewing industries. Also, by the late 1800s, New York State had as many as a thousand distilleries at its peak, distilling whiskey from rye, corn, or wheat, and brandy and other stronger spirits from excess fruit and other imported ingredients. Beer and spirits were an integral part of a typical New Yorker's diet, and prior to the Croton Aqueduct's construction in 1842, it was sometimes considered safer to drink than New York City–area water. Alcohol had a longer shelf-life than other beverages, and even children were given watered-down alcoholic beverages.[6] Further, distilling excess grain and fruit that couldn't be sold at market was a good way to enhance profits and give farmers additional revenue or goods to trade. New York State distilleries also made rum from molasses imported from the West Indies[7] and exported as far away as Africa or sold or shared locally. These distilleries flourished until Prohibition, which abruptly shuttered all legal means of making spirits, and after 1920 the drop-off in legal distilling radically changed the agricultural landscape of New York State, with fields of wheat, hops, and other ingredients that went into beer and spirits soon replanted with apples, hay for livestock, and other crops.

After Prohibition was repealed, however, the distillation industry did not return, in part because the state never changed the law to allow it. Eventually large distilleries could get a license, but for a hefty $50,000 fee.[8] It took until 1976 when the farm winery law passed, which allowed grape growers to sell their wine directly to the public, that small-scale retail production of alcoholic beverages was again legal and accessible. Prior to this act's passage there were fewer than twenty wineries in the state, and soon thereafter, the number multiplied exponentially.[9] This law greatly simplified (and made more affordable) the prior impediments to producing wine in New York State. The same was done for the alcoholic spirits industry in 2002: the A-1 license was modeled on the farm winery bill and reduced the distillery permit fee to $1,500 for three years. With this new law, distillers could legally make up to 35,000 gallons of spirit products, which the distiller could then sell through licensed bars, restaurants, and retailers. Then in 2007 the Farm Distillery Act was signed into law, which permitted the farm distiller the right to sell to consumers at the distillery and required the use of a minimum of 70 percent New York–grown agricultural raw materials. Both licenses permit the distiller to self-distribute his goods. Since 2007, forty-five new Farm Distilleries have opened in New York. Retailer placement can be harder for small-batch or unproven products to break into in New York, which has the more competitive "private distribution," unlike Oregon, which has state distribution of alcoholic beverages.[10] However, in 2012, New York State's governor, Andrew Cuomo, signed a bill that opened up even more opportunities for small distillers to gain a foothold in the retail market by allowing them to easily obtain permits to sell at farmers markets or other offsite locations.

So what is interesting about alcoholic spirits in New York State is that the products made by the new small-batch producers are, because of the farm distillery laws, mostly—but often almost entirely—made from locally sourced products. The result of these laws is such that distillers are becoming more creative within the law's strictures and more interesting—and New York State terroir–based products are being developed, redefining many customers' expectations of whiskey, bourbon, rye, gin, and other spirits.

OREGON DISTILLING HISTORY

In the 1800s, Oregon was still considered the wild west, and a frontiersman, do-it-yourself attitude firmly took hold among the population. There was plenty of distilling happening at home for personal consumption, as many residents were homesteaders and living subsistence lives, often in small towns or even more remote rural areas. Oregon went "dry" in 1916, a few years before Prohibition became national law. Thus there was already a strong system in place for bootlegging and moonshining when the penalties for producing and selling alcohol became stiffer under federal law. When alcohol was once again legal in the state in 1933, lawmakers placed a high priority on regulating alcohol production and sales. Then Governor Julius Meier appointed a committee headed by Dr. William Know that suggested a method similar to Canada's. They created the Oregon Liquor Control Committee, which still exists today and whose duty it was, in part, to collect tax revenue from alcohol production while keeping alcohol abuse under control.[11] According to the OLCC's website, "Oregon is a control state with the exclusive right to sell packaged distilled spirits, which are dispersed statewide from a distribution center in Portland and sold in 242 retail liquor stores operated by contracted agents."[12] This means that only state-licensed stores can sell liquor and that the state, in essence, serves as the only statewide distributor, with the exception of distilleries that can sell from their place of production. While it is illegal to distill without a license, the OLCC has embraced the Oregon Distilling Guild, seeing a benefit in having more distilleries for consumers to visit, try, and ultimately, purchase from. Portland, in particular, is supportive of Distillery Row, which helps to consolidate distillers into one area of the city, allowing them to collaborate on marketing, promotions, and consumer traffic.

Spending equal amounts of time in the Boston and New York City areas in the last few years, I couldn't help but notice—and sample—the newly (re)emerging cocktail culture and the subsequent boom in small-batch alcoholic spirits. The American Cocktail Revolution, first noted around the mid-aughts—with 2006 being dubbed "The Year of the Cocktail" by *USA Today*—mostly focused on revivals and reinterpretations of classic cocktails, or using nearly forgotten spirits, liquors, and bitters. Cocktail bars with serious commitment to the craft of their drinks became the evening activity of choice for many hip New Yorkers, and a classic silver shaker or a leather-bound flask was a favorite holiday or birthday gift for many young and fashionable urban dwellers who sought out unmarked speakeasy-type bars with such draws as hand-carved "artisanal" ice cubes.

That consumers were looking to the past to inspire their cocktails shouldn't be surprising, as this was mirroring what was happening in the food industry. As we have seen, the rise in traditional recipes and methods of food preparation and preservation also was gaining traction around this time, as was the demand for locally sourced and artisanal food. The interest in classic cocktails and local spirits was, of course, not far behind. The allure of a good cocktail has only become more entrenched within the culture, and continues to become a jumping-off point for artisans who wish to take some of these classic or niche spirits and reinvent them. It shouldn't be surprising that in Brooklyn, where a collective artisanal food revolution was taking place at the same time, that well-crafted cocktails were being revived; local artisans were thinking: I can make that from scratch. As of mid-2012 Brooklyn boasted twelve distilleries, with the city being host to another thirteen in Manhattan and one in the Bronx.[13] And so has craft or small-batch distilling grown nationally from six micro-distillers in 1996 to over four hundred today.[14]

THE DISTILLING PROCESS

Distillation of alcoholic spirits is a method that depends first on fermentation—spirits can be made from any number of raw materials including various grains, corn, and fruit. The first step is beginning the process that creates alcohol from these raw materials by making a mash of ground grain, corn, or fruit and adding water and, sometimes, sugar, malt, or yeast depending on the spirit.[15] When this mash is fermented and then added to the still, it then becomes known as the wash. The wash is slowly heated in the still for a set amount of time, where evaporation of the alcohol occurs at a lower temperature than water and the alcohol heads upward through the

still, separating alcohol from the wash and creating a stronger distilled spirit. Beer, on the other hand, is not distilled, and what is
consumed is the result of the fermentation of the grain, sugar, and
yeast.

There are basically two types of stills used in the micro-distiller-
ies in New York and Oregon (and elsewhere, of course): pot stills
and column stills. In a column still, the wash is heated and the
evaporated alcohol (mixed with only a small amount of water—pure
distillation or distillation at 100 percent removes all water; distillation of less efficiency, e.g., 90 percent, means that the spirit is 90
percent alcohol, etc.) heads up the tall column, and the distiller can
choose at what proof or "efficiency" of distillation he or she wants
for the spirit. Thus alcohol can be distilled at a very high proof with
column stills, and such stills are necessary for making vodkas and
gins. The resulting alcohol comes out more pure and clear, but also
distills out much of the subtlety of flavor from the raw ingredients.
With a pot still, the alcohol cannot be distilled at such a high proof,
and thus more of the color, texture, and flavor is retained (think
brown spirits like whiskey). Most distillers choose column stills
because they offer more flexibility in what can be made in them.
However, with a pot still there is more opportunity for the distiller
to achieve nuanced flavor from the process. In a pot still, the distilled vapors head through a condensing coil rather than up the
column to cool. The first distillation liquid is at a lower proof—
generally 25 percent to 35 percent—and is called the "low wines."
The low wines are collected and redistilled to a higher proof liquid,
of about 70 percent. Distillers sometimes choose to combine some
of the low wines with the second distillation to adjust the taste of
their end product. After distillation, the spirit can be bottled or put in
barrels for aging.

Barrel aging can add both color and flavor to a spirit and federal
designations of different spirits include laws on how long and in
what kinds of barrels various spirits are aged. Focusing on whiskey—for the majority of the distillers with whom I spoke were
making that spirit—the term refers to any spirit made from a mash
of grain between 40 percent and 95 percent alcohol. Yet within the

Figure 5.1.   Column still. Photo by the author.

whiskey category, there are distinctions by the main ingredient used in the mash. For example, bourbon is made from at least 51 percent corn and "stored in charred new oak containers" for an unspecified amount of time. Rye whiskey is made from at least 51 percent rye, wheat whiskey from at least 51 percent wheat, and so forth. However there is also corn whiskey, which is also made from at least 51 percent corn, but is stored in used or uncharred new oak containers. The term "stored" however, is not regulated by any length of time, so as long as the spirit touches charred new oak barrels, in can be considered whiskey. "Straight" whiskey or bourbon basically means that the spirit was aged for a minimum of two years in a charred new oak barrel. While there are many more distinctions to the laws and definitions of various spirits, and nuances to the distilling process, this is a basic overview that can help with understanding of the distillers' and spirits' narrative.

NEW YORK STATE: LOOKING BACKWARD
TO MOVE FORWARD

Perhaps it was only fitting that I was walking over centuries-old cobblestones in a corner of Brooklyn that would feel positively small town if it weren't for the distant hum of traffic on the nearby Manhattan Bridge. I was headed to King's County Distillery, located in the old paymaster building on the edge of the Brooklyn Navy Yard, within spitting distance of where 1869's "Whiskey War"— when the government sent fifteen hundred troops with a goal to decimate the black market distillers in the Vinegar Hill neighborhood—took place. To experience their tour and tasting I had to give my name to the guard at the gate, who allowed me through. Just beyond the gate is the beautiful brick distillery built more than a hundred years ago. Fittingly, Colin Spoelman and David Haskell found a location that appropriately represented their status as the new oldest continually operating distillery in New York City—in business since 2010. But for those who aren't aware of the interesting story of the state's distilling laws, it would be easy to buy into the distillery's historic narrative. And in many ways, that isn't too far from the truth.

I met with Nicole Austin, the master blender, who first took me out front of the distillery to show me a small patch of dirt, a rarity in this corner of Brooklyn. It was their intention, she said, to grow crops here to make, even symbolically, a spirit completely local to Brooklyn. We circled back to the aging room, which had recovered from being mostly underwater during Hurricane Sandy. They distilled using a pot still (although they were awaiting the arrival of new copper stills when I visited) in a process that is not much different from any other small distiller. But the beauty of their product lies in the details—namely the raw ingredients they use to create their mash, and the aging process. By law they must use at least 70 percent New York State–grown ingredients, but they generally use almost exclusively local products, in part to align with their philosophy of supporting local business and working with farmers they know and trust, and in part because it is simply cheaper to ship quality grain from closer farms than from farther away. They also make a delicious chocolate whiskey made with the husks from Mast Brothers chocolate, their neighbors in Williamsburg, in a process that she said was secret. The result, tasted at the end of the tour in the upstairs retail area, was enlightening. Not at all sweet, but imbued with dark, almost bitter chocolate flavor, I found it a whiskey worthy of sipping on its own, straight up or on the rocks. [16]

Next we went upstairs to the aging room where dozens of barrels were laid out in perfect rows. King's County ages their whiskey in five-gallon barrels, which are smaller than the industry standard. These age quicker and are also easier for the staff to move. Nicole explained how one of the main aspects of her job is to taste the barrels, making judgment calls on which ones should be blended— or which ones might be of the highest quality and suited for single-barrel bottling. It would make sense that the art of distilling and

Figure 5.2. Aging room at King's County Distillery.

aging would benefit from a long history of instinct and information that could only be learned through time and experience—especially gained from working in a specific space. Climate, especially in an unheated building like theirs, can alter the aging process, as can where the barrels are situated in the aging room—such as closer to the window, or more toward the interior. Relatively little has changed with the technology of distilling since Prohibition brought a booming industry to a standstill almost a century ago. "Craft" distilling has always been, like cheese and other artisanal industries, a combination of science and art, and while there may be a few more advanced ways to monitor the science of distilling, the art is still very much the same. While Nicole has a background in engineering and has learned as much as she can about the science of her job, she remarked that the art of blending is "still a bit magic." She is still learning about her space, while keeping meticulous notes, and while King's County has already received accolades including "Best in Category" for corn whiskey at the 2011 American Distilling Institute's Craft Spirits Conference and silver medals for both whiskeys at the 2013 Conference, their tenure as the oldest continually operating distillery in New York City is just beginning.

So it is keeping in line with their narrative that their whiskey is packaged in small, flask-like bottles sold in their upstairs retail space displayed alongside old apothecary bottles on rough-hewn shelves. Artifacts from the area's long history are displayed throughout the space and the walls are mostly unadorned. This aesthetic, along with the century-old brick, gives a sense that it could be a century earlier. King's County—through their name, location, and physical and narrative packaging, is taking on the trappings of history, as if trying to erase the near-century of missing distilling tradition in the state, to create a direct connection to their modern artisanal work. And it is here that the modern trappings meet the traditions they are striving to invoke, as Nicole said that King's County's story is "different" than that of other larger distillers because they are "more in touch with their ingredients" and their spirits are "made with care." Just like the original distillers, who were often distilling using their own crops, but so different from the large distillers who have controlled the market since Prohibition ended. So they are unique because they are doing things the traditional way, because they are smaller, because they are local—picking up the craft distilling industry right where it left off... in 1919.

I also spoke on the phone with Colin, founder of King's County Distillery, who said that his company started when he outgrew making whiskey in his bathtub (technically illegally). When he began King's County Distillery he noted that the legal hurdles he faced were reflective of the industry's tumultuous past. "The industry was completely shaped by Prohibition," he said, "and a lot of laws and practices continue to define the movement." And in fact, the specter of the past looms large over the artisanal—or craft or small batch— alcoholic spirits industry. As Colin notes, his product—and many small-batch products like his—aren't always that easy to differentiate from those produced by the larger corporate distilleries that also focus on high-end spirits. Where he can spend his time and energy is focusing on high-quality ingredients—he sources what he needs organically and locally but always with an eye toward quality—and the distilling process itself. However, being an urban distiller, he does not have the capacity, space, or time to allow his product to age like many corporate distillers who have been in the business for decades or longer, hence the smaller barrels that Nicole spoke about. Colin considers his product very smooth, but notes that people buy King's County Whiskey for many reasons—not all of which are focused on flavor. Colin recognizes that people are drawn to the company's identity as a the new "oldest distillery in New York City," to the allure of the "made in Brooklyn" distinction, and even the historical significance of whiskey being made in urban centers again, where it had originated centuries ago. And of course the narrative of the (re)birth of an industry: New York State microdistilling. [17]

Despite King's County Distillery's strong Brooklyn connection, that was not the reason that Colin was attracted to making whiskey. He grew up in a dry county in the South and said he had a particular cultural connection to visiting the local moonshiner or bootlegger. This Appalachian culture of liquor making has a long history and tradition, and his initial efforts at making whiskey were to connect to the culture of his childhood. Colin, who, when I spoke to him in late 2012 still worked a part-time job in addition to running the distillery, has clear but modest goals for the company. They had grown exponentially during their first two years—going from making a half-gallon a month to fourteen gallons of whiskey a day—but he recognizes that small-batch whiskey has a natural limit on expansion. Colin's goals include "establishing our place in the industry—and a place that is reasonably secure." Hopefully this will not be difficult, as Colin notes "the enormous appetite for craft spirits"—especially in urban centers with strong "foodie" scenes. Like Brooklyn, of course.

However, when I asked him about the terms, he resisted the word *artisanal* and even *craft* to describe his approach, noting that the definitions for these terms have been overused and diluted. "Our country has gotten to a place where there is no other word for a small business that isn't 'artisanal,'" he said, while acknowledging that the term, to him, "sort of suggests that the person who is making it is conscientiously making something." He describes his approach as "inspired by the past" with a focus on "quality not quantity."

Colin noted that he didn't have a clear business philosophy or approach when he started his business, except for the focus on quality and continual improvement in technique and flavor. Like many other artisanal businesses, his initial goal was to connect with—or celebrate—culture from his past. He also noted some benefit, and perhaps inspiration, from being in Brooklyn, although not as strong as Mast Brothers, who seemed to really thrive on the community. The ultimate goal, too, seemed to be finding a job that he was excited about—although this is somewhat conjecture. He implied that this was a hobby that had kept expanding until he got to the place where he could become licensed and turn it into a business. That he lived in a place and time where there was a demand for his product very likely helped King's County become successful enough to employ people to keep production moving seven days a week. Colin's influences pair the sense of history—as in his own history with distillation in Appalachia as well as the history of New York State spirits—with distillation's relationship with the land. For as fellow distiller Ralph Erenzo of Tuthilltown Distillery in upstate New York has said, "Distilling *is* farming." These values and the larger narrative in which they are expressed are both representative of a return to the simpler, some may say authentic, traditions of the past, and are also speaking to the same consumer of artisanal goods that prefers to identify with the narrative of the artisan, desires sustainably sourced, often local ingredients, and is willing to pay a premium for the preservation of traditional processes. Thus with Brooklyn being ground zero for the new artisanal food (and drink) revolution, it is no surprise that King's County has led the way for more than a dozen new distillers, with its well-honed narrative, passionate workers, and high-quality, locally sourced spirits.

Other distillers in New York City and around the state are also overtly making the connection to history to blur the line between their modern artisanal business and the nearly lost local tradition of spirit making. Breuckelen Distilling is also located in Brooklyn and is using an old spelling of the borough as their moniker. While their space is more modest—and modern (they have a similar distilling setup in an industrial section of Sunset Park)—they make a similar connection between history and their new forays into the industry, while also nodding to the modern consumer interest in local and sustainable sourcing. They highlight the traditional connection between agriculture and distilling, with the farmer who provides most of their grains being profiled in greater detail than even the distillers. They also call to mind the farmer/distiller narrative with the old-timey font used for their labels and the provenance of the spirits noted as part of their name: New York Wheat and Local Rye & Corn being two of their offerings. [18]

    Cacao Prieto, a distillery in Red Hook, Brooklyn, also evokes a similar sense of history and tradition with their small-batch Widow Jane Straight Bourbon Whiskey. They claim that even the water comes from Rosendale, New York (a source that is infused with more limestone mineralization than even Kentucky); its narrative and packaging evoke a similar sense of the past to sell the present. Its website notes: "The greatest structures in New York . . . from the gargantuan caissons that allowed the Brooklyn Bridge to soar, to the Statue of Liberty's 27,000 ton pedestal, to the Empire State Building itself are all held fast and strong by that Rosendale stone. . . . Widow Jane Whiskey is a true New York City whiskey, evocative of both the rock that created the foundation for this city of skyscrapers and the forward looking, DIY spirit that has made Brooklyn the center of a new artisanal food and beverage movement."[19]

Yet, like the other food artisans discussed here, many of whom also rely on a connection to tradition and history to package their product, there is also a strong influence of innovation among the new distillers. King's County may be reclaiming whiskey for Brooklyn, but they are also producing a chocolate whiskey inspired by the artisanal connections so ingrained in their hometown to produce a completely modern product. Likewise, Brooklyn Gin is seeking to reclaim their eponymous spirit from the ubiquitous London Dry varieties that had for so long been the only options at the bar or liquor store. Their narrative focuses on the farm-fresh, "locally purchased" fruit (for there is no citrus—a key ingredient in their gin flavoring—growing in the state, of course), "hand-cracked juniper," and doing "everything by hand" with "creativity and originality." Their packaging is reminiscent of the past with squat embossed antique bottles, and the labeling is as simple as law will allow, evoking pre-Prohibition cocktail culture. It is looking to the past, but repackaging it for the modern consumer, who, like the founders Emil Jattne and Joe Santos, "believe[s] in the American tradition of happy hour."[20]

UPSTATE NEW YORK DISTILLING CULTURE

But New York State is more than skyscrapers and trendy cocktail bars. The large agricultural area where Brian McKenzie, one of the founders of Finger Lakes Distilling, grew up in upstate New York was among grape vineyards, and he remembers watching the wine industry—and wine tourism industry—grow up around him. While he enjoyed the local libation, he preferred drinking whiskey, which eventually brought him to a craft distiller conference in Alabama in 2007. Brian had business experience and was interested in starting his own, and at the conference he met Thomas Earl McKenzie (no relation) who had grown up among Southern alcoholic spirit culture, and had experience consulting with distilleries and wineries. They decided to go into business together in upstate New York, using the built-in wine tourism destination to help garner customers and visibility for what would be a novelty among the vineyards. [21]

Finger Lakes Distilling is located on a hill overlooking Seneca Lake—a spot that evokes New York State's agricultural history as much as the Brooklyn Navy Yard represents its urban past. They began by making whiskey, bourbon, gin, and vodka, and have expanded their line of spirits to include grappa and liqueurs, inspired by the local wine industry, of course. With a philosophy that focuses on high-quality ingredients and personal attention to every batch of spirits, the approach is similar to the other artisanal distilleries that have been opening over the past few years—especially in the northeast. Brian notes that he has had obstacles starting his business—but no more than the typical small business that deals with alcohol production. While Brian's stated philosophy of "taking raw, locally grown grains and turning them into high-quality distilled spirits" is very much aligned with that of other "craft" distilleries, he does bristle a bit at the terms *artisan* and *craft*. He believes that these distinctions are "more about the methods being used to distill the spirit, rather than the size" of the distillery, nodding to the fact that many small distilleries are called artisan or craft regardless of their methodology or philosophy. He prefers his legal distinction of "farm distillery," which does certainly point to the local and hands-on nature of his business.

Finger Lakes Distilling has grown relatively quickly and now supports the equivalent of about seven full-time positions. As they have grown, they have stayed true to their original focus and have only seemed to use their growing size and volume to their advantage. Otherwise, their marketing and publicity has been through the

Figure 5.3.   Finger Lakes Distilling amidst the vineyards.

Finger Lakes wine trail, word of mouth, and some publicity due to their unique story—two similarly named whiskey lovers distilling in the heart of New York State wine country. While their "meet the distillers" approach works well for selling their product and narrative to the many consumers who will find them through the wine trail, the packaging of their products—particularly their whiskey—also conforms to many of the urban distillers' connection to the past. Their three signature whiskeys are bottled in a squat bottle reminiscent of a pot still, and named after the distillers, McKenzie: Rye Whiskey, Pure Pot Still Whiskey, and Bourbon Whiskey, all with a classic font and a corked top. And almost all of their products are named and described via their connection to the land—Seneca Drum Gin, Vintner's Vodka (made from local grapes) among others. Even the quote and photo that they choose to feature on their home page evoke the state's agricultural legacy: they show the grape vineyards that surround the distillery and their view of the lake and highlight a *New York Times* quote: "On the more lavish side of the craft . . . Finger Lakes Distilling . . . juts like a sleek white liner among 100-year-old vineyards on a hillside above Seneca Lake."[22]

Brian has certainly acknowledged the growth of small distilleries promoting their craft spirits in the past five years and likens it to the microbrewery beer boom of a few decades ago. As he noted, the market will eventually reach saturation, and not everyone will survive. But he feels confident in his product, philosophy, and rate of growth. Finger Lakes Distilling products are now available in four states and counting, and even five hours outside of New York City, they have found that many urban consumers connect with their story of local agriculture even with the city's own distillers competing for sales.

But if there is a distiller who embodies the rich history of New York State distilling, it is Ralph Erenzo from Tuthilltown Spirits in the Hudson Valley. He was the first to legally distill whiskey since the end of Prohibition with the A-1 license and is instrumental in continually lobbying for changes in the law to make it easier for micro-distillers to sell their products. Erenzo was also instrumental in the passage of the Farm Distillery Act, and many look to him for guidance as he continually supports small distillers in the state. In addition, his entire business narrative is reflective of the area's agricultural and distilling history, representing the larger identity of the industry north of the city. His website sets the scene of pastoral Hudson valley:

> Before Prohibition more than 1,000 farm distillers produced alcohol from New York grains and fruits. Tuthilltown Spirits brings the tradition of small batch distillation back to the Hudson Valley, distilling whiskeys which were the first legally distilled and aged grain spirits produced in New York since Prohibition. . . . For 220 years Tuthilltown Gristmill, a landmark which is listed on the National Register of Historic Places, used water-power to render local grains to flour. . . . Today, Tuthilltown

Spirits distills vodkas from apples grown at orchards less than 5
miles away and whiskeys using grain harvested by farmers less
than 10 miles away."[23]

Ralph told me that he got into distilling because he wanted to
start a business—but also wanted to distinguish himself from the
microbreweries and wineries so prevalent in New York State. As a
fan of distilled spirits, he decided upon opening a distillery—which
coincided with the state lowering the barrier for distilleries in the
state. Tuthilltown is now both a farm distillery and an A1 distillery[24]—both of which have been made significantly less expensive
in the past few years. As Ralph notes, supporting distilleries is only
a positive thing for the state—as this will "add taxes that haven't
been collected since Prohibition" noting as well that supporting
state farmers' shift to grains for alcohol production can only be a
positive thing as "it's a whole lot easier than growing fruit." Ralph,
personally, sources almost 100 percent of his ingredients locally,
and has even had a farmer remove an apple orchard to grow rye—
which he says is a bonus for both of them. Not only is growing
grains easier than produce, but the weather is well-suited for it and
there are significantly fewer weather-related issues that arise. Ralph
also notes that his decision to use all local ingredients is not just a
philosophical one—it's cheaper for him to drive a truck across town
to pick up corn than to have it shipped from Iowa. But he also has an
agreement with the farmers where he has much more control over
what goes in the ground, rather than just buying products after
they've been grown. This gives him more control over quality of
ingredients—something he finds extremely important—especially
for a craft distiller.[25]

Thus, we can see through these stories of New York State distillers how they have built their business narrative upon the rich history of distilling in the state—both the urban traditions and the rural
ones. But also what is happening directly because of the farm distillery law is that New York State spirits are embodying the area's
terroir—by the use of almost exclusively local produce as well as
through the connection of the distillers' craft and values to the prod-

uct itself. Thus New York State whiskey from these distillers is now seen as deeply connected to a revived tradition, handmade, and from local corn and grains. How does this terroir taste different from Kentucky's or Oregon's? Perhaps an expert taster like Nicole Austin can speak to that. Or, I argue, it is as much about the narrative as the mouth feel or the fire in your belly.

PORTLAND, OREGON'S DISTILLERY ROW

While cheap rents and large warehouse spaces brought many of the distilleries to the same industrialized area of southeast Portland, it wasn't until 2010 that a new website and marketing campaign made the "Distillery Row" moniker official. Proud of their homesteader, DIY identity, tracing back to the days when Oregon was still the wild west, Portland also prides itself on the artisanal food and drink culture that has helped to nurture the popularity of these distilleries. Further, unlike New York and numerous other states, distillers have long been able to distill legally, offer tastings, and sell directly to the public from their production site, with the city and state supporting these businesses rather than setting up legislative hurdles.

I was surprised a bit by how spread out Distillery Row was— some distillers were walking distance from each other, but generally it was best to drive. Perhaps my assumptions were based upon what I had experienced in New York—walking distance to the subway, close quarters with other businesses, or conversely, a rural outpost amid farms and vineyards—but these businesses were spread out over a few miles. The first stop was Eastside Distilling, which seemed more like clubhouse in the front with a wood-paneled tasting bar, an overstuffed couch and lounge chairs beyond that, with a few tattooed twenty- and thirty-somethings sitting around and chatting in the mid-afternoon, rock and roll on the stereo. A desk was in the corner, indicating this was the office space for the distillery as well. In the closed-off room behind the office/lounge was a modest, but productive, distillery. They have been rapidly growing since they first began distilling in 2009, initially focusing on rum (which has won numerous awards), but have been branching out to include flavored liquors, vodka, and whiskey in the past few years. Their products include award-winning coffee rum, ginger rum, and eggnog liquor—interesting considering that the sourcing for most of these ingredients is not local, nor, by Oregon law, does it have to be. The contrast between Oregon and New York State micro-distilling appears stark. Eastside's product line of more than a dozen spirits and liqueurs can best be described as fun and festive. The packaging of their various rums is reminiscent of pirate booty, their potato vodka celebrates the spud. Made in Portland, Oregon, and "handcrafted" were their two most prominent selling points—that and the connection to local produce, where applicable. Or, as the person who gave my brief tour and led my tasting said, their products were inspired by "social food culture." Yes, Eastside's spirits were made very much in the same fashion as most other craft distillers, but yet their narrative as a company focuses less on the spirits' connection to place and more upon their handmade aspect—even indicating on some of their aged spirits the batch and bottle number. Thus their identity is less focused on the past and more on the present craft revolution. Which is fitting, given the state's less tenuous relationship with Prohibition and its aftermath as compared to New York State.[26]

While Distillery Row is a relatively newly branded destination, the current wave of distillers has been making Portland their home starting with New Deal Distillery in 2004. Tom Burkleaux's New Deal Distillery is one of the oldest in Oregon, and is the grandfather of Distillery Row. I met with Tom in his open and bright warehouse space (that he would soon be vacating), arriving just as the sun was setting. Not only first among his peers in Portland, he was also among the first in the distillery revolution, as he remembers others noticing what he was doing and eventually being inspired by his hard work and initiative. He said he started New Deal because he sensed that we were heading into a recession and he loved making things—"good things," he noted. He also credits Portland with being the appropriate incubator for his distilling. By his account, it has never had a big boom or bust, and has a longtime commitment to

Figure 5.4. Tom Burkleaux at New Deal Distillery.

"keeping it weird," as well as a cohesive small business community
that nurtures others to start their own, or try their hand at artisanal
products, through example. It's also a good size for these start-ups,
he pointed out. And that makes sense—not too big to get lost or too
small to not have a strong enough customer base, it is a city that is
scalable, where indie products are prized, and a little rough around
the edges in a casual West Coast, DIY kind of way, the same qualities that inspired Charley and Jessica of Woodblock Chocolate. He
started his distillery in a small room with $5,000, and slowly grew
over the past decade. His goal from the beginning was to create a
sustainable business, although he admits he didn't have a business
plan. Rather, he was committed to learning the craft of distilling, not
to take himself too seriously, and to embrace experimentation.
When he was later able to hire help, he was also dedicated to paying
employees a living wage.

When I visited in early 2013 he was about to move to a building
he had just purchased across the street from the space where we

met—a sign of his success, although he laughed when I asked if distilling was his full-time job (he still has a day job). Tom sees quality liquor as an affordable luxury—"thrift store elegance" he called having accessibility to some of the finer things in life, but on a recession-era budget. His first product was also a reflection of this idea—he started distilling vodka, which could combine value (it was relatively quick and easy to make) and craft (he could still express himself through it creatively). Since then, he has expanded to include gin and flavored liqueurs, but looks forward to growing further into wine and brandies at the new location. [27]

As we tasted his efforts at a bar amid his distilling equipment, Tom recounted the history of Portland distilling with reflection and authority. He has been in the industry long enough that he recalls that craft or artisanal distilling didn't, at first, have a name. He sees craft brewing as having created the customer for craft distilling by reinforcing the idea that small batch, done well, was worth the money, and gave credence to the consumer who sought out different, new, and well-crafted potables. Now he sees the craft distilling industry as growing quickly—and not all newcomers are as passionate about the art of distilling as he is. He believes that truly artisanal distillers should focus on quality, but also be able to speak to the process of distilling and be proud of that process. This nods toward the importance of story associated with artisanal products, but he applies that to the producer as well as the consumer. He also believes that with the influx of new distillers—much like the craft brewing industry of the 1990s—there will be an inevitable shakeout of those who have adapted to survive. "It takes a lot to control the supply chain," he noted, but being able to source the best, whole ingredients is what he believes makes spirits taste better. In the meantime, he is focusing on his own products and sustainable growth—perhaps someday getting rid of his day job—even as he has watched a few craft distilling contemporaries be tempted with corporate investments. To this, he gave me perhaps one of the best definitions of the term *artisanal* by any producer: To be an artisanal producer, the one who makes the product is also the one who controls the money, he said. Which makes a lot of sense. Once the person responsible for the bottom line becomes too far removed from the product, that's when compromises are more likely to be made with process or ingredients.

New Deal Distillery's product narrative is much like Tom's own—closely aligned with their identity as a small, artisanal business in Portland—and their Portland 88 Vodka is reflective of this. As the marketing copy says, the spirit is "dedicated to Portland's old DIY spirit and its openness to new ideas, Portland 88 Vodka is a nod to the decade we discovered and fell in love with our city." Besides vodkas and flavored liqueurs, New Deal also makes two styles of gin, both presented as innovative takes on the classic spirit and both also presented as truly "Portland." Gin No. 33 is said to be made in the "Portland Dry Style" and "Distilled and Bottled in Portland, Oregon," is proudly printed on the front of all labels. But Tom sees himself as more than just distilling high-quality spirits in the manner of other Portland DIY-ers—he also has a manifesto highlighted on his website that outlines his modern take on craft

Figure 5.5. Botanicals used in Aviation Gin.

distilling, "made for local folks, by local folks." He goes on to reflect on his narrative of the artisan in the world today, seeking sustainable sourcing and fighting corporate greed, rather than looking to the past to find his identity. His stance goes further than other distillers like Distillery Row's Stone Barn Brandyworks, which uses primarily local fruit, and Eastside, which notes local produce in certain products, New Deal states their commitment to using local and sustainable whenever possible—and pushes for that to be a challenge for all artisanal products regardless of the industry. But still, considering what makes these sprits "craft"—at least by Portland's standards—seems to lie in size. They are small enough where they are just employing a small team—most of these distillers started with one person, or as a two-man operation—and few owners are able to forgo their day job to distill full-time. They all do have goals to expand, but with varying philosophies on how.

Perhaps the most notable exception is House Spirits Distillery. Christian Krogstad founded House Spirits Distillery in 2004 and teamed up with Ryan Magarian to help create their first product, Aviation Gin. Their rise was aided by the increasing interest in cocktail culture and their main product shared a name with a classic cocktail. Gin was one of the areas where distillers could, relatively easily, express some creativity through various botanical blends. Gin, classically heavy on juniper (in fact the definition of gin in the United States is an alcoholic beverage of at least 80 proof, flavored with juniper berries), is typically a dynamic spirit, which can be flavored with a number of botanicals. Ryan and Christian wanted to change the consumer understanding of gin and began playing with this botanical mix to produce something more nuanced and unique. Walking through House Spirits Distillery, it was clear that there was more money at play judging by the large warehouse space, the variety of stills being used, and even the number of employees performing various distilling and office jobs. Throughout their partnership they had established that Ryan was in charge of the distilling and Christian the business side, but when I visited House was a distillery at a crossroads: they were entertaining an offer from investors who wanted to provide capital for them to expand. They had

already grown from twenty cases a month five years ago to exponentially more in early 2013 when I visited, and they assert that with
this new capital their production and dedication to quality wouldn't
change. But it does make one wonder—can it stay the same?[28] At
the time I was thinking about how the story would change—they
would no longer be the two guys, passionate about gin, who helped
found gritty Distillery Row. Is working with an investor the culmi-
nation of all of this hard work—or will their vision be compromised? And, at what point can they still be considered artisanal?
Checking their website a year later there was no mention of either
founder by name; their philosophy merely noted "Using ethically
sourced ingredients, our award winning spirits are created under the
watchful eye of our head distiller and our talented bartender."[29]

House Spirits Distillery's narrative does nod to their home in
Portland—they note that 94 percent of the botanicals in Aviation
Gin are locally sourced and their aquavit, their other signature spirit,
is aged in pinot noir barrels from the nearby wine region of Willa-
mette Valley. The barrels add viscosity because of the oils, and this
is a more natural way of creating a quality product, as opposed to
many mass-produced versions that add glycerin. As one of the first
domestic producers of aquavit, their goal is to introduce people to a
new spirit, in line with many craft distillers' goal of reimagining
classic spirits. House was also aging whiskey that wasn't ready for
bottling when I visited, but is now for sale as Westward Oregon
Straight Malt Whiskey. Once again, with whiskey, their goal is to
help consumers reimagine their perceptions, with a version that is
oaky and not as sweet. Further, this is their only spirit notably
packaged as being reflective of the area's terroir, and their packaging and pithy name both speak to the adventurous spirit of those
who headed west more than a century ago seeking something new,
the next frontier.

Portland's distilling culture is inspired by the lingering West
Coast, adventuresome spirit that brought settlers across the country
and founded "weird," "DIY" Portland, but is also certainly influenced by the laws that allowed distillers to enter the industry cheaply and easily and the state-run alcohol distribution that enables new

distillers to take part in the state-wide market with relative ease. But even Portland has not forgotten Prohibition. While nearly every New York distillery mentions the impact that law had on the industry, I only found one mention of this dry decade-plus of American history in Portland. House Spirits Distillery makes a Volstead Vodka—a "refreshingly sober approach to vodka" that is "drily dedicated to Andrew Volstead, father of Prohibition."

SO, WHAT IS A CRAFT DISTILLER?

Unlike other industries, craft distilling has somewhat of a legal definition, although this varies state to state. In New York State, there are a few classes of distilleries. An A1 distillery has fees that cost around $1,500, and allow distillation of up to thirty-five thousand gallons per year, (considerably larger than a "small batch" distiller) packaged in containers no larger than one quart. A class D distillery license—known as a farm distillery license and modeled after the farm winery distinctions granted in the 1970s, also allows up to thirty-five thousand gallons a year, but requires that 70 percent of the ingredients are New York State produced. However, only farm distilleries may operate a tasting room and sell directly to the public; thus some distillers choose to pay the fees to possess more than one license.

In Oregon, the distilling laws have long been more hospitable to small craft distillers. Because the state controls the distribution of alcohol, a small distiller could more easily get their product into the hands of Oregon liquor stores. Marketing within the state—and selling out of state—was up to the individual distiller, but this flexibility was crucial for helping small distillers grow. In 2008, a new law was passed that allowed for tasting rooms and sales of product on premises,[30] and in early 2013 Oregon passed another new law intended to help their local craft distillers, allowing them to open up to five additional tasting rooms beyond their distillery—the only place they could sell their product besides the state-supplied liquor stores operated by the Oregon Liquor Control Commission. They must still purchase their own liquor from the state, however, just as other liquor stores do. This law is intended to help "craft" distillers—a popular and growing product category as evidenced by the statistic that locally made spirits now make up a full 12 percent of Oregon liquor sales.[31] There are also some additional labeling and packaging requirements as well for Oregon-based distilleries. Craft is not defined by the law, but seems to be embraced by those whose narrative involves their status as a local artisan.

These disparate laws, from one coast to the other, are emblematic of the wide variety of laws governing both small and larger distilleries in every state. For small distillers, one state may allow up to thirty-five thousand gallons on a permit, while another may allow sixty thousand gallons. Some states require a certain percentage of locally produced ingredients, while others have no such law. Some cities have been impediments to burgeoning craft distillers as well. Bully Boy Distillery in Boston was the first to open in the city post-Prohibition and they noted that there was no template for a permit. Further, some of these laws exclude NDPs—or non-distiller producers, who purchase base spirits from another distillery and infuse or flavor them to create a more refined final product. There is, in fact, debate within the craft distilling community about whether NDPs should be considered a part of their ranks, and what exactly determines the category of craft distiller. Ian Cameron from the alcohol lifestyle magazine *Diffords Guide* notes that the term "craft" is becoming a marketing term, with little in the way of regulation or distinction of quality.[32] While some states do define craft distilleries for licensing purposes, there is no regulation on using the term for descriptive or promotional purposes.

Likewise, the term *small batch* was initially referencing the distiller's pick of their aged spirits, intended to indicate the best of the barrels. However, the term has been co-opted by other industries, and while some distillers continue to use that term, *artisanal* and *micro-distillery* are also in use as well. The American Distilling Institute noted that craft distillers doubled from twenty-four to fifty-two from 2000 to 2010, but then grew to 234 by the end of 2012,[33] with others putting that number at closer to 400. With such exponential growth, some are calling for a voluntary certification that would help indicate quality and integrity to the consumer. Voluntary certifications or mandatory laws aside, the distillers with whom I spoke indicated what they thought made a craft distiller. Like the other industries, most distillers spoke of quality raw ingredients—although some did note that highly distilled liquors like vodka and gin can stand cheaper raw materials due the process of distilling, which, by definition, strips out most of the impurities. Gin gains its flavor from the infused botanicals, which by all accounts were very thoughtfully sourced, but despite the flavor they impart, they are actually a small percentage of the total ingredients used. Other spirits, like whiskey, are reliant on the flavor of the raw materials, including the grain that is used to create the spirits, as well as the barrels used for aging.

While quality raw ingredients, often local by law or preference, are necessary to the making of craft spirits, technique and attention to detail are what the distillers use to set themselves apart from one another. Some measure processing times to the second, while others obsessively study the climate of different zones within their aging room. Myriad factors—and not all of them able to be controlled—add up to create an artisanal spirit, and the distillers I met were serious students of their craft, continually working to create better products, experiment with more interesting flavors, and often find innovative ways to move their craft forward, including changing the public perception of common spirits like whiskey and gin.

Yet, as even some distillers themselves note, what ultimately sells the product and helps to differentiate it in the minds—and even palates—of consumers is the narrative around the spirit. The New York State distilling scene seems to be focused on its identity in terms of its relationship to Prohibition. Perhaps because distilling culture in the state can be divided into pre-Prohibition and contemporary efforts, that these new distilleries are the first in almost a century is a selling point as well as often a way to define themselves in relation to the past. The names—King's County, Breuckelen Distilling—conjure New York from a century ago, and the packaging—Tuthilltown's old-timey font, King's County's flask-like bottles—

intend to evoke classic cocktail culture. Even on many of the company information pages, being among the first distilleries since Prohibition, use of classic recipes, or adherence to tradition are primary claims of identity. While many of these distilleries are reclaiming New York State's place as a major force in craft distilling from its prominence in the 1800s, there is also a streak of moving the industry forward. Interestingly, many of the less-traditional spirits are described using different selling points—"off-the-beaten-track" or "zippy and fresh" and both names and packaging that seem contemporary and lighthearted. Conversely, more traditionally made spirits are so entrenched with history that even their names—like Tuthilltown's Half Moon Orchard Gin, named for Henry Hudson's boat—reinforce the connection with history. Thus, while there are products from New York State distilleries that are pushing new boundaries, these are the ones that are packaged as outliers, while the core branding seems to be reliant on historical references to add authenticity to these relatively new products.

In Oregon, by contrast, there hasn't been a substantially longer history of distilling—Rogue Spirits in Newport, Oregon, was established in 2003 and is considered by many to be the state's first craft distillery of the new wave of artisanal spirit makers—yet there doesn't appear to be a reliance on history or classic cocktail culture to brand or identify products, Aviation Gin being the exception. Rather, the focus is upon quality, innovation, freshness. New Deal Distillery evokes the "DIY spirit of Portland" as central to their identity, and Eastside Distillery highlights its Portland connection and the products that do use local produce as well, even as many of their ingredients cannot be sourced locally. The cocktail culture of Portland is also very supportive of locally made spirits, with popular drinks that mirror the innovative approach of the spirits themselves, inspired by the past, but reimagined for the future.

The idea that "small-batch" distilling can stay at a thousand gallons or below and retain economic sustainability is also waning, although some distillers may offer occasional single offerings of that size. Distilling is an industry where, unlike pickles or cheese, one needs to have a relatively high upfront investment in equipment, if one wants to become self-sustainable. Tom Burkleaux notes two hundred cases a week as, roughly, the lowest output a distiller can have to stay a sustainable business. And this number is formulated with Portland rents in mind. The market for craft spirits is growing, even as the industry is becoming vastly more competitive. Thus, whether the craft distiller packages its spirits looking to the past or the present as inspiration, it better be one good story to capture the attention—and highball glasses—of the new artisanal food consumer.

6

DEFINING THE MOVEMENT, ONE BITE AT A TIME

A year after I visited lower Manhattan for 2012's Pickle Fest, I returned to the Lower East Side Pickle Day to visit a few of the artisans with whom I had spoken over the previous year. The location had changed to a street not far from, perhaps fittingly, Little Italy and a neighborhood that had formerly been the home of many Jewish immigrants more than a century ago. I looked forward to sampling some pickles and spending a minute or so chatting with the pickle makers as I had the year before. But when I turned onto Orchard Street, I almost turned right back toward the subway. Throngs of people were crowded around every booth, with more jammed onto the sidewalk behind them, making even walking down the street a slow-moving affair. Those lined up for pickle samples could only grab one and then move along, any chance of conversing with the artisan likely to be met with angry glares from the long line behind them.

As I made my way down the street, the crowd this year looked as much hipster as it did just a typical New York assemblage—blonde girls taking selfies while holding their half sours high in the air, families braving the crowd with a stroller or small child in tow, tourists who had cheered at their luck of visiting the city on Pickle Day—I marveled at how much had changed in the past year. Maybe it was this slightly more accessible location (although the previous year's Fest was next to the popular New Amsterdam market), maybe it was better publicity (although I had heard about both through numerous New York foodie blogs and news sources), or maybe many of these twenty thousand-plus people[1] had discovered artisanal pickles in the past year.

I decided to head into the fray anyway—I had made it this far after all. And after slowly moving against the tide of pickle fanatics, I finally found the one artisan to whom I most wanted to say hello— Robert Schaefer of Divine Brine—the only local pickler with whom I had only spoken on the phone. I edged my way into the crowd in front of his table, hoping to thank him for his time a few months prior. Elbowing my way to the front of the line, I could see Robert, smiling widely, and handing out one pickle sample after another. Empty boxes that once held his jars were strewn haphazardly in the booth behind him, and even the pickle samples were waning as well. I introduced myself and Robert paused just long enough to shake my hand.

"It's been like this since we opened. I sold out in the first few hours!" he said, motioning to the detritus behind him. Any fears that the artisanal pickle market—in New York City, at least—was saturated, were likely put to rest that day for the artisans attending.

That story of continual growth has been similar among the artisans with whom I spoke at the start of my research in late 2012 and caught up with in one way or another as I was finishing this project in early 2014. Even in the span of a year and a half, for many so much had changed for the better. Brooklyn Brine opened their pickle and beer shack with Dogfish Head Brewery to great acclaim, Alex Whitcome of Taza Chocolate is beginning a separate but complementary business sourcing sustainable cacao, Bully Boy Distillery finally brought their aged whiskey to market with excellent reviews, First Light Creamery began selling yogurt and started a wildly popular dairy CSA in western New York. More and more often I recognize the label of an artisan I visited or interviewed in a retail outlet and smile at the pride they must have felt as their distribution began to grow.

Admittedly, the artisans I interviewed cannot be seen as a fully representative sample from each industry from around the country. Living in both Boston and Brooklyn during this research meant that it was easiest to discover and meet those in close proximity. Visits to Vermont, western New York, and the West Coast allowed me to discover and meet a larger, but not completely illustrative group of artisans. Some of my research was through opportunity. I contacted cheese makers by e-mail from all over the country via various states' cheese councils or other regional artisanal groups and used the data from those who replied. Repeated efforts to contact certain artisans whose input I wanted because of their location or public business narrative went unanswered. I'd like to think that if they were much like so many of the other artisans with whom I did speak, they were extremely busy managing the business and production that even a half hour was a lot to ask. There were artisans who talked to me as they walked from their "day" job to their work at their food production site, and one who called me right after she dropped her kids off at school. I am very thankful for the time so many artisans gave me to tell me their story and talk about their business influences and challenges. But, also, as I sought artisans from various regions, I found that so many of these craftspeople are deeply entrenched in their region—and that it was hard for an outsider to know who to contact without a visit to the area or a conversation with a local in the know. Those I found online had to have a web presence—something many start-ups might not put their efforts toward right away, especially if their main form of distribution was via local markets where the selling was face to face. Some artisans I found through the Internet, others through in-person research like Pickle Fest, a few more from browsing the product selection at the local cheese shop or asking the liquor store owner or cocktail maven about their favorite local spirits. And in an effort to paint a snapshot of this fast-evolving movement, I also had to work quickly. Thus I am certain that I left out many, many interesting producers whose stories and perspectives deserve to be heard.

As I reflect on the overall story, however, of each of these industries, what I found was that each business had a specific narrative or adaptation of a specific narrative that helped to define its industry and how it presented its industry to the consumer. And each industry represents an element of the artisanal food revolution as a whole that is apparent in various industries. The brined and fresh-pack picklers embrace their role as de facto representatives of the new artisanal food revolution: their product is handmade and connects to a deeper regional or ethnic tradition, and the artisans themselves are the poster children for the new "hip" entrepreneurs who are reclaiming a product that had, for many, turned into an afterthought. The fermented picklers in particular have an ethos more akin to the counter-cuisine traditions of a generation earlier, with a focus on health and community and environmental sustainability. Yet we see these same values illustrated among the other industries as well. Most of the artisans I met were in their twenties and thirties—or at least were when they began their business—and did so for reasons similar to their counter-cuisine counterparts of a generation ago: they wanted control over their professional lives and they wanted to feel connected to making a quality product and doing so by hand and with care. While the pickle makers may be the quintessential "hip entrepreneurs" of the moment, in part because of their visibility at (often urban) events like Pickle Fest, the distillers, chocolate makers, and cheese makers, among other artisanal industries, are certainly gaining visibility with so many consumers interested in the personal story of the people who make their food. Most share the concerns about an increasingly mass-produced and industrialized food chain and how it affects the environment, the workers, and the consumers. Yet these hip entrepreneurs are also updating the role of counter-cuisine and are broadening this new movement and making it all their own.

The cheese makers' narratives, especially as primarily rural artisans, reflect the artisanal connection to the land—where, of course, all of the raw materials used by the craftspeople across the industries are from. They also represent the evolution of the pastoral narrative that so many back-to-the-landers embraced in decades past toward the *post*-pastoral—or how the combination of tradition and modernity and science are becoming an integral part of how we view food artisans today. Further, they illustrate how American originality is an important characteristic of this movement, in contrast to the standardized traditional approach we see in so many other countries. This is of particular importance as both the collective and personal narratives that are so important to each of these industries include a deep connection to the land and the people who work the land. Chocolate makers are striving to educate consumers about the farming and fermentation of cacao—a step in the chocolate-making process that is almost always done by workers local to the source—and make their sustainable approach to working with these farmers a key component of their marketing and packaging. All of the pickle makers emphasized the importance of relationships with farmers in sourcing their produce, with many connecting the traditions of pickling with the need to preserve seasonal bounty— and are committed to bringing these ideas to the modern consumer. And as the distiller Ralph Erenzo said, "Distilling *is* farming." Particularly in New York State, but apparent around the country, the modern distiller is working with the land to (re)create the traditional connection between farming and spirit distillation.

Further, chocolate makers are helping to redefine the idea of terroir—by using the connection of flavor and ethical business and environmental practices and craftsmanship to define their industry. This is seen throughout the artisanal movement through the connection of place to product and value and production. Scholars speak about terroir when discussing particularly farmstead cheese, and how the climate and season, and of course the cheese maker's vast input, helps to differentiate each wheel. And while distilling is differentiated by region, with some distillers defining themselves in relation to the rich history of their home region and others looking to their area's current trends to tell their products' story, the embracing of so many local ingredients, particularly in New York State as we have seen, is creating a new category of spirits as tied to the land as they were a century ago. The story—the *terroir*—of New York whiskey, for example, has become known, and for good reason. It is a completely local product whose nuances are apparent because of the raw ingredients used, as well as the personal manipulation and production values imbued by the distillers themselves. Picklers are also promoting the connection between their product and the land, with some of the artisans noting they embrace how different a batch can taste from one season to the next because of the inherent inconsistencies of nature. The homogenization of previous decades is now being seen as a negative attribute rather than a positive one.

Finally there is the common thread of narrative—and particularly history—as a way to define one's product and add value beyond the nutritional or recreational enjoyment of it. The distillers' narratives are deeply reflective of their region's history regarding alcohol production and consumption and have helped to differentiate these artisans from each other and their mass-produced competitors, as well as to connect with the consumer. But, as has been made apparent, every industry uses authentic narrative to connect the consumer with its traditions—pickling with its urban and immigrant and even subsistence-farming past, chocolate with its ancient history of the Mayans and Aztecs, and cheese with its European and American roots. Narrative is one of the key ingredients in each of the products, for artisans must tell their story and the story of their industry to add value to the products that for so long have been available in cheap, lower-quality, mass-produced versions. We are on the cusp of redefining these and other industries for the consumer, in regard to taste and value, worker rights and environmental stewardship, and it is these artisans that are working hard to move us forward.

THE NEW COUNTER CUISINE MOVEMENT AND HOW IT HAS AFFECTED THE VALUE OF FOOD

As noted in chapter 1, food scholar Warren Belasco asserts the tradition of celebrating handmade, artisanal foods in American culture during times of particular political progressive thinking, as could be seen during the "Progressive Era," the 1930s, and the counterculture movements of the late 1960s and early 1970s. During the latter, regional food traditions and cuisine became particularly prized, as did foraging and local and traditional food values.[2] Thus, it makes sense that this new artisanal food revolution was starting to reach a broader consumer audience in the first decade of the new millennium, with a recession on the horizon, increasing fear over the state of the environment, and the seeming corporate influence upon the government and consumer sector. Similar to the counter-cuisine movement of a few decades ago, there is still a thinking that workers' and animals' rights are important enough to source raw ingredients more ethically, and the resistance to foods seen as anti-environmental—whether because of the miles they have traveled to reach the consumer's plate, or the chemicals used to grow them—are generally common among artisanal producers, as is the general critique of the increasingly industrial food system. However, where the counter-cuisine movement of the 1960s and 1970s prized the process of the handmade products over the end product, I would argue that today's artisan is concerned with *both* the process and the product, making a shift from their artisanal forbearers.

I argue that this change is reflective of how consumers and artisans alike are considering the "quality" of the artisanal foods in new ways during this current counterculture movement, which also reflects the larger set of values that are inherent in artisanal foods today. Alain-Claude Roudot notes that the notion of "quality" in regard to food is experienced by different groups in different ways, and can, in fact, change. Unsurprisingly, food scientists cite food safety as being the number one concern when considering the "quality" of food. Yet consumers often disagree. In 2001, at the height of the bovine spongiform encephalitis scare in France, French consumers cited "taste" and "pleasure" as the premier qualities they look for in food, with food safety being number three.[3] While a similar study has not been done among American food consumers today, I can speak for myself and for many similar-minded people I have met as sharing these values with the French. Conversations, most often with fermented picklers and cheese makers, noted that their perception of food safety sometimes differed with that of the federal or state regulators and was shaped more by the flavor and experience of the end product than by science. For example, on the topic of raw milk, one farmstead cheese maker said that her family grew up drinking raw milk from her cows and goats and that she would have no problem selling it (illegally) to local farmers or neighbors. But she said she would hesitate to sell it to someone from outside of her rural region because she believed that they didn't possess the same physical familiarity with the land that her family did. Thus she was recognizing the benefits of raw milk for some, but not for everyone, and in a way that used intuitive knowledge, rather than laboratory testing. This is all beyond the realm of strict scientific "proof," which, at least according to government interpretations of scientific studies, asserts that pasteurized milk is always of the best quality for consumption. This also discounts the consumers' reasons for wanting a product like raw milk (or raw milk cheeses, which are illegal unless aged more than sixty days). Many argue that raw milk preserves the flavor of the land, and can intensify the experienced terroir. Others cite their own beliefs about health or a desire to eliminate as much exterior influence upon their food as necessary. Regardless of the reason, "safety" as understood by science is in the background.

This conflict between science and taste began more than a century ago and parallels the histories given in this book on the movement from a handmade, "artisanal" food society to an industrialized one. Because of admitted issues with food safety and "quality" control, as well as advances in technology at the end of the nineteenth century and into the twentieth, this era saw consumer perception of quality move from gustatory satisfaction toward safety and homogenization. As Roudot notes, "No longer were people nourished by products from neighboring fields and gardens, or even by food at the village tavern; rather, edible goods were now fabricated in factories created precisely to sever the connection between food and local environment."[4] Nature was seen as wild and unpredictable and fostering illness; industrialization was increasingly believed to be healthier, more consistent, of higher quality than the products' handmade, traditionally preserved or produced, more "natural" equivalents. Modern food science now is acknowledging that taste is once again becoming more important to consumers. I argue that it is, in part, this relatively new movement toward taste as an indicator of quality—in addition to the postmodern return to ingredients and processes that are as natural and traditional as possible—that is characterizing today's counter-cuisine movement.

Also, this idea of "quality" is increasingly becoming (re)embedded in "nature"—in opposition to the trend of the last century and a half that asserted that industrialization made food safer. In particular, the distinction of "local" and farmstead, the narrative of knowing one's farmer, and the benefits of organic produce are all becoming increasingly important to the modern consumer—a stark change from the previous century's focus on globalization. "Quality has come to be seen as intrinsically linked to the supposed 'localness' of production" and has become part of the larger value system intrinsic in assessing one's food choices.[5] For example, one study found that consumers in Wales considered local, small batch, farmstead, organic—and even socially linked—cheeses to be of a higher "quality" than those that did not fit these qualifications.[6] Thus consumers' perception of quality is moving beyond safety and even beyond taste itself, but becoming inclusive of a larger value system—inclusive of the narrative of the artisan and food product itself. Now people don't just want pickles made in the traditional methods from local, organic cucumbers; they also want delicious pickles, interesting pickles, pickles with a story made by a passionate pickler. And with this understanding of how consumers value products come producers who strive to market themselves, authentically, in line with this new definition of quality. Thus today's counter-cuisine is more commercialized than its predecessor, and most of these artisans want to work with the system, rather than against it. They want to change the system from the inside rather than work outside of it. And they want to be sustainable economically, in addition to their commitment to environmental stewardship, community building, and the myriad values that food artisans are now expected to publically embrace.

In Heather Paxson's *The Life of Cheese*, she cites her conversation with Karen Weinberg, who owns a farm in eastern New York, talking about what it takes to make her farm economically sustainable. Weinberg notes that it constantly changes with the market and that she has great ideals of environmental sustainability. However, "if you can't survive, then it's all sort of out the window."[7] This reflects the comments of many artisans across the industry. Shamus Jones would like his products to be organic, but he notes that the industry does not support the added cost at this time. So he sources his ingredients as thoughtfully as he can, but with cost and his economic sustainability in mind. Like Jones, most artisans note that, yes, environmental issues are important, as are local sourcing and strong relationships with farmers and others within the larger community. However, many noted that despite these ideals, sometimes economic sustainability dictated using nonorganic or nonlocal raw ingredients (like Shamus Jones or Michaela Hayes), or discontinuing a relationship with a farmer (like Uri Laio), or other similar issues.

Further, the artisans of today—and the consumers who support them—also find value in the product beyond its nutrition, or even the pleasure derived from its taste. The cheese maker Joe Widmer "eagerly embraces the new artisanal movement as an opportunity to enhance the value—both symbolic and economic—of the same cheese that his father and uncles and grandfather produced."[8] While much has been discussed about cheese being a value-added product—as in its economic benefits for the maker—cheese and other artisanal products are also reinforcing a deeper value system that includes the connection between the maker and the familial or traditional processes they are following, the narrative behind the product, or the shared value system between the artisan and the consumer. For example, while I believe it is an easy argument to say that Taza or Woodblock Chocolate has better flavor than its mass-produced dark chocolate counterparts, consumers are also buying into the ethical values of direct trade with the cacao growers and the preservation of traditional cacao culture. Yet consumers would not know about, say, the chocolate maker's relationship with the growers if they did not make this narrative an important part of their marketing and packaging. As Paxson noted concerning the importance of packaging in today's artisanal food movement: "Quality is not there to be discovered: those attributes which define things are made explicit, even superadded, in the course of the marketing process."[9] The narrative told by the artisan is also a value-added component of the product itself—by telling their (authentic) story, they can better connect to the consumer and increase the perceived value of the good itself, allowing the artisan to command significantly higher prices than the good's mass-produced counterpart.

Yet for all of the positives that were apparent through my research regarding the new artisanal movement, which include a stronger connection among the land, the artisan, and the consumer; greater awareness of environmental issues inherent in various forms of farming and food production; and increased interest in preserving traditional preservation and preparation methods, to name a few, food artisans do tend to be romanticized by the consumer, which can lead to unrealistic expectations regarding the artisans' "moral purity."[10] This sometimes leads consumers to hold artisans to an unfair standard and judge them harshly when they make compromises. One such example is Uri Laio's decision to change to a producer who is certified organic versus keeping his relationship with his local, but not certified organic, farmer. He recognized that he would have drawn criticism from different factions whether he changed his sourcing or not, and in the end he had to do what was best for the business. Or consider Jasper Hill's co-branded cheese efforts. They have found this to be the best route to their own sustainability; would their business be as controversial if all of the cheeses in their vaults were made by their cheese makers? Often the narrative perpetuated by artisans is that of a small and independent artisan who supports local sourcing, is organic, and has close working relationships with the farmers who provide the raw materials. When any of these expectations is upended, even for valid reasons, this change of the consumer's own narrative of what they are choosing to spend money on and consume can cause a disillusionment with the perceived added value of the artisanal food item, potentially diluting the entire industry.

Such is the potential case of the rampant use of the term *artisanal* by decidedly non-artisanal food producers. Artisanal crackers, pizza dough, and even bacon jerky may fetch a higher price than an otherwise identical product that isn't labeled as such, with a potential upside of introducing a larger consumer base to the idea of artisanal goods as embodying a broader narrative that includes a positive connection to preservation of the land and traditional knowledge as well as the value of skilled work done by hand. However, not holding the term to any standard definition dilutes its power of narrative among all consumers and it has the potential to end up as a meaningless marketing term like "natural" has become. This pushback on the term *artisanal* was already becoming apparent among a number of the craftspeople with whom I spoke. Some were reluctantly admitting that their products were "artisanal" but preferred "craft" or another descriptor, or resisted any term altogether, with the cheese industry being an exception, likely in part because of the accepted (although not regulated) definition of artisan as proposed by the American Cheese Association. For the most part it was artisans in Brooklyn who most embraced the term, perhaps indicating that it still has cachet in this epicenter of artisanal food production.

DEFINING THE MODERN FOOD ARTISAN

So who is the modern food artisan in America? It is easy at first to define the American artisan in relation to the idealized European artisan that seems to have captured the imaginations of consumers via the transmittal of various narratives, including savvy marketing. Perhaps someone who learned their craft from a previous generation, someone who lovingly molds the cheese by hand, or stirs the whiskey mash, a butcher's apron tied around their waist. They are proud of their skill, and pack every jar of pickles with a smile on their face. While the pride may be there, as well as the skill, most of today's artisans in fact switched careers, and learned how to perform their craft through a rag-tag method of schooling. Today's new bean-to-bar chocolate makers had few mentors to teach them how to best roast or temper, and many are learning by doing and passing along their knowledge informally. Distillers, in particular in the many states that made distilling difficult or illegal, also had little in the way of an ongoing tradition to learn from and are looking to gain knowledge from just a few more seasoned distillers as well as learning heuristically. Many cheese makers took up their craft as a way to add value to their milk and help make their farm more economically sustainable, turning to mentors like Peter Dixon in Vermont to learn the process. The spirit of "coopetition" (or "cooperatition" as Tom Burkeaux from New Deal Distillery calls the same concept) is alive and well among these artisans, as can be seen through mentors like Dixon choosing to share his knowledge with his peers rather than see them as his competitors. The Craft Chocolate Makers of America banded together to increase their buying power, share advice, and help promote their value system. And there was a surprising amount of bi-coastal mentoring happening among many of the picklers with whom I spoke, from the process of pickling to the ins and outs of running a food business. This building of community[11] among those in the industry as well as between artisan and consumer has also helped to characterize the new artisanal food movement and crystallize the artisans' goals for turning to artisanal food businesses, often changing careers in their late twenties, thirties, or even later.

"Coopetition" is also helping establish American traditions among these industries, despite being only a fraction as old as those from the Old World. Thus what truly characterizes most modern American artisans today is their originality. While it would be easy to compare American cheeses with their European counterparts, it is hard to do so on an industry level because while the European model is to create a single standard by which to judge all others, the American artisanal interest lies in creative expression and making unique products. Some artisans did turn to European producers to help learn their craft, but they returned to America to adapt it to their own region or interest. It was a jumping-off point for their own interpretation, not a method of producing something identical. It is this instinct to express one's creativity while paying attention to quality and craft that I believe helps to define *artisanal* by today's standards. For we look to artists to reflect our individual and collective values, to nourish us inside and out, to inspire us to try new things, to go new places. And all of these can be—are being—experienced through artisanal food.

So what is artisanal? David Pye speaks to the telltale indicators of craftsmanship: "the quality of the result is not predetermined, but depends on the judgment, dexterity, and care which the maker exercises as he works" allowing for potential for error and risk.[12] Thus artisanal work involves thinking, adapting, the practical application of knowledge, and, potentially, the instinct to push yourself forward, the space to try something new, the room to experiment thoughtfully, to take risks for the possibility of reward. Nearly all of the artisans with whom I spoke mentioned their future plans. Some were aging whiskey—a great risk as it sits in a barrel, often for years, before one knows if it is any good. Others spoke of new products. Shamus Jones said he and his team were always thinking up new pickling ideas and trying them out. Charley Wheelock was constantly tinkering with his chocolate-making process and seeking new cacao beans to sample, Liz Alvis wanted eventually to make cheese from her own goat herd in Portland proper. The American artisanal movement is continuing to adapt and grow and provide new experiences for themselves and for the increasingly curious and growing artisanal food consumer.

What we are seeing grow so rapidly in the past decade (or less) really is a new artisanal food revolution, but one that didn't come by accident or convenience. These artisans have helped shape these industries, with many of these areas of craftsmanship nearly rising from the dead in recent years. And while it is easy to say that the economy inspired these artisans to take a risk and turn to artisanal food production, one cannot discount how this movement has, in part, "come about by necessity, not merely because of opportunity."[13] Paxson notes how many dairies had to find new streams of revenue to survive, and many turned to artisanal cheese making, in essence creating the product and trusting that consumer would come. But other industries did the same thing, in essence. The local craft distilling industry did not exist in New York State until about a decade ago, and local distillers had to trust that their product would find consumers who would support this new endeavor. The same can be said about bean-to-bar chocolate in America; consumers had few to no options for flavorful, single-origin chocolate bars, let alone ones that were organic or ethically sourced. These innovators had to sell consumers on the added value of their product over a Hershey bar—or even Lindt or Godiva—with almost no model on which to rely.

Yet in the end, what or who can be considered artisanal? Some may question how automated an artisan can be—can they use an automatic stirrer, like some cheese makers employ for their curds? May they hire someone else to pack their pickle jars? Can they conch and temper their chocolate using machines? One may argue that each industry has its own technological advances, and logistics would dictate that only the processes integral to the overall quality of the product need be done by the artisan themselves. Would we ask a distiller make his own fire from logs in order to be considered artisanal? Would we begrudge a hardworking farmstead cheese maker hiring someone to help her milk her goats or package her cheese? I'm also fond of Tom Burkeaux's definition of artisanal as when the person handling the product is also the person who handles the money. For, as Vince Razionale of Jasper Hill asked, "How much does it have to hurt?" I believe that David Pye's distinctions for craftsmanship are also strong guidelines for defining artisanal work today. But in the end it is also about the whole package. A product must be high quality and taste good, but the authentic story must also be compelling. The modern artisanal food producer has redefined the value of food through the increasing inclusiveness of values inherent in terroir, or this new definition of "quality"—environmental stewardship, artisanal human interactions, ethical business practices—so food has come to represent not merely nourishment, but also a way of life. And this makes sense. So many of these artisans came to this business to change their life, to create community, to change the world. And we, as consumers, strive for the same thing. One bite at a time.

NOTES

I. ARTISANAL FOODS

1. Trudy Eden, "The Art of Preserving: How Cooks in Colonial Virginia Imitated Nature to Control It," *Eighteenth-Century Life* 23, no. 2 (May 1999): 13–23.

2. Alan Davidson, *The Oxford Companion to Food* (Oxford: Oxford University Press, 1999).

3. Harold McGee, *On Food and Cooking: The Science and Lore of the Kitchen*, 2nd edition (New York: Scribners, 2004).

4. Harvey Levenstein, *Revolution at the Table* (New York: Oxford University Press, 1988).

5. "The Bronx in Brief," Bronx Historical Society, www .bronxhistoricalsociety.org/bxbrief (accessed February 27, 2014).

6. Alain-Claude Roudot, "Food Science and Consumer Taste," *Gastronomica* 4, no. 1 (Winter 2004).

7. Jonathan Rees, *Refrigeration Nation* (Baltimore, MD: Johns Hopkins University Press, 2013), 163.

8. Katherine J. Curtis White, "Population Change and Farm Dependence: Temporal and Spatial Variation in the U.S. Great Plains, 1900–2000," *Demography* 45, no. 2 (2008): 363–86.

9. Roudot, "Food Science and Consumer Taste," 44.

10. See Laura Schenone, *The Lost Ravioli Recipes of Hoboken* (New York: Norton, 2008); Simone Cinotto, "Sunday Dinner? You Had to Be

There!" in *Italian Folk: Vernacular Culture in Italian American Lives*, ed. Joseph Sciorra (New York: Fordham University Press, 2010); and Simone Cinotto, "Leonard Covello, the Covello Papers, and the History of Eating Habits among Italian Immigrants in New York," *Journal of American History* (September 2004).

11. Warren Belasco, *Appetite for Change* (New York: Pantheon Books, 1989); Michael Pollan, "Food: But Not As We Know It," *Independent*, June 15, 2003, 48, 49.

12. John Mariani, *How Italian Food Conquered the World* (New York: Palgrave Macmillan, 2012).

13. See Mariani, *How Italian Food Conquered the World*; Cinotto, "Sunday Dinner? You Had to Be There!"; and "Leonard Covello, the Covello Papers, and the History of Eating Habits among Italian Immigrants in New York"; as well as Hasia Diner, *Hungering for America: Italian, Irish, and Jewish Foodways in the Age of Migration* (Cambridge, MA: Harvard University Press, 2003).

14. John Leland, *Hip: The History* (New York: HarperCollins, 2005); Jesse Scheidlower, "Crying Wolf," *Slate*, December 8, 2004.

15. Belasco, *Appetite for Change*, 94.

16. Ibid., 96.

17. Ibid., 46–47.

18. Ibid., 203–4.

19. Heather Paxson, "Cheese Cultures," *Gastronomica* 10, no. 4 (Fall 2010): 35–47.

20. Belasco, *Appetite for Change*, 167–68.

21. Warren Belasco discusses the counter-cuisine movement in detail in his excellent work *Appetite for Change*, but Michael Pollan and others have also written about this era in our food history and have equated it with the present-day food movement that similarly focuses on environmental sustainability, local sourcing, worker rights, and other values.

22. Belasco, *Appetite for Change*, 172.

23. Ibid., 194.

24. Ibid., 202–3.

25. Ibid., 204–17.

26. Ibid., 245–46.

27. U.S. Department of Agriculture, "Farmers Markets and Local Food Marketing," www.ams.usda.gov/AMSv1.0/ams.fetchTemplateData.do? template=TemplateS&leftNav=WholesaleandFarmersMarkets&page=

WFMFarmersMarketGrowth&description=Farmers%20Market%20
Growth&acct=frmrdirmkt (accessed August 3, 2012).

28. Warren Belasco, *Meals to Come: A History of the Future of Food* (Berkeley: University of California Press, 2006), 229.

29. Ibid.

30. As quoted in Ibid., 230.

31. Josh Sanburn, "Things We Buy in a Bad Economy," *Time*, October 19, 2011, moneyland.time.com/2011/10/21/12-things-we-buy-in-a-bad-economy/?iid=pf-article-mostpop2#gardening-seeds.

32. Meghan Casserly, "The 11 Hottest Industries for Start-Ups," *Forbes*, February 6, 2012, www.forbes.com/sites/meghancasserly/2012/02/06/11-hottest-industries-for-start-ups-foodtrucks-wineries-booze/.

33. Sarah Muller, "Tom Colicchio Dissects Rise of Artisanal Food," *Culture WNYC*, February 3, 2010, culture.wnyc.org/articles/features/2010/feb/03/tom-colicchio-dissects-rise-artisanal-food-new-york/; Mr. Cheese, "Artisan Cheese Demand Is on the Rise," *All Things Cheese*, January 6, 2010, www.allthingscheese.com/artisan-cheese-demand-on-rise/.

34. Mark Engler, "Hijacked Organic, Limited Local, Fault Fair Trade: What's a Radical to Eat?" *Dissent* 59, no. 2 (2012): 20–25.

35. Bruce Horovitz, "Marketers Use Artisan Label to Evoke More Sales," *USA Today,* October 10, 2011.

2. PICKLES

1. V. Mars, ed., *Food in Motion: The Migration of Foodstuffs and Cookery Techniques*, vol. 1, Oxford Symposium (London: Prospect Books, 1983), 81–83.

2. Jane Zeigelman, "Immigrant Identities, Preserved in Vinegar?" *New York Times*, August 3, 2003.

3. Judy Levin, "Salty, Sour and Controversial: A Quick History of the Pickle," *Tenement Museum*, January 20, 2012, tenement-museum.blogspot.com/2012/01/salty-sour-and-controversial-quick.html.

4. Sue Shepherd, *Pickled, Potted, and Canned* (New York: Simon & Schuster, 2006), 197.

5. James Matterer, "To Pickle Cucumbers to Look Very Green," *Gode Cookery*, www.godecookery.com/engrec/engrec59.html.

6. "Heinz 57," Heinz History Center, 2014, www.HeinzHistoryCenter.org.

7. Levin, "Salty, Sour and Controversial: A Quick History of the Pickle"; "Heinz 57."

8. "A Modest Beginning," Mt. Olive Pickles, www.MtOlivePickles.com (accessed March 1, 2014).

9. Meghan Casserly, "The 11 Hottest Industries for Start-Ups," *Forbes*, February 6, 2012.

10. Holly H. Garner, Elizabeth L. Andress, and Anne L. Sweaney, "An Updated Look at Home Canning," National Center for Home Food Preservation, July 29, 2002, nchfp.uga.edu/pres_papers.html.

11. Ana Campoy, "Putting Up Produce: Yes You Can," *Wall Street Journal,* October 15, 2009.

12. Camilla Sterne, "The Pickling Revolution Takes Boulder," *Boulder Weekly*, July 18, 2013.

13. Adam Davidson, "Don't Mock the Artisanal-Pickle Makers," *New York Times*, February 15, 2012.

14. Mark Garrison, "More Sour to You," *Slate*, June 20, 2013.

15. Sam Addison, personal interview, January 30, 2013.

16. Amy Trubek, *Taste of Place: A Cultural Journey into Terroir* (Berkeley: University of California Press, 2009), 15.

17. Matthew B. Crawford, *Shop Class for Soul Craft* (New York: Penguin, 2009), 8.

18. Michaela Hayes, personal interview, November 28, 2012.

19. Lourdes Martinez, Suzanne Thornsbury, and Tomozaku Nagai, "National and International Factors in Pickle Markets," *Agriculture Economics Report*, October 2006.

20. Shamus Jones, personal interview, November 29, 2012.

21. Howard Becker, "Arts and Crafts," *American Journal of Sociology* 83, no. 4 (1978): 866.

22. Jordan Champagne, personal interview, January 9, 2013.

23. Shamus Jones interview.

24. "About," Crock and Jar, www.crockandjar.com (accessed March 1, 2014); Michaela Hayes, personal interview, November 30, 2012.

25. Heather Paxson, *The Life of Cheese* (Berkeley: University of California Press, 2013), 17.

26. Ibid., 18.

27. Warren Belasco, *Appetite for Change* (New York: Pantheon, 1989), 94.

28. Ibid., 96.

29. Travis Grillo, personal interview, October 18, 2012.

30. Alex Hozven, personal interview, January 8, 2013.

31. Citizen, "Cultured Pickles," Vimeo, 2013, vimeo.com/38476352.

32. Uri Laio, personal interview, January 11, 2013.

33. Julie O'Brien, personal interview, January, 25, 2013.

34. Becker, "Arts and Crafts," 864.

35. Betsey Walton, personal interview, January 4, 2013.

3. CHEESE

1. "Amazing but True Facts about Marin County Agriculture," University of California Cooperative Extension, cemarin.ucanr.edu/files/30457.pdf (accessed March 1, 2014).

2. Donna Pacheco, personal interview, January 7, 2013.

3. "Grown in Marin," Division of Agriculture and Natural Resources, University of California, 2014, ucanr.edu/sites/Grown_in_Marin/.

4. "Our Family Tradition," Achadinha Cheese Company, 2012, www.achadinha.com/Home.html.

5. American Cheese Society, "Cheese Glossary," www.cheesesociety.org (accessed February 5, 2014).

6. Heather Paxson, *The Life of Cheese: Crafting Food and Value in America* (Berkeley: University of California Press, 2012).

7. V. H. Holsinger, K. T. Rajkowski, and J. R. Stabel, "Milk Pasteurisation and Safety: A Brief History and Update," *Review of Science and Technology* 16, no. 2 (1997): 441–51.

8. H. P. Bachmann et al., "Interlaboratory Comparison of Cheese Making Trials: Model Cheeses Made from Raw, Pasteurized and Micofiltered Milks," *Lebensmittel-Wissenschaft und-Technologie* 31 (1998): 585–93.

9. Heather Paxson, "Cheese Cultures," *Gastronomica* 10, no. 4. (Fall 2010): 35–47.

10. Wisconsin Milk Marketing Board, "2013 Dairy Data," www.wmmb.com/assets/images/pdf/WisconsinDairyData.pdf.

11. Paxson, *The Life of Cheese*, 9.

12. Wisconsin Milk Marketing Board, "2013 Dairy Data."

13. Paxson, *The Life of Cheese*, 66.

14. Ibid., 75.

15. Ibid., 11.

16. George Miller, personal interview, February 13, 2013.

17. See Heather Paxson's work.

18. "Jericho Hill Farm," Vermont Cheese Council, 2010, www
.VTCheese.com.

19. Ibid.

20. "About Our Tarentaise," Thistle Hill Farm, www.thistlehillfarm
.com/aboutthecheese.htm (accessed March 1, 2014).

21. John Putnam, personal interview, February 13, 2014.

22. "Our Story," First Light Farm, 2014, first-light-farm.com/.

23. Jill Basch Giacomini, personal interview, January 7, 2013.

24. Paxson, *The Life of Cheese*, 20.

25. Terry Gifford, *Reconnecting with John Muir: Essays in Post-Pastoral Practice* (Athens: University of Georgia Press, 2010), 173.

26. Giffords discusses how the post-pastoral incorporates the environmental justice movement—"environmental needs for people and planet" (174), which include both the needs of a larger, modernized population, as well as their necessity to learn to live more lightly upon the earth to reduce the negative environmental effects such as pollution and global warming.

27. Paxson, *The Life of Cheese*, 188; Amy Trubek, *Taste of Place: A Cultural Journey into Terroir* (Berkeley: University of California Press, 2009).

28. "Red Hawk," *Culture*, www.culturecheesemag.com/cheese-library/red-hawk (accessed March 1, 2014).

29. See Trubek, *Taste of Place*; Susan J. Terrio, "Crafting Grand Cru Chocolates in Contemporary France," in *The Craft Reader*, ed. Glenn Adamson (New York: Bloomsbury, 2009).

30. Paxson, *The Life of Cheese*, 211.

31. "Welcome to the Center for an Agricultural Economy," The Center for an Agricultural Economy, 2014, www.hardwickagriculture.org.

32. Vince Razionale, personal interview, February 14, 2013.

33. "Barely Buzzed," Beehive Cheese Company, www.beehivecheese
.com/cheese/ (accessed March 1, 2014).

34. Heather Paxson and others have noted the tendency of cheese makers to use the language of childrearing when speaking about their cheese and cheese making.

35. Liz Alvis, personal interview, January 6, 2013.

36. "About Us," Portland Creamery, www.portlandcreamery.com (accessed March 1, 2014).

37. Elizabeth Blair, "'Child Prodigy' Film Revives Question: What Is Art?" NPR, originally aired October 31, 2007, www.npr.org/templates/story/story.php?storyId=15811817.

38. Paxson, *The Life of Cheese*, 55.

4. CHOCOLATE

1. Alex Whitmore, persona interview, August 10, 2011.

2. N. Spielmann and C. Gélinas-Chebat, "Terroir? That's Not How I Would Describe It," *International Journal of Wine Business Research* 24, no. 4 (2012): 254–70, doi: dx.doi.org/10.1108/17511061211280310.

3. Bernard L. Herman, "Drum Head Stew," *Southern Cultures* 15, no. 4 (Winter 2009): 37.

4. Heather Paxson, "Locating Value in Artisan Cheese: Reverse Engineering Terroir for New-World Landscapes," *American Anthropologist* 112, no. 3 (2010): 444.

5. Spielmann and Gélinas-Chebat, "Terroir?"; Paxson, "Locating Value in Artisan Cheese," 444–57.

6. Paxson, "Locating Value in Artisan Cheese," 449.

7. T. J. Tomasik, "Certeau à la Carte—Translating Discursive Terroir in the Practice of Everyday Life: Living and Cooking," *South Atlantic Quarterly* 100, no. 2 (2001): 519–42.

8. Ibid., 525.

9. "Chocolate Consumption," *The World Atlas of Chocolate*, www.sfu.ca/geog351fall03/groups-webpages/gp8/consum/consum.html (accessed March 1, 2014).

10. David Stannard, *American Holocaust: Conquest of the New World* (New York: Oxford University Press, 1993).

11. Ken Albala, "The Use and Abuse of Chocolate in 17th-Century Medical Theory," *Food and Foodways* 15, nos. 1–2 (January–June 2007).

12. S. Coe and M. Coe, *The True History of Chocolate* (London: Thames & Hudson, 2007), 42.

13. Carol Off, *Bitter Chocolate* (New York: The New Press, 2008), 50–51; Wendy A. Woloson, *Refined Tastes* (Baltimore: Johns Hopkins University Press, 2002).

14. Coe and Coe, *The True History of Chocolate*, 245.

15. Off, *Bitter Chocolate*, 73–82.

16. "Who Consumes the Most Chocolate?" *The CNN Freedom Project*, January 17, 2012, thecnnfreedomproject.blogs.cnn.com/2012/01/17/who-consumes-the-most-chocolate/.

17. Off, *Bitter Chocolate*, 207.

18. Ibid., 272–78.

19. Charley Wheelock, personal interview, January 3, 2013.

20. Nat Bletter, personal interview, November 15, 2012.

21. "Welcome to the World of Chocolate Straight from Its Origins," *Madre Chocolate*, madrechocolate.com/Home.html (accessed March 1, 2014).

22. Susan J. Terrio, "Crafting Grand Cru Chocolates in Contemporary France," in *The Craft Reader*, ed. Glenn Adamson (New York: Bloomsbury, 2009), 257.

23. "Craft Chocolate Makers of America," craftchocolatemakers.org (accessed March 1, 2014).

24. Derek Herbster, personal interview, October 18, 2012.

25. Cameron Ring, personal interview, January 7, 2013.

26. "The Chocolate of Tomorrow," KPMG, June 7, 2012, www.kpmg.com/global/en/issuesandinsights/articlespublications/pages/chocolate-of-tomorrow.aspx.

27. "About Us," *Dandelion Chocolate*, 2014, www.dandelionchocolate.com.

28. Terrio, "Crafting Grand Cru Chocolates in Contemporary France," 33.

29. "Sales of Fair Trade Certified™ Products Up 75 Percent in 2011," *Fair Trade USA*, March 6, 2002, fairtradeusa.org/press-room/press_release/sales-fair-trade-certified-products-75-percent-2011.

30. See Elizabeth Barham, "Translating Terroir: The Global Challenge of French AOC Labeling," *Journal of Rural Studies* 19 (2003): 127–38; Paxson, "Locating Value in Artisan Cheese"; Terrio, "Crafting Grand Cru Chocolates in Contemporary France"; and Amy Trubek, *Taste of Place: A*

Cultural Journey into Terroir (Berkeley: University of California Press, 2009).

31. Barham, "Translating Terroir."

32. "In the Beginning . . . There Was Homemade Chocolate," *Chocolate Alchemy*, January 6, 2004, chocolatealchemy.com/2003/10/01/in-the-beginningthere-was-homemade-chocolate/.

5. SPIRITS

1. Larry Olmstead, "George Washington's New Whiskey: Founding Father of American Distilling Is Back!" *Forbes*, April 4, 2012, www.forbes.com/sites/larryolmsted/2012/04/04/george-washingtons-new-whiskey-founding-father-of-american-distilling-is-back/.

2. Gary Regan and Mardee Haiden Regan, "History of Spirits in America," *Distilled Spirits Council of the United States*, 2014, www.discus.org/heritage/spirits/.

3. David Kyvig, *Repealing National Prohibition* (Kent, OH: Kent State University Press, 2000).

4. Ibid.

5. Andrea K., Zimmermann, "Nineteenth-Century Production of Wheat in Four New York State Regions: A Comparative Examination," *Hudson Valley Regional Review* 5, no. 2 (1988).

6. "What Was In Colonial Cups Besides Tea? Cider, Water, Milk, and Whiskey!" *O Say Can You See?* blog of the National Museum of American History, December 6, 2012, blog.americanhistory.si.edu/osaycanyousee/2012/12/what-was-in-colonial-cups-besides-tea-cider-water-milk-and-whiskey.html.

7. Eve Turow, "The Distant Past and Recent Rise of New York's Brewing and Distilling Industry," *Fork in the Road*, blog of the *Village Voice*, June 27, 2013, blogs.villagevoice.com/forkintheroad/2013/06/the_distant_pas.php.

8. "Distilleries Return to Brooklyn," CBS New York, newyork.cbslocal.com/video/7177121-distilleries-return-to-broo/ (accessed March 1, 2014).

9. "On the Vine Trail," *Song of the Vine: A History of Wine*, 2008, rmc.library.cornell.edu/ewga/exhibition/winetrail/.

10. Devin S. Morgan, "An Introduction to New York's Farm Distillery Law," *Farmshed*, December 2, 2012, farmshedcny.com/an-introduction-to-new-yorks-farm-distillery-law/.

11. "Oregon Whiskey History," *Cultural Oregon*, February 12, 2013, culturaloregon.com/oregon-whiskey-history/.

12. "About the OLCC," Oregon.gov, www.oregon.gov/olcc/pages/about_us.aspx (accessed March 1, 2014).

13. "Distilleries Return to Brooklyn."

14. "Interview: Tuthilltown Spirits Co-Founder Ralph Erenzo," *Shanken News Daily*, July 24, 2012, www.shankennewsdaily.com/index.php/2012/07/24/3605/interview-tuthilltown-spirits-co-founder-ralph-erenzo/.

15. "Class and Type Designation," chapter 4 in *The Beverage Alcohol Manual (BAM) Practical Guide: Basic Mandatory Labeling Information for Distilled Spirits*, vol. 2, www.ttb.gov/spirits/bam/chapter4.pdf (accessed March 1, 2014).

16. Nicole Austin, personal interview, November 17, 2012.

17. Colin Spoelman, personal interview, October 19, 2012.

18. "Around the Distillery," Breuckelen Distilling, brkdistilling.com/around-the-distillery/ (accessed March 1, 2014).

19. Cacao Prieto, "Our Liquor Products," cacaoprieto.com/liquor/products/ (accessed March 1, 2014).

20. Brooklyn Gin, "About," www.brooklyngin.com/about/ (accessed March 1, 2014).

21. Brian McKenzie, personal interview, October 22, 2012.

22. Finger Lakes Distilling, 2013, fingerlakesdistilling.com/.

23. "Distilling at Tuthilltown," Tuthilltown Spirits, 2014, www.tuthilltown.com/about.

24. "N.Y. ABC, LAW 61: NY Code—Section 61: Distiller's Licenses," 2013, codes.lp.findlaw.com/nycode/ABC.

25. Ralph Erenzo, personal interview, October 25, 2012.

26. Tour guide at Eastside Distilling in discussion with the author, January 3, 2013.

27. Tom Burkleaux, personal interview, January 4, 2013.

28. Andrew Tice, personal interview, January 4, 2013.

29. "The Spirits," House Spirits, 2014, housespirits.com/spirits/.

30. Oregon Liquor Control Commission, "Starting Your Own Craft Distillery," www.oregon.gov/olcc/pages/craft_distilleries.aspx (accessed March 1, 2014).

31. Jacob Grier, "Craft Distilleries and the Commerce Clause," *Liquidity Preference*, May 31, 2013, www.jacobgrier.com/blog/archives/6063 .html.

32. Ian Cameron, "The Fall and Rise of Craft Distilleries," *Diffords Guide*, May 30, 2012, www.diffordsguide.com/class-magazine/read-online/en/2012-05-29/page-7/craft-distilleries.

33. Ibid.

6. DEFINING THE MOVEMENT, ONE BITE AT A TIME

1. "Lower East Side Pickle Day," Lower East Side NY, www .lowereastsideny.com/events/lower-east-side-pickle-day/ (accessed March 1, 2014).

2. Warren Belasco, *Appetite for Change* (New York: Pantheon Books, 1989), 64.

3. Alain-Claude Roudot, "Food Science and Consumer Taste," *Gastronomica* 4, no. 1 (Winter 2004): 41.

4. Ibid., 42, 44.

5. J. Murdoch, T. Marsden, and J. Banks, "Quality, Nature, and Embeddedness: Some Theoretical Considerations in the Context of the Food Sector," *Economic Geography* 76, no. 2 (2000): 107–25.

6. Ibid.

7. Heather Paxson, *The Life of Cheese: Crafting Food and Value in America* (Berkeley: University of California Press, 2012), 79.

8. Heather Paxson, "Cheese Cultures," *Gastronomica* 10, no. 4 (Fall 2010): 45.

9. Paxson, "Cheese Cultures."

10. Paxson, *The Life of Cheese*, 7–8.

11. See Paxson's research on why this second wave of artisans choose to change careers and turn to handmade goods in *The Life of Cheese*.

12. David Pye, "The Nature and Art of Workmanship," in *The Craft Reader*, ed. Glenn Adamson (New York: Bloomsbury, 2010), 342.

13. Paxson, *The Life of Cheese*, 89.

BIBLIOGRAPHY

Albala, Ken. "The Use and Abuse of Chocolate in 17th-Century Medical Theory." *Food and Foodways* 15, nos. 1–2 (January–June 2007).

"Amazing but True Facts about Marin County Agriculture." University of California Cooperative Extension. cemarin.ucanr.edu/files/30457.pdf. Accessed March 1, 2014.

American Cheese Society. "Cheese Glossary." www.Cheesesociety.org. Accessed February 5, 2014.

Bachmann, H. P., et al. "Interlaboratory Comparison of Cheese Making Trials: Model Cheeses Made from Raw, Pasteurized and Microfiltered Milks." *Lebensmittel-Wissenschaft und-Technologie* 31 (1998): 585–93.

Barham, Elizabeth. "Translating Terroir: The Global Challenge of French AOC Labeling." *Journal of Rural Studies* 19 (2003): 127–38.

Becker, Howard. "Arts and Crafts." *American Journal of Sociology* 83, no. 4 (1978): 866.

Belasco, Warren. *Appetite for Change.* New York: Pantheon Books, 1989.

———. *Meals to Come: A History of the Future of Food.* Berkeley: University of California Press, 2006.

Blair, Elizabeth. "'Child Prodigy' Film Revives Question: What Is Art?" NPR, October 31, 2007. www.npr.org/templates/story/story.php?storyId=15811817.

Bronx Historical Society. "The Bronx in Brief." www.bronxhistoricalsociety.org/bxbrief. Accessed February 27, 2014.

Cameron, Ian. "The Fall and Rise of Craft Distilleries." *Diffords Guide*, May 30, 2012. www.diffordsguide.com/class-magazine/read-online/en/2012-05-29/page-7/craft-distilleries.

Campoy, Ana. "Putting Up Produce: Yes You Can." *Wall Street Journal*, October 15, 2009.

Casserly, Meghan. "The 11 Hottest Industries for Start-Ups." *Forbes*, February 6, 2012.

"Chocolate Consumption." *The World Atlas of Chocolate.* www.sfu.ca/geog351fall03/groups-webpages/gp8/consum/consum.html. Accessed March 1, 2014.

"The Chocolate of Tomorrow." KPMG.com, June 2012.

Citizen. "Cultured Pickles." Vimeo, 2013. vimeo.com/38476352.

"Class and Type Distinction." Chapter 4 in *The Beverage Alcohol Manual (BAM) Practical Guide: Basic Mandatory Labeling Information for Distilled Spirits*, vol. 2. www.ttb.gov/spirits/bam/chapter4.pdf. Accessed March 1, 2014.

Coe, S., and M. Coe. *The True History of Chocolate*. London: Thames & Hudson, 2007.

Crawford, Matthew B. *Shop Class for Soul Craft*. New York: Penguin, 2009.

Davidson, Adam. "Don't Mock the Artisanal-Pickle Makers." *New York Times*, February 15, 2012.

Davidson, Alan. *The Oxford Companion to Food*. Oxford: Oxford University Press, 1999.

"Distilleries Return to Brooklyn." CBS New York. newyork.cbslocal.com/video/7177121-distilleries-return-to-broo/. Accessed March 1, 2014.

Eden, Trudy. "The Art of Preserving: How Cooks in Colonial Virginia Imitated Nature to Control It." *Eighteenth-Century Life* 23, no. 2 (May 1999): 13–23.

Engler, Mark. "Hijacked Organic, Limited Local, Fault Fair Trade: What's a Radical to Eat?" *Dissent* 59, no. 2 (Spring 2012): 20–25.

Garrison, Mark. "More Sour to You." *Slate*, June 20, 2013.

Garner, Holly, Elizabeth Andress, and Anne Sweaney. "An Updated Look at Home Canning." National Center for Home Food Preservation, July 29, 2002.

Gifford, Terry. *Reconnecting with John Muir: Essays in Post-Pastoral Practice*. Athens: University of Georgia Press, 2010.

Grier, Jacob. "Craft Distilleries and the Commerce Clause." *Liquidity Preference*, May 31, 2013. www.jacobgrier.com/blog/archives/6063.html.

"Grown in Marin." Division of Agriculture and Natural Resources. University of California, 2014. ucanr.edu/sites/Grown_in_Marin/.

"Heinz 57." Heinz History Center, 2014. www.HeinzHistoryCenter.org.

Herman, Bernard L. "Drum Head Stew." *Southern Cultures* 15, no. 4 (Winter 2009): 36–49.

Holsinger, V. H., K. T. Rajkowski, and J. R. Stabel. "Milk Pasteurisation and Safety: A Brief History and Update." *Review of Science and Technology* 16, no. 2 (1997): 441–51.

Horovitz, Bruce. "Marketers Use Artisan Label to Evoke More Sales." *USA Today*, October 10, 2011.

"In the Beginning . . . There was Homemade Chocolate." *Chocolate Alchemy*, January 6, 2004. chocolatealchemy.com/2003/10/01/in-the-beginningthere-was-homemade-chocolate/.

"Interview: Tuthilltown Spirits Co-Founder Ralph Erenzo." *Shanken News Daily*, July 24, 2012. www.shankennewsdaily.com/index.php/2012/07/24/3605/interview-tuthill town-spirits-co-founder-ralph-erenzo/.

Kindstedt, Paul. *American Farmstead Cheese: The Complete Guide to Making and Selling Artisan Cheeses*. White River Junction, VT: Chelsea Green, 2005.

Kyvig, David. *Repealing National Prohibition*. Kent, OH: Kent State University Press, 2000.

Leland, John. *Hip: The History*. New York: HarperCollins, 2005.

Levenstein, Harvey. *Revolution at the Table*. New York: Oxford University Press, 1988.

Levin, Judy. "Salty, Sour and Controversial: A Quick History of the Pickle." *Tenement Museum*, January 20, 2012. tenement-museum.blogspot.com/2012/01/salty-sour-and-controversial-quick.html.

"Lower East Side Pickle Day." Lower East Side NY. www.lowereastsideny.com/events/lower-east-side-pickle-day/. Accessed March 1, 2014.

Mariani, John. *How Italian Food Conquered the World*. New York: Palgrave Macmillan, 2012.

Mars, V., ed. *Food in Motion: The Migration of Foodstuffs and Cookery Techniques*, vol. 1, Oxford Symposium. London: Prospect Books, 1983.

Martinez, Lourdes, Suzanne Thornsbury, and Tomozaku Nagai. "National and International Factors in Pickle Markets." *Agriculture Economics Report*, October 2006.

Matterer, James. "To Pickle Cucumbers to Look Very Green." *Gode Cookery*, 2002. www.godecookery.com/engrec/engrec59.html.

McGee, Harold. *On Food and Cooking: The Science and Lore of the Kitchen*. New York: Scribners, 2004.

Morgan, Devin S. "An Introduction to New York's Farm Distillery Law." *Farmshed*, December 2, 2012. farmshedcny.com/an-introduction-to-new-yorks-farm-distillery-law/.

Mr. Cheese. "Artisan Cheese Demand Is on the Rise." *All Things Cheese,* January 6, 2010. www.allthingscheese.com/artisan-cheese-demand-on-rise/.

Muller, Sarah. "Tom Colicchio Dissects Rise of Artisanal Food." *Culture WNYC*, February 3, 2010. culture.wnyc.org/articles/features/2010/feb/03/tom-colicchio-dissects-rise-artisanal-food-new-york/.

Murdoch, J., T. Marsden, and J. Banks. "Quality, Nature, and Embeddedness: Some Theoretical Considerations in the Context of the Food Sector." *Economic Geography* 76, no. 2 (2000): 107–25.

"N.Y. ABC. LAW 61: NY Code—Section 61: Distiller's Licenses," 2013. codes.lp.findlaw.com/nycode/ABC.

Off, Carol. *Bitter Chocolate*. New York: The New Press. 2008.

Olmstead, Larry. "George Washington's New Whiskey: Founding Father of American Distilling Is Back!" *Forbes*, April 4, 2012.

"On the Vine Trail." *Song of the Vine: A History of Wine*, 2008. rmc.library.cornell.edu/ewga/exhibition/winetrail/.

Oregon Liquor Control Commission. "Starting Your Own Craft Distillery." www.oregon.gov/olcc/pages/craft_distilleries.aspx. Accessed March 1, 2014.

"Oregon Whiskey History." *Cultural Oregon*, February 12, 2013. culturaloregon.com/oregon-whiskey-history/.

Paxson, Heather. "Cheese Cultures." *Gastronomica* 10, no. 4 (Fall 2010): 35–47.

———. *The Life of Cheese*. Berkeley: University of California Press, 2012.

———. "Locating Value in Artisan Cheese: Reverse Engineering Terroir for New-World Landscapes." *American Anthropologist* 112, no. 3 (2010): 444–57.

Pollan, Michael. "Food: But Not as We Know It." *Independent*, June 15, 2003, 48, 49.

"Red Hawk." *Culture*. www.culturecheesemag.com/cheese-library/red-hawk. Accessed March 1, 2014.

Rees, Jonathan. *Refrigeration Nation*. Baltimore, MD: Johns Hopkins University Press, 2013.

Regan, Gary, and Mardee Haiden Regan. "History of Spirits in America." *Distilled Spirits Council of the United States*, 2014. www.discus.org/heritage/spirits/.

Roberts, Jeffrey P. *The Atlas of American Artisan Cheese*. White River Junction, VT: Chelsea Green, 2007.

Roudot, Alain-Claude. "Food Science and Consumer Taste." *Gastronomica* 4, no. 1 (Winter 2004): 41–46.

"Sales of Fair Trade Certified™ Products Up 75 Percent in 2011." *Fair Trade USA*. March 6, 2002. fairtradeusa.org/press-room/press_release/sales-fair-trade-certified-products-75-percent-2011.

Sanburn, Josh. "Things We Buy in a Bad Economy." *Time*, October 19, 2011.

Scheidlower, Jesse. "Crying Wolf." *Slate*, December 8, 2004.

Shepherd, Sue. *Pickled, Potted, and Canned*. New York: Simon & Schuster, 2006.

Spielmann, N., and C. Gélinas-Chebat. "Terroir? That's Not How I Would Describe It." *International Journal of Wine Business Research* 24, no. 4 (2012): 254–70.

Stannard, David. *American Holocaust: Conquest of the New World*. New York: Oxford University Press, 1993.

Sterne, Camilla. "The Pickling Revolution Takes Boulder." *Boulder Weekly*, July 18, 2013.

Terrio, Susan J. "Crafting Grand Cru Chocolates in Contemporary France." In *The Craft Reader*, ed. Glenn Adamson. New York: Bloomsbury, 2009.

Tomasik, T. J. "Certeau a la Carte—Translating Discursive Terroir in the Practice of Everyday Life: Living and Cooking." *South Atlantic Quarterly* 100, no. 2 (2001): 519–42.

Trubek, Amy. *Taste of Place: A Cultural Journey into Terroir*. Berkeley: University of California Press, 2009.

Turow, Eve. "The Distant Past and Recent Rise of New York's Brewing and Distilling Industry." *Fork in the Road* blog of the *Village Voice*, June 27, 2013. blogs. villagevoice.com/forkintheroad/2013/06/the_distant_pas.php.

United States Department of Agriculture. "Farmers Markets and Local Food Marketing." www.ams.usda.gov/AMSv1.0/ams.fetchTemplateData.do?template=Template S&leftNav=WholesaleandFarmersMarkets&page=WFMFarmersMarketGrowth& description=Farmers%20Market%20Growth&acct=frmrdirmkt. Accessed August 3, 2012.

"Welcome to the Center for an Agricultural Economy." The Center for an Agricultural Economy, 2014. www.hardwickagriculture.org.

"What Was in Colonial Cups Besides Tea? Cider, Water, Milk, and Whiskey!" *O Say Can You See?* blog of the National Museum of American History, December 6, 2012, blog.americanhistory.si.edu/osaycanyousee/2012/12/what-was-in-colonial-cups-besides-tea-cider-water-milk-and-whiskey.html.

White, Katherine J. Curtis. "Population Change and Farm Dependence: Temporal and Spatial Variation in the U.S. Great Plains, 1900–2000." *Demography* 45, no. 2 (2008): 363–86.

"Who Consumes the Most Chocolate?" *The CNN Freedom Project*, January 17, 2012. thecnnfreedomproject.blogs.cnn.com/2012/01/17/who-consumes-the-most-chocolate/.

Wisconsin Milk Marketing Board. "2013 Dairy Data." www.wmmb.com/assets/images/pdf/WisconsinDairyData.pdf.

Woloson, Wendy. *Refined Tastes*. Baltimore, MD: Johns Hopkins University Press, 2002.

Zeigelman, Jane. "Immigrant Identities, Preserved in Vinegar?" *New York Times*, August 3, 2003.

Zimmermann, Andrea K. "Nineteenth-Century Production of Wheat in Four New York State Regions: A Comparative Examination." *Hudson Valley Regional Review* 5, no. 2 (1988).

INTERVIEWS

Sam Addison. January 30, 2013.
Liz Alvis, January 6, 2013.
Nicole Austin, November 17, 2012.
Nat Bletter. November 15, 2012.
Tom Burkleaux, January 4, 2013.
Jordan Champagne, January 9, 2013.
Ralph Erenzo, October 25, 2012.
Jill Basch Giacomini, January 7, 2013.
Travis Grillo, October 18, 2012.
Michaela Hayes, November 28, 2012.
Derek Herbster, October 18, 2012.

Alex Hozven, January 8, 2013.
Shamus Jones. November 29, 2012.
Uri Laio, January 11, 2013.
Brian McKenzie, October 22, 2012.
George Miller, February 13, 2013.
Julie O'Brien, January, 25, 2013.
Donna Pacheco, January 7, 2013
John Putnam, February 13, 2014.
Vince Razionale, February 14, 2013.
Cameron Ring, January 7, 2013.
Colin Spoelman, October 19, 2012.
Andrew Tice, January 4, 2013.
Tour Guide at Eastside Distilling, January 3, 2013.
Betsey Walton, January 4, 2013.
Charley Wheelock, January 3, 2013.
Alex Whitmore, August 10, 2011.

WEBSITES

Achadinha. www.achadinha.com/Home.html
Beehive Cheese Company. www.beehivecheese.com/cheese/
Breuckelen Distilling. brkdistilling.com/
Brooklyn Gin. www.brooklyngin.com
Cacao Prieto. cacaoprieto.com
Craft Chocolate Makers of America. www.craftchocolatemakers.org
Crock and Jar. www.crockandjar.com
Dandelion Chocolate. www.dandelionchocolate.com
Finger Lakes Distilling. fingerlakesdistilling.com/
First Light Farm. first-light-farm.com/
House Spirits. www.housespirits.com
Jericho Hill Farm. www.VTCheese.com
Madre Chocolate. madrechocolate.com/Home.html
Mt. Olive Pickles. www.MtOlivePickles.com
Oregon Liquor Control Commission. www.oregon.gov/olcc/pages/about_us.aspx
Portland Creamery. www.portlandcreamery.com
Thistle Hill Farm. www.thistlehillfarm.com
Tuthilltown. www.tuthilltown.com

INDEX

ABOUT THE AUTHOR

Suzanne Cope is a writer and scholar of food studies and creative writing studies. She earned both her MFA and PhD from Lesley University and has recent and upcoming personal essays and articles in literary journals and magazines including *Edible Boston, Edible Cape Cod,* and *New Plains Review,* and academic publications including the *Italian American Review* and *Encyclopedia of Food Issues.* She teaches writing at Manhattan College, New York, and in the MFA program at the University of Arkansas at Monticello. She lives in Brooklyn, New York.